T5-AGO-845

After Politics

After Politics

The Rejection of Politics in Contemporary Liberal Philosophy

Glen Newey
Reader in Politics
University of Strathclyde

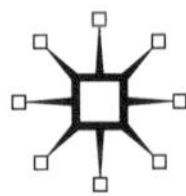

First published 2001 by
PALGRAVE
Houndmills, Basingstoke, Hampshire RG21 6XS and
175 Fifth Avenue, New York, N. Y. 10010
Companies and representatives throughout the world

PALGRAVE is the new global academic imprint of St. Martin's Press LLC Scholarly and Reference Division and Palgrave Publishers Ltd (formerly Macmillan Press Ltd).

ISBN 0–333–77813–8

This book is printed on paper suitable for recycling and made from fully managed and sustained forest sources.

A catalogue record for this book is available from the British Library.

Library of Congress Cataloging-in-Publication Data
Newey, Glen.
After politics : the rejection of politics in contemporary liberal philosophy / Glen Newey.
p. cm.
Includes bibliographical references and index.
ISBN 0–333–77813–8
1. Liberalism. I. Title.

JC574 .N49 2000
320.51'3—dc21

00–052442

10 9 8 7 6 5 4 3 2 1
10 09 08 07 06 05 04 03 02 01

Printed and bound in Great Britain by
Antony Rowe Ltd, Chippenham, Wiltshire

To
Linda, Liam, and this time Laura, too

Non est potestas super terram quae comparetur eis ...

Philosophers regard the passions by which we are afflicted as vices, into which men fall by their own fault; and, as a result they are wont to ridicule, bewail, or censure them, or – if they want to appear more righteous – to abominate them. For they regard this as god-like behaviour, and think that they have attained the pinnacle of wisdom when they know how to praise in any number of ways a human nature which exists nowhere, and to denounce that which really exists. For they conceive of men not as they are, but as they would like them to be; and hence they produce satire rather than ethics, and have never managed to devise polities which could be called into use; but which are mere phantasms, or could only be instituted in the poets' golden age, where they were least needed. So, while in all practical sciences theory is held to diverge from practice, this is nowhere more true than in politics, and nobody is thought to be less fitted to rule a state than are the theoreticians or philosophers.

Spinoza, *Tractatus Politicus* 1

Contents

Acknowledgements

I would like to record my thanks to a number of anonymous referees who have commented on the book in whole or in part. I am also grateful to participants at the following forums, where I aired some of the views expressed here: the University of Sussex's Philosophy Society, at its Philosophy graduate/faculty work-in-progress seminar, and at its Social and Political Thought graduate/faculty seminar; the Political Theory workshop, University of London; the Political Thought conference at St Catherine's College, University of Oxford, 1997; the Political Theory graduate/faculty seminar at the University of Edinburgh; the Political Theory seminar at the London School of Economics; the Political Studies Association annual conference at Glasgow University, 1996. I am also duly grateful to the University of Sussex, which awarded me periods of paid and unpaid leave to write the book.

I am particularly grateful to my former doctoral supervisor, John Horton, for his generosity and intellectual companionship, as well as for more specific comments on some of the issues raised in the book. I also wish to express my thanks to the anonymous readers at Palgrave who have commented on the whole typescript, to my editor Alison Howson for her help and advice and to Chase Publishing Services for meticulous editing.

Once again my largest debt is to my wife Linda. The gestation of the book has been considerably longer than that of our daughter Laura Calypso (who was born while I was taking one of my numerous breaks from writing it), and has caused me a lot more work. The dog, as ever, provided sterling support.

Introduction

In the title of a famous essay published in 1962, Isaiah Berlin asked, 'Does Political Theory Still Exist?'[1] That Berlin answered the question in the affirmative was less startling than the fact that so notable a practitioner of the discipline thought it a question worth asking. Six years earlier, Peter Laslett had ruefully concluded that 'political theory, at any rate for the time being, is dead'.[2] Few, if any, of those practising the discipline today would question its existence, or viability. Terence Ball's recent verdict on its progress since Berlin's article appeared is representative of many practitioners' current views:

> As it turned out, however, all reports of the death of [political] theory proved to be premature if not perhaps wholly unwarranted in the first place. By the mid-1970s academic political theorists were wont to quote Mark Twain's remark upon reading his own obituary. 'The reports of my death,' Twain cabled to his distraught editor, 'have been greatly exaggerated'.[3]

According to Ball's narrative, and that of others since the appearance of *A Theory of Justice* in 1971,[4] the pessimism prevalent in the 1950s and early 1960s concerning the discipline's prospects, and its intellectual point, have been largely dispelled. Ball himself locates this in the obsolescence of a motivationally reductive behaviourism in the academy (itself the progeny of now discredited scientistic verificationism about meaning), which seems to allocate an attenuated, if not non-existent, role for theory in shaping political practice.[5] For given behaviourism or functionalist approaches to the mental it is harder to see how the normative content of propositional attitudes is capable of guiding action. While this factor should not be underestimated, some of the secular causes behind the 'death of theory' claims in the 1950s and 1960s also, I believe, lie in earlier versions of the impossibilist and rejectionist attitudes which I isolate in Chapter 1.[6]

But reports of the discipline's *survival* may have been exaggerated. In a purely institutional sense, of course, it not only survives, but thrives. There are probably more professional political philosophers at work now than ever before. Perusal of academic publishers' catalogues also indicates that, if anything, the discipline is suffering from a crisis of *over*-production of new monographs. Some of these indeed address substantive normative questions. However, the theoretical strictures to which I believe these efforts are subject (for which I argue in Chapter 5), and the more general concerns about the intellectual and political context within which political philosophy is written, stand regardless of this – particularly the concentration on normative rather than descriptive analysis. Political philosophers' productivity should not forestall reflection on the *content* of the discipline; a new definitive theory of justice may be but the outworking of a near-exhausted paradigm. I shall suggest below that, while the situation may not be quite as grave as this, the remit of political philosophising, as currently practised, is unduly narrow.

In the next section, I set out synopses of the subsequent chapters, which in my view expose political philosophy's failure to engage with politics.

The main argument

I advance two main claims about the relation between liberal political philosophy and politics in this book. These claims are as follows:

(a) few works of modern liberal political philosophy attempt to address the real world of politics, often applying inappropriate theoretical models to it when they do; and
(b) liberal political philosophers aim at the supersession of the ostensible subject-matter of their discipline – that is, politics; they aim at a post-political order.

Because liberal political philosophy[7] is usually looking past politics and towards something else – the implementation of a particular conception of the right, or of the good – it proves incapable of understanding political phenomena. Often theory is avowedly normative. But, as I argue, political philosophers find themselves pulled towards normative theorising even when they are attempting to provide explanatory theory. Thus we are often left with an *explanatory deficit* in philosophical attempts to account for political phenomena, since the explanation of political behaviour, like other forms of behaviour, requires an account not of the reasons on which agents *should* act, but those on which they in fact do act.[8] This, as I argue with regard to some key debates within political philosophy, has led to widespread confusion about the discipline's methods, as well as its aims.

As regards the second claim, the aim of the most considerable and widely discussed contributions to political philosophy since the publication of *A Theory of Justice* (and indeed in a tradition going back much further) has been to describe a state of the world in which politics as we know it no longer exists.

The link between claims (a) and (b) is as follows. Since philosophers usually take it as their business to purvey theory, they have sought theorised explanations of the (practical and theoretical) reasoning engaged in by participants in political action. The quest for theoretical explanations usually involves a search for *best* reasons for belief or action. But very often a reconstruction of the actual reasoning involved diverges sharply from that which, according to the theoretical account, is optimal – in some cases (as I argue with respect to the essential contestability thesis, for example), necessarily so. This then leaves a gap between the actual reasons on which political agents act, and those on which, according to theory, they ideally should act; the result is an *esoteric* theory, as I suggest in Chapter 5 – one whose truth-conditions include its being disbelieved by those agents to whom it purportedly applies. So even where theory sets out to be explanatory – to provide a descriptive philosophical account of politics as it is – theorists find themselves pushed towards idealisation, that is, towards a (b)-like form of philosophical endeavour. More clearly still, the pursuit of ideal theory is likely to marginalise, or indeed supplant entirely, a more descriptive approach to the subject.

As already noted, the subtitle of the book is to be taken at face value. My focus is on contemporary philosophical liberalism, the currently dominant anglophone political philosophy. I do not discuss at any length how far the rejection of politics which I detect in philosophical liberalism is made good elsewhere on the ideological spectrum. Some forms of anti-liberalism have been better than others at avoiding this rejection. 'Communitarianism', for instance, has been notoriously bad at developing a convincing account of politics, not least because it so often counterposes to the 'fragmentation' or 'atomism' of liberal social theory a stress on normative consensus. This is less true of feminism, and some forms of Marxism and (perhaps) conservatism.[9]

I now set out claims (a) and (b) in more detail.

(a) My fundamental claim here is one of *explanatory insufficiency*: because political philosophy has not been concerned to analyse politics, but rather aimed at its supersession, at describing, in other words, the normative conditions requisite for a post-political state of the world – it proves incapable of understanding political practice, and not infrequently, the status of its own theorising. The detailed arguments of Chapters 1–4 are intended to demonstrate how this thesis of explanatory inadequacy applies to specific debates within political philosophy set out below, while Chapter 5 provides theoretical reasons – mainly drawn from modern ethical theory – explaining why recent political philosophy has taken this form. In addition, political theorists are apt to impose on political phenomena structures which purport to set out *theoretical* truths about value, conflict, or agency, without linking these to the deliberation of real political agents.

The result is often misunderstanding, or even incoherence, in political explanation. Real political phenomena – such as the pervasiveness of political conflict – are ignored, or transmuted into material which is more amenable to theory. Once this condition is recognised, the move is made from explanation to claims about how rational political agents *should* act. The move from description to normativity opens an explanatory gap.

'Political philosophy and politics' (Chapter 1). Most of this book is devoted to analysis of misunderstandings in political philosophy, and as such is theoretical in content. Each chapter deals with specific issues and theorists in the discipline, as they are relevant to this theme. But in Chapter 1 I consider more generally the nature of this misunderstanding, and the reasons why it has arisen. Apart from reasons internal to the practice of political philosophy and related disciplines such as ethics, there are in my view wider cultural reasons for the turn away from politics by political philosophers. These include mistrust of politicians, scepticism about the ability of politics to bring about the good, and in particular distaste for power and its exercise.

'Philosophy, politics and contestability' (Chapter 2). The essential contestability thesis purports to explain the causes of political disagreement. Far from explaining political disagreement, it is doubtful whether the thesis is even coherent and, if it is, whether the charge of incoherence can be rebutted without the thesis's forfeiting its explanatory efficacy. Commentators on the thesis have relied on over-theorised accounts of actual political behaviour, assuming that disagreement must admit of a *conceptual* explanation. The thesis is threatened by incoherence, and the best responses to this threat sacrifice the thesis's explanatory power by relying on an *esoteric* account of disagreement: that is, one whose truth requires that it is not believed in by the protagonists. But even if it were coherent, it would remain to be shown why different interpretations of a given concept *matter* politically. There is assumed to be a certain kind of linkage between theory (in particular, that which is held to deliver the thesis itself) and deliberation, as it occurs in the opinion-formation and arguments of political disputants. But the most it can show is not that the conceptual structures *in fact* explain the contrary opinions of these people, but how they might have arrived at a particular view of the concept's extension *if* they were being rational.

'Political obligation' (Chapter 3). Political philosophers have confused or conflated two distinct kinds of theoretical enterprise. The first is that of justifying the state, which many writers have taken to be synonymous with solving 'the problem of political obligation'. The second is that of providing a credible descriptive account of the deliberative route by which proto-citizens might rationally arrive at an acknowledgement of the state's legitimacy. Given that these enterprises begin from opposite ends of what may or may not be the same problem, there is little reason to assume that they will meet in the middle. Junction is thought to be effected by means of the notion of *obligation*.[10] But, as I argue, the attempt comes to grief when we cast about for entirely general, obligation-justifying reasons. Either these fail to be reasons *for* the allegedly obligated agents, or else their motivational grip is bought at the cost of their failing to ground anything recognisable as an obligation. I conclude that the conflation is prompted by the importation of a *sui generis* category of purported reasons for action, namely *obligation*. These are purportedly reason-giving, and apply categorically, but (having been thus identified) they are also beyond grounding in more basic sorts of reasons for action. We either occupy an ideal realm, in which obligations can be conjectured to apply categorically, or proceed from the all-too-contingent reasons for action of real agents, in which case there is no reason to think that the reasons in question will ground a categorical requirement such as an obligation. I suggest that this is not merely the regrettable deficiency of a sub-optimal world, one remediable in principle by greater practical rationality. The conjectured obligations are essentially groundless. Hence this category of purported reasons for action proves incapable of explaining citizens' relation to their state.

Distortion has been created, I suggest, through the importation of conceptual apparatus from moral theory. Treating the question of state justification as 'the problem of political obligation' misleads us into thinking that there must be a single problem, whereas in reality theorists have addressed under this label a plurality of loosely related questions. And the term *obligation* itself has misled theorists into mistaking, or unjustifiably limiting, the nature of the reasons which these questions sought as justifications. In the case of the 'conceptual' argument,[11] the patently false claim – that substantive questions about citizens' reasons for obeying the state or the law, or about the justification of state power, can be disposed of lexicographically – is lent credibility by the fact that statements of obligations (unlike rights) essentially impute reasons for action to their bearers. But when it comes to justifying the state, this merely defers answering the question whether or not there is reason for citizens to act on the obligations which their state imposes on them.

'Politics and the limits of pluralism' (Chapter 4). Much discussion in contemporary liberalism centres on value-pluralism.[12] The meta-ethical thesis that the truth about value is that it is plural rather than singular, null, or unknowable, is confounded with a descriptive thesis, also going by the name 'pluralism', about cultural diversity in large modern cosmopolitan societies – and then it is the latter thesis which is taken to have normative political weight.[13] One explanation for this conflation is that it may appear to reduce controversial theoretical commitments – in particular, those which pronounce certain conceptions of the good as superior, or truer, than others. There is however no reason in general to think that the values which those subscribing to the meta-ethical thesis regard as values must find their reflex in the conceptions of the good prevalent in society at large, either internally or *vis à vis* one another. Here, as with political obligation and essential contestability, theorists begin from observations about modern political circumstances – in this case, the fact of diversity – then work out from there the normative implications, from the presumed meta-ethical 'facts' to which the fact of diversity corresponds.[14]

But it is far from clear how the protagonists are supposed to deliberate from their particular conceptions of the good to the desired conclusion. The most we could get is something like Rawls's 'overlapping consensus', but then it is what the different conceptions have in common that is doing the justificatory work, not the fact of diversity. Even if this diversity were somehow explicable by the 'facts' about value, they would still leave open the political question what should be done about it.[15] What in fact underpins the normative response to diversity (such as a version of neutrality), as I argued, is a unitary principle consistent with the rejection of meta-ethical pluralism, such as that of equal respect. But this may be a principle which the groups espousing conceptions of the good in society reject. There is then no deliberative path for members of these groups to the proposed normative resolution.

My aim here is not to argue for a particular theoretical line on the philosophical foundations of liberalism. The point is that a metaphysical thesis, namely value-pluralism, has been thought first to explain a political fact, and second to support a certain normative conception of how political theory should respond to it. But value-pluralism does not explain civil society pluralism: it is neither a necessary nor a sufficient condition of the latter that value is metaphysically plural. Nor does value-pluralism demand any specific conception of how to deal with civil-society diversity. It is hard to resist the conclusion that its supposed relationship to the metaphysical 'fact' of pluralism explains why this question bulks so large in their current concerns. It is, no doubt, a professional failing of philosophers to overestimate the significance of certain constructions of theory (in this case, the metaphysics of value) for theory elsewhere. But even if 'facts' in the metaphysics of value explained the existence of civil-society diversity, they would still leave entirely open the question of what politically should be done about it. Perhaps the most curious feature of the current concern among political philosophers with pluralism in the metaphysics of value is that it is often used to *support* a reductivist attitude towards politics. Often the underlying argument, where there is one, relies on a form of insufficient-reason claim – that there is no reason to favour one conception of the good over another. But if there really are plural moral values, it seems hard to resist the conclusion that they may issue in equally reasonable – if not equally true – but conflicting conceptions of what politically ought to be done (undue concentration on the metaphysics of pluralism has obscured the fact that the same situation may even arise in a *monistic* system, given only that reference to the unitary value may by itself under-determine the decision between alternative presented policies, and so on). This spells trouble for those conceptions of discourse ethics which, when applied to politics, hope that practical conflict (for example, over policy) will admit of a purely dialogic resolution, or that dialogic procedures will provide a means of rationally resolving it.[16]

I now return to claim (b) above, that political philosophers aim at the supersession of the ostensible subject-matter of politics in a post-political order. Contemporary analytical political philosophy is not concerned with the philosophical analysis of politics. It is rather *anti-political*, to the extent that it aims at deriving philosophically a set of principles, enacted through institutions and procedures, which if implemented would herald the end of politics. As argued in Chapter 2, this does not presuppose a fully articulated conceptual model of the political, but only some uncontroversial empirical observations about political life. First, politics is characterised by endemic disagreement over what counts as a political question, and this has its normative aspect, since such disputes are about what *ought* to be a matter of public concern.[17] Any descriptive model of the political has to take account of this normative dimension in public debate over what itself qualifies as politically controversial. This need not mean that such a model cannot after all be descriptive – there may be room for a purely descriptive account of the criteria on the basis of which a given subject-matter is held to be political. But it suggests that theory which relies on an implicit model of the political is liable to broach issues which are themselves the subject of political dispute.

Second, more generally, politics is characterised by endemic disagreement over issues which are by common consent a matter of public concern. There are a number of possible explanations of this, some of which are discussed in the text (particularly Chapters 2 and 4). One explanation, which abstains from making the theoretical commitments (such as value-pluralism or essential contestability) criticised later, is that there is room for reasonable disagreement about the matters with which politics deals. Of course, much recent political theory has sought to address this possibility. It is however unlikely, given that this scope for reasonable disagreement exists, that there will not also be disputes about what resolutions of the disagreement are justifiable; the state of current political philosophy provides an existential proof of this.

Third, politics essentially involves the use of power. It is fair to say that very little recent liberal political philosophy has dealt with this fundamental aspect of political life. It is fairly obvious why ideal theory would seek to abstract from questions of power – that, after all, is part of what it is to be ideal theory. But producing such theory incurs a theoretical debt to address the existence of political power, rather than to ignore it. Partly that is because what ideal theory finds to be wrong with the existing state of things consists essentially, rather than merely accidentally, in aspects of the use of power. There is also a question to answer about how theory would even in principle be implemented. More fundamentally, there is a need to distinguish between the different ways – and degrees of justification with which – power may oppose implementation, and how far strategic modifications to ideal theory are possible or desirable.

In saying this I am not arguing that there is no place for first-order normative theorising in political philosophy. As I argue below, however, even – indeed especially – 'ideal' theorising incurs theoretical debts in respect of political practice. For looking past that practice towards ideal theory is presumably worthwhile only if it in the relevant respects falls short of the theoretically articulated ideal. But then, assuming the aim is to amend practice to conform more nearly to the ideal, we need to know both how and why the status quo is inadequate, and in the light of this how we might get from it to conformity with the prescriptions of theory.

'Moral theory and political philosophy' (Chapter 5). It may be said that these examples are selective, and indeed they are. To this extent my claims about the *overall* state of political philosophy are as vulnerable to sceptical objection as is any inductive argument. In Chapter 5, however, I offer a general theoretical explanation of the misunderstandings discussed in Chapters 1–4. Without reprising the argument in any detail, its most relevant conclusion for current purposes is that the dominant methodology in the discipline assumes the truth of controversial, and quite possibly false, positions in the philosophy of action and ethics. These are *the sovereignty of morality*, and *cognitivist internalism*. I argue against both, on the grounds that externalism is a less implausible account of the motivational antecedents of moral agency, and that there is literally *no* reason to think that the sovereignty doctrine is true – a conclusion which I argue is strengthened, rather than vitiated, if the 'categorical' status of morality is insisted upon.

But there is a second layer of argument, which is that each position pulls against the other. That both are presupposed by current practice provides a plausible explanation of the argumentative incoherence exposed in the book. If this argument succeeds, there is a *general* problem with attempts to structure politics via normative analysis, which if the remarks in this introduction are right, is the dominant mode of current political philosophy. It would apply, for example, to attempts to derive political structures from reflection on the value of autonomy, as in works such as Raz's *Morality of Freedom*, or from that of rights, as in Gewirth's *Reason and Morality* or Nozick's *Anarchy, State and Utopia*. In succumbing to the pull of a normative account of reasons for action, theory fails to provide adequate explanations of political phenomena, as witnessed in the discussion of political obligations, or essential contestability. Pluralism provides a hybrid example, to the extent that what is often thought of as a descriptive thesis about modern political circumstances (the fact of cultural diversity) is taken, when conflated with meta-ethical pluralism, to have normative force. But equally, more avowedly normative theory fails to justify its own methodological assumptions.

'Neutralising politics' (Chapter 6). The doctrine of political neutrality deviates from the pattern outlined above to the extent that its original rationale is not explanatory but normative.[18] It should however be noted that the neutralist programme is meant to be carried through with minimal normative commitments. Even so, at critical points in the argument the impetus is to turn away from the problems in implementing neutrality and towards ideal theory. So, given the problems facing an outcome-based conception of neutrality, its defenders resort to a procedural conception. What this does not do, however, is model actual political procedures, and there are clear reasons why it *could* not do so – because the politics would have already to have been done before the politics began. Thus we move from real political processes to an idealised conception in which (as in Habermas's work) substantive conclusions are supposedly *generated* by political procedures, but the procedures themselves are already determined extra-politically. The rationale for this, I argue, is an avowedly normative conception of moral persons as equal.

But neutrality cannot provide this resolution. I distinguish two broad types of argumentative role for neutrality – between, on the one hand, neutrality as a condition or side-constraint *on* justification, and on the other, as an object *of* justification – that is, as an attribute of political outcomes. According to the side-constraint view, what is required is not merely that political outcomes be neutral, but that there is a neutral *justification* for these outcomes. I shall argue that side-constraint neutrality is presupposed by object neutrality: there is little point in trying to justify political design unless the justification respects neutrality as a side-constraint on acceptable forms of argument. Neutrality seeks to secure the non-partiality advantage by respecting the neutralist side-constraint, and this means employing forms of insufficient-reason argument. I shall however suggest that this by itself is not enough to ground a neutralist political order: it is not clear at which point the demand to respect the neutral *status* of the protagonist is meant to apply. Neutralists are faced with a dilemma. Either they keep faith with neutrality as a side-constraint, but cannot justify a neutral form of political design. Or they forgo the non-partiality advantage by rejecting the insufficient-reason form of argument, thus violating side-constraint neutrality, and justify neutral political design by values controversial between conceptions of the good, which is tantamount to abandoning neutrality itself. As I shall argue, prominent advocates of neutrality vacillate between a purely insufficient-reason-based argument, and one based on substantive (and controversial) moral commitments. What began as an attempt to avoid the use of disputed philosophical doctrines, by achieving a purely *political* justification ends by resorting to them.

There is the further possibility that a given neutralist justification will be deemed controversial and rejected precisely *because* it justifies conclusions which political antagonists reject. Any neutralist justification of political design would have first to eliminate from conceptions of the good a vital area of contention between them – their account of politics itself; they have to limit the content of the eligible conceptions of the good so as to exclude explicitly *political* conceptions of value. The world within which neutral political design is justified is a world after politics.

'Rawls and Habermas: liberalism versus politics' (Chapter 7). This chapter examines political justification with particular reference to the work of Rawls and Habermas. It may be said that since Rawlsian and other theory envisages the 'well-ordered'[19] society as democratic, it remains political. This impression is misleading. The well-ordered society does indeed contain certain kinds of constitutionally entrenched rights and duties. But this interpretation of the political content of the well-ordered society is open to two objections. First, either the nature of these constitutional entities – their practical force – is the subject of political dispute or it is not. If they are, then the disputes characteristic of politics will remain, and may surface in radically disparate understandings of the rights' and duties' practical force; but politics is then reinstated at the cost of practical indeterminacy in the content of the theory itself. If not, they will presumably be interpreted judicially, and to this extent questions of implementation are removed from the political to an alternative arena within the public sphere. There will be scope for such conflict just to the extent that the rights and duties leave it indeterminate what policy should be. Second, more fundamentally, the belief that philosophy can both leave room for politics and arrive at practically determinate constraints within which political engagement occurs ignores the possibility that the nature of the constraints themselves may be the subject of attritional political dispute. It is not however enough, even as far as this aspect of the critique goes, to advert to the need for (in Rawlsian terminology) a 'partial compliance' theory.[20] For (given an account, say, of what the ideally just society would be like), we lack not only an understanding of how to behave in a world which falls short of the ideal. We also lack an understanding of the fact that different individuals may be motivated by different conceptions of what ideals such as justice require, rather than (as the notion of partial compliance apparently envisages) the fact that many people will simply be indifferent to the demands of justice. The point is that *to the extent that* society is well-ordered in Rawlsian terms, it will lack even well-intentioned disputes over the requirements of ideals such as justice. But such disputes seem to be of the essence of politics, rather than mere effluvium to be dispersed by the application of theory.

Thus, even within a broad commitment to normative theorising rather than description, there is the need – one which requires satisfaction for theory to stand any chance of implementation in practice, and not merely the demand for theoretical coherence – to justify ideal theory *politically*. For it needs to be shown (among other things) why, given that alternative conceptions of justice (and so on) have reasonable and well-intentioned partisans, the particular conception favoured should be implemented by those in power. Given the unlikelihood of instantaneous mass conversion to the favoured conception, its votaries will have to engage with those of the other conceptions. This process will, I suggest, be essentially indeterminate in advance. But if so, it is gratuitous to suppose that this process can be pre-empted or second-guessed by a partial compliance theory which is devised in advance of negotiation. But this model of determining principles will then be something much less like abstract philosophising, and more like real-world political argument. If this is right, political philosophers who engage in normative theorising will require a different form of self-understanding. That will involve acknowledging the lack of discontinuity between their justificatory enterprise and the forms of rationalisation which, in prospect or retrospect, seek to justify actual political practice.

Nonetheless, this approach still remains firmly within the realm of the prescriptive. Beyond this, first-order normative theory needs supplementation by a qualitatively different kind of political philosophy – one concerned with philosophical *description* rather than with prescription, and not merely because it might provide useful information for the purposes of formulating partial compliance theory, or something similar. There may be cognitive gain in redescription, and presumably this is what philosophy aims to provide elsewhere. But there is little reason to think that the news which this redescription conveys must be good.

Both Rawls and Habermas have latterly moved under Kantian influence towards a more avowedly neutralist style of theory. In the case of Rawls, his more recent work has attempted to move away from the consensual moral conception on which the argument of *A Theory of Justice* based itself. In fact, however, as Rawls acknowledges repeatedly in *Political Liberalism*, this does not mean that the theory dispenses with normative assumptions – far from it. As a result, given that the clash between the comprehensive doctrines sets the terms of the problem, there is liable to be a plurality of views as to how best it should be resolved; there is simply no warrant for the claim that the values of moral personhood on which the 'political conception' of justice is modelled will command the universal assent that it requires. Merely adverting to the *possibility* that the political conception will make possible an 'overlapping consensus'[21] on the basis of the differing perspectives of incompatible comprehensive doctrines does not establish that it will. The political workability of Rawls's theory depends on its acquiring a degree of motivational force which there is no reason to believe that it will possess for the partisans of particular comprehensive doctrines. It may be there is some argument which shows that it should; but even if that were so, there would still be a question about how to implement it in a world where the partisans of certain evaluative doctrines remain implacable.

Similarly, in his recent writings, Habermas has sought to lay down universal discursive principles on the basis of which initial discord can be procedurally channelled into politically ratified decisions. Certain aspects of the procedural strictures which Habermas imposes on this process mirror the apparatus of the Original Position in *A Theory of Justice*. It is however unclear why we should accept the strictures themselves, and the meta-ethical priorities which they explicitly embody. Since there is no available-to-inspection test of reasonableness analogous to tests for theoremhood in formal systems, it is open to the participants to object to procedures which in their view are unreasonable precisely because they foreseeably ensue in outcomes which the participants do not accept. In these circumstances subjecting the participants to epistemic constraints appears to be a device to bind them to sanction outcomes which in a state of full knowledge they would regard as unreasonable. Moreover, since the epistemic constraints are, as in Rawls's work, generated by certain normative commitments, it needs to be shown why different normative commitments, or other views of the conditions appropriate to political design, are ruled out. Though Habermas proposes his discursive conditions as a means of *determining* substantive moral principles, it turns out that they have moral commitments already written into them. Here again I conclude that Habermas's theory seeks to pre-empt outcomes which are determinable only politically.

'Political philosophy without foundations?' (Chapter 8) deals mainly with the work of Richard Rorty and John Gray. Rorty explicitly rejects the 'foundationalist' philosophical project of Rawls and other recent theorists, arguing that a philosophical commitment such as liberalism is 'prior' to philosophy. As I argue, however, Rorty's target is really *normative* forms of foundationalism: he in effect accepts the methodological assumption which I have detected in his more traditionally minded adversaries, that the philosophical task is to determine normative foundations, or it is nothing. Given Rorty's espousal of a broadly descriptivist view of the philosophical enterprise elsewhere, this seems strange. If however Rorty means to argue (as often appears) that any form of redescription is as good as any other, that position is hard to square with his view of philosophy as futile attempts to write undergirding 'meta-narratives'. The truth-predicate has its origins in ordinary discourse, and certain kinds of politically relevant judgements are, in the judgements of the discourse's practitioners, highly impervious to redescription. Rorty (perhaps unwittingly) perpetuates the very schism between philosophy and practice which forms the basis for much of his critique of foundationalism. By contrast, John Gray uses the methodology of foundationalism in political philosophy to show that political philosophy's main aim – to establish a particular form of political design – cannot be achieved. Gray's understanding of politics, and the relation of philosophy to it, is a good deal closer to that defended in this book. Gray believes that the 'fact' of pluralism dooms the liberal foundationalist project. As it is argued in Chapter 4, the grounds for belief in pluralism are less compelling, and its consequences for political design less far-reaching, than many philosophers believe. But insofar as the anti-foundationalist arguments succeed, they subvert philosophy's claims to legislate for politics. For without the prospect of a rational resolution, the project of political design loses its authority over politics, and disputes between philosophers about the projects become more like everyday political disputes. What results is a conception of political philosophising more akin to everyday political argument than orthodox foundationalism envisages.

The work of Rorty and Gray has the merit, lacking in many of the other thinkers mentioned above, of methodological reflectiveness. Their post-philosophical anti-foundationalism prompts salutary questions about the role of philosophy, and the conception of politics with which it works. What is needed, in my view, is more political philosophy, and less political theory.[22] The contrast is intentional. It countenances the possibility that political philosophy may be practised without purveying theory, where 'theory' is interpreted as a rational construction intended to guide practice or provide a more systematised understanding of it. The best to be hoped for may be merely a better understanding of why a credible philosophical theory of politics is unavailable. Even within a broadly normative style of theorising, however, the assumptions informing current theory are questionable.

Chapter 1 asks why this failure has come about.

1
Political Philosophy and Politics

Post-politics and political philosophy

Modern political philosophy has little to say about politics as an activity. This is perhaps not quite as odd as would be the case if philosophers of science had nothing to say about scientific activity, or philosophers of language nothing about linguistic practice – or, for that matter, if philosophers of ethics found nothing of relevance to their inquiries in the phenomena of the moral life (even Kantians can apply a just savings principle to some of the latter). But it is still fairly odd. I shall first seek to substantiate this claim.

Most political philosophers are currently not providing very much philosophical reflection on politics – at least not on politics as it is.[1] The central concern of political philosophy since the publication of *A Theory of Justice*[2] has been to arrive at a set of ideal prescriptions rather than attempting to provide a descriptive account of politics as it non-ideally exists. Not that the latter is the only fit subject for political philosophers to address. For example, we can ask whether there are any general conditions under which the existence of the state is justified, and what these conditions may be, or (differently) under what conditions the state's requirement that its citizens perform certain actions is justified. Again, we can ask what justice is, how important it is in relation to ethical and other concerns, and how much heed an account of justice should take of what is politically possible. Recent political philosophy has addressed some, though not all, of these prescriptive issues.

There is a shared pattern in normative political philosophy, which remains despite disagreements about the nature of justice or other kinds of concern. As I argue in Chapter 5, this has its roots in disputes about normativity and the demands it makes on practical rationality; an important aspect of this is the relatively low importance enjoyed by given motivational patterns in agency, with a concomitant loss of psychological realism. The shared pattern turns away from explanation of real-world political phenomena, even though the latter provides the starting-point for theory. This is not surprising, since it is not plausible to think that the presumably heterogeneous reasons on which real political agents act are those which would conform to any interesting normative specification of how they ideally should act.

The normative bias in contemporary political philosophy consists partly in its failure to establish methods and aims distinct from those of ethical theory. But it is also due to the fact that political philosophy has been largely given over to normative theorising, or what is often called 'applied' ethics. I do not deny that this form of theorising has its place within the discipline. But there can also be cognitive gain in description, and the discipline as currently practised is perhaps disproportionately concerned with normative theory. Just as moral philosophers can usefully address the moral life in all its imperfection, so political philosophers can, and should, address that of the political life.

This is not merely the familiar charge that political philosophers theorise under ideal conditions, ignoring questions of practical implementation. However, even within a broadly normative conception of political philosophy – indeed, especially within it – there is room to ask how ideal principles should be implemented. Presumably the point of engaging in an idealised form of normative theorising is the belief that real conditions exhibit a normative deficit. But it seems that there is only a purpose in that if theory can survive to implementation. Then it is incumbent on these theorists to explain how theory comes to be implemented. Crucially, that may mean that the principles of justice (and so on) laid down in theory need to be modified during implementation – not least because the latter process, which is too often identified with administration, will involve negotiation with those who believe in other conceptions of justice. So, as well as knowing what the principles are, we need to know how far they will be accepted politically. An answer to these questions will require, if only implicitly, a conception of the political.

This point is not satisfactorily dealt with, in my view, by the notion of what Rawls calls 'partial compliance theory'.[3] In Rawls's presentation, partial compliance theory is concerned with the just society's appropriate response to acts of particular injustice, through punishment, just-war theory, and so on. Again, this already presupposes substantive agreement on principles of justice, and the likeliest recipients of punishment or for the prosecution of a just war may not be people who hold a radically different conception of the good. The oddity consists in thinking that divergence can simply be contained within the theory, rather than encountering other and rival conceptions of justice.

Much political philosophy is written as if there is nothing of philosophical interest in politics, or that whatever is of interest is reducible to something else – usually ethics, or theoretical controversies in the philosophy of action. Insofar as political philosophy has aimed at articulating the guiding principles and institutional matrix of the ideally just society, it has had little to say philosophically about politics.

This is a form of reductivism. As such, its appeal consists in seeming to reach beyond appearances to considerations which are explanatorily more basic. Why do I claim that this reductivism is so strange? After all, there presumably has to be some distinction between any given practice or area of human endeavour, and philosophical reflection upon it – even when the practice is that of philosophising itself. The alternative to this reductivist position in political philosophy, then, can hardly be (it may be said) simply to drop everything and start doing politics. This might be disputed by some, such as those readers of Marx who take seriously his admonition that philosophy should stop trying to understand the world, and start trying to change it[4] – itself a form of reductivism, to which Marxism is anyway committed on other grounds. But those who think that Marx did well in his own work to reject the dichotomy between thought and action which this seems to assume, will need to find their bearings elsewhere. What is strange is to believe that there is no space between these reductivisms.

One peculiarity of recent political philosophy has been that it takes the discipline's aim to be, in a certain sense, its own elimination – or at least the elimination of the arena of human concerns which ostensibly provides its subject-matter. As I suggest below, this propensity may be due in part to the desire to maintain disciplinary boundaries, coupled with the fear that in political philosophy they are more vulnerable to insurgency than elsewhere. Political philosophy seems threatened by Polandisation, menaced on the one side by merely descriptive (and, on some views, methodologically under-powered) political science, and on the other by the theoretical apparatus offered by deontological, consequentialist, and other currently debated theory-guided conceptions of the ethical. This worry itself seems slightly puzzling, in that other areas of philosophy remain uncowed by the danger of mere description where the subject-matter also admits of normative correction – for example, philosophers of action usually take themselves to be providing a philosophical account of what agents are doing when (or at any rate before) they act, regardless of the normative assessment of the act itself. Even where the theory allows in normative content – as with some theorists of action who make room for *akrasia*[5] – the phenomena are faced squarely rather than wished away; and surely this exercise in saving the phenomena is itself a philosophical one. Meanwhile, even (perhaps especially) first-order normative theory needs to explain why real-world agents so often fail by the theory's own lights.[6]

Nonetheless, faced with what, according to this view, is a choice between theoretical naivety and theory – albeit imported from outside the discipline – it is doubtless understandable that philosophers, many of whom take themselves to be nothing if not purveyors of theory, elect to err on the side of the latter. Even so, the importation of theory where inappropriate may itself be naive. This is not only because currently dominant styles of ethical theory, such as those just mentioned, have a highly theorised conception of the ethical, and of practical rationality.[7] It also, as I shall argue, demands an unwarrantedly theory-friendly conception of the material on which theory sets to work.

I shall suggest below that the anti-political reductivism prevalent in current political philosophy expresses a view of politics characteristic of liberal democratic societies. This stance towards politics has not, however, been confined to liberal theory. It is equally to be observed in Marxist (and indeed much non-Marxist socialist) thinking about politics, and is most eloquently summarised by Engels's well-known remark that under communist society the government of people would give way to the administration of things. This again is unsurprising, given some of the other theoretical commitments made by Marxism. In particular, if relationship to the means of production determines class membership, and if class membership determines identity of interest – that is, persons belonging to the same class have *ipso facto* identical interests – then the advent of post-revolutionary classless society will, by communising the means of production, bring with it a fundamental identity of interests.

The notion of an identity of interests can bear more than one interpretation, and the mere fact that you and I have, under some description, an interest in (getting) the same thing does not rule out, and indeed may precipitate, conflict between us. But in the sense in which Marx and Engels seem to have understood the identity of interests which they held to ensue upon common membership of the proletariat, there would have been no conflicts in communist society. In Marx's vision of post-revolutionary society, the political disputes of the past were to be supplanted by fine-tuning at the margin. Politics would cede to administration, or (as Trotsky put it) the rule of man over man would yield to that of man over nature. [8]

The rejection of politics is the more puzzling, given that many of those already mentioned subscribe to the pluralist doctrine that there is a multiplicity of reasonable conceptions of the good, such that dispute between them is rationally interminable, each of which is supported by a defensible conception of what is reasonable, and is so related to its preferred policy objectives that its support for those objectives is, in its own terms, reasonable. As I note in Chapters 6 and 7, this is the starting-point for some recent contributions to political theory – but then a philosophical resolution, in the form of principles determining political design, will have to be carried through in spite of pluralism rather than with its help. If pluralism in this sense – that there is a plurality of equally reasonable conceptions of ultimate principles to structure political design – is true, the prospects for any very general account of distributive justice look poor. This is Gray's point,[9] to which I return in Chapter 8.

Other methodological assumptions have contributed to shaping the discipline's current profile. Notable among these is the implied relation of current practice in political philosophy to its own history. In the past two or three decades the work of many historians of political philosophy has been more methodologically self-aware and contextualist in approach, especially that of the contextualist or 'Cambridge' school of historians of political thought.[10] The contextualist school has held the positivist view that there is a uniquely right, or at least best, interpretation to be recovered from studying historical texts (such as texts in the history of political thought). This methodological turn has largely bypassed political philosophers. This may, in itself, be a good thing: there is reason to doubt that contextualism not only can, but even ideally could, achieve a uniquely correct interpretation. Apart from familiar questions of hermeneutic circularity, there is also the problem of determining non-circular criteria for fixing contextual relevance. Intractable difficulties also attend the strong form of semantic realism which Skinner's approach demands – not because there are problems in defending a truth-conditional semantics, but because it is far from clear, even in principle, what the relevant truth-conditions would consist in. Given that, the theoretical space exists for radical disagreement over what counts as hermeneutic success, even within a blankly realist view of truth-conditions.

More notable for present purposes, however, is that the project of political design, if viable, would leave it quite unclear why present-day political philosophers should take any professional interest in their discipline's history (assuming that on this approach there was something with sufficient institutional or thematic integrity to constitute such a history). My aim is not to endorse the contextualist approach, but to suggest that divergence in practice between historians and contemporary practitioners of political philosophy itself betokens a form of reductivism. Contextualists are wont to claim that the historical specificity of the texts' production makes them inapplicable to the very different political circumstances of modernity; but, in reaffirming that these texts are applicable to modern political conditions, contemporary political philosophers do not implicitly claim that these conditions are, after all, relevantly similar to those of ancient Athens, or seventeenth-century England. What underlies this sharp difference between historians of political thought and contemporary political philosophers is unlikely to be disagreement about the similarity between the circumstances of modern politics and those in which the classic texts were produced. Few contemporary political philosophers influenced by earlier thinkers believe that the warrant for writing political philosophy as they do lies in resemblances between contemporary political conditions and those of Kant's Prussia, or classical Athens. And indeed any plausible comparative analysis between modern politics and those of eighteenth-century Königsberg, or fourth-century BC Athens, will disclose major cultural differences.

This does not make most political philosophers believe that their discipline's history is irrelevant to their concerns – on the contrary. But the classic texts bequeathed to the present are taken on the whole to be hermeneutically transparent. Perhaps there is no thought behind this at all. But if there is any thought, it is likely to be that (as historians of political thought once believed) the 'transhistorical' or 'timeless' truths in the canon forestall problems of interpretation. Thus political philosophers who use historical texts in this way implicitly claim that what guarantees the applicability of these texts to modern times is their implementation of a suitably timeless body of truths. But since political conditions are *ex hypothesi* subject to historical mutability, that timeless content must lie somewhere else – usually, in the timeless truths of morality, or of practical rationality.[11]

To the extent that a text qualifies for the canon by memorably addressing a set of timeless concerns, it comes ready-interpreted. These concerns are not, however, usually taken to be political. In practice they amount to the implicit belief that there are 'truths' of ethics or human nature which transcend the contextual particularity of the texts' production. Since this is taken to comprehend the political circumstances in which the texts were written, it is inferred that their philosophical value lies not merely outside these circumstances, but outside politics *tout court*. Thus there is a dichotomy between politics, as the sphere of historically conditioned particularity, and an apolitical set of concerns, and the works' philosophical merit consists in their account of the latter.

It is noteworthy that Machiavelli, for example, seldom features among the avowed historical influences of modern-day political philosophers. Machiavelli points repeatedly at the force, contingency and mutability of politics. He affirms the political, and in doing so cuts back the room for ethical concerns – at least where these provide an independent set of practical reasons which are then simply imposed on politics. This Machiavellian stance is not, however, the basis on which teaching and research in the subject proceeds. Contemporary political philosophers do not take theirs to be a discipline without a history, or whose historic texts are now of no more than antiquarian interest. If anything, the resurgence of interest in political philosophy has been marked by a sharply increased interest in its history. The influence of Kant on Rawls,[12] of Hobbes on Gauthier, Mill on Gray, Locke on Nozick, Aristotle on Galston, Marx on Cohen, Hegel on Taylor[13] – to name but a few – testifies to this. Indeed, the political philosophy syllabuses of many (probably most) anglophone universities are largely given over to historical texts, with a coda for the study (again, usually text-based) of 'contemporary' work.

These curricular idiosyncracies may not be due to the fact that modern political philosophers reject Machiavelli's analysis of politics. While there are certainly major differences between the political circumstances of sixteenth-century Florence and the modern world, the relapse into normative theorising may be explained not by the thought that Machiavelli's view of politics is no longer applicable, but that it is all too applicable. The desire to eliminate contingency from ethics is a dominant strand in much current (particularly Kantian) moral theory.[14] In this respect real-world politics is apt to appear irrational, and requiring rational control. Insofar as it figures at all, politics is taken to require historical inquiry rather than philosophical analysis. This assumption reinforces the demarcation between political philosophers and historians of political thought.

Anglophone political philosophy is nowadays largely practised as a branch of 'applied' ethics. Discussion occurs at what I shall call the level of *political design* – that is, the level at which political structures, institutions and procedures, are determined philosophically. This generality of approach is inherited from Rawls. But it is not obvious that the philosophy of politics should merely concern itself with normative questions. Even if it does, it need not be, or aim to be, prescriptive. And even if it is prescriptive, it is not obvious that political design should be the object of the prescriptions. There are other ethical dispositions, than conformity to rules prescribed institutionally, which even a theory of justice may judge worthwhile. Indeed it may be thought worthwhile to cultivate the ethical dispositions (for example, that to act justly) directly, rather than mediately, by way of institutions, principles, procedures, and so on.

It is fair to ask why this reductivist programme in political philosophy is so widely pursued, if it is as odd as I allege. I address this question below.

The rejection of politics

My major explanation of the reductivist tendency will invoke politics itself, and not just theorising about it. The rejection of politics is a phenomenon witnessed well beyond academic political philosophy. The most basic reason for the rejection of politics is mistrust of it, and the distaste which political practice, and political professionals, so often engender.

There are also academic reasons. One is based on fear that the discipline may degenerate into something less respectable – something tainted by empirical considerations, such as political science. So, faced with two possible directions of collapse, political philosophers have stuck to pure analysis, although many distinguished political philosophers in the canon have been engaged one way or another in a form of descriptive enterprise. This is true of, among others, Aristotle, Machiavelli, Hobbes, Harrington, Burke, Herder, Hegel, Marx and Mill. It is implausible to think that in the *Politics*, for example, Aristotle believed himself to be simultaneously pursuing two quite distinct forms of intellectual inquiry; one 'pure', the other part-empirical.

As Ball[15] has indicated, political philosophy over the past generation or so has felt a forceful reaction against unduly scientistic assumptions about the analysis of politics – particularly where the view of science informing those assumptions was verificationist (itself a hangover from a longer-standing empiricist tradition of thought about science), with its dualism of 'fact' and 'value'. Since verificationism was hard to defend, so also were the characteristic philosophical positions (for example, emotivist analysis of the semantics of moral terms such as *good, ought,* and so on) which were held to entail it, including the positivist duality of normativity and description. This reaction, however, has its double-minded aspect. In one direction, the blurring of the fact/value distinction has perhaps curbed political philosophers' diffidence about normativity, while in the other, description has become the domain of 'political science', to be sharply distinguished from the inquiry in which political philosophers engage themselves – the latter move being apparently motivated by the very distinction which the first regards as discredited.

Whatever the explanation for this may be, the effect has been to clear a space between empirical study of politics and the discipline of political philosophy. What that space would contain, were it filled, would be philosophical reflection on the nature of politics as it is practised. This is not to say that this reflection would take the form of pure description – though certainly not because the activity of philosophising precludes description.[16] Like metaphysics, politics provides materials for descriptive philosophical analysis, some of which I shall consider later in this chapter. This is not to say that philosophers can look on the phenomena with the normatively unclouded eye of classical empiricism. There is a familiar Davidsonian argument to show that it is a condition of intelligibility that observers, *qua* visiting anthropologists, impute to their subject beliefs which they, the observers, regard as reasonable – and that extends to normative beliefs.[17] But even if there is no descriptive project which can coherently dispense with normative assumptions, that project will still be quite different from that of most current disciplinary practice. The further step, which is to be challenged, moves from the inescapability of normative commitment to the current philosophical conception of the project itself, and particularly that version of it which proceeds via meta-ethical foundationalism.

One reason for the temporary 'death' of political philosophy in the 1950s[18] was, as noted above, that the methods of philosophical analysis then fashionable seemingly left little room for this approach to the discipline. While contemporary political philosophers engage far more with texts in the history of their discipline than do their colleagues in other branches of philosophy, they still proceed on hermeneutic assumptions dismissed by many practising historians of political thought as philosophically naive. I also noted earlier that the belief, to which political philosophers practising in this way are usually committed, that there are transhistoric concerns or truths contained in the classic texts, assumes that the task of interpretation has already been accomplished.

In practice this has meant that political philosophers have theorised about what they *could*. The thinking runs roughly as follows. Philosophical inquiry about a subject-matter such as politics essentially involves theorising about it; a condition of theorising in this philosophical way is the analysis of concepts current in the subject at hand; so, unless the subject admits of such analysis, the inquiry will not be a philosophical one. Exponents of the discipline purvey analyses of politics' conceptual content, and those concepts held to be most analytically interesting or important are usually ethical ones. The possibility that this kind of analysis might not be the only mode of theorising about politics, let alone that theorising might not be the only mode of philosophising about politics, has been largely ignored.[19]

There is a further reason for the reductive tendency in political philosophy, related more closely to the themes of this book. As a methodological stance, this reductivism itself expresses assumptions about the nature of politics which, as I shall argue, are widespread both in the academy and among professional politicians – a view I shall label *instrumentalism*. This is the view that political reasoning is means-end; that political objectives are determined extra-politically; and that individual-level practical rationality is to be taken as the model for collective (that is, political) rationality. Political instrumentalism holds that politics exists to serve ends which are prior and external to it, and that political deliberation raises no special problems not to be found in individual practical reasoning.

Instrumentalism implies a certain relationship between political activity and civil society, which also invites the form of methodological reductivism I have outlined. The implied relationship is that politics merely fills two complementary roles – negatively, to referee civil society conflicts when they occur, and positively, to facilitate the pursuit of civil society interests or conceptions of the good by using appropriate managerial techniques. As a result, philosophical reflection on politics is attenuated, or transformed into something else.

There are a number of reasons for this reductivism. First, instrumentalism's implied conception of practical rationality is borrowed from well-known positions in the philosophy of action, making reductivism in this direction attractive. Where these are not explicitly Humean, they are at least of a recognisably *zweckrational* form. This instrumentalism need not result from the view that politics is regarded as merely being a vehicle for producing certain kinds of good, otherwise unavailable, such as those dependent on central coordination of agents' preferences. Second, since politics is held by instrumentalism to serve ends which are determined extra-politically, politics itself is made to appear a non-autonomous and externally driven activity – a service industry with occasional (and hard to sustain) ethical pretensions. There is as a result little acknowledgement that the ends to be pursued may be rationally modified in the course of political engagement, let alone that politics itself might constitute a non-instrumental good. In consequence, the managerialism described by MacIntyre[20] tends to hold sway.

Third, and perhaps in part because of this, politics is apt to look at best like jobbery, in which competing interests vie. At its worst it may seem like a consuetudinary outlet for psychopathy. With this conception of politics in mind, theorists going back as far as Plato have thought that politics had better be brought within a set of regulative, if not constitutive rules, and ethical norms seem fit for this task. Fourth, once individual rationality has been taken as the model for its collective counterpart, it is hard to see why there is anything special about politics. On one particularly clear form of instrumentalist model, the 'world-agent' version of utilitarianism devised by Hare, politics simply is the aggregating of desires for and against presented courses of action – political conflict turns out to be a form of individual-level desire-conflict. Here, again, the pull towards reductivism is strong.

So, seen like this, reductivism is the natural progeny of instrumentalism. Like all forms of reductivism, it offers simplification, by showing that one subject-matter can be translated, without remainder, into another. But this can only seem possible given an over-simplified view of the original subject-matter. My goal in this book, accordingly, is to offer both a non-instrumentalist view of politics and, in doing so, to question current methodological commitments within the discipline.

I have suggested that there are clear theoretical reasons why recent political theory has taken the course it has. There are also good reasons in political practice why this should have been so. This should not be surprising, if political philosophers' conception of the proper remit of their discipline is coloured by wider assumptions about the nature of politics. In part the latter issue from expectations which it is in the interest of politicians themselves to promote.

The anti-political bias of political philosophy is partly a result of instrumentalist thinking by those involved in politics. The methodological assumptions informing the dominant style of contemporary political theory derive from a view of politics which holds that it aims at its own supersession. This is a view which democratic politicians have an interest in reinforcing. For democratic political cultures necessarily project a view of politics as instrumental to the wishes of those, the electorate, responsible for having put the politicians into power. To emphasise the autonomy of political processes, particularly in circumstances such as those of most modern states, where the opportunities for direct participation by citizens in political decision-making are very limited, is to expose the contradiction within democratic culture itself (and to court future electoral disaster). Circumstances in which the electorate habitually fails to exercise power can be concealed only by subordinating the rationale of politics to those occasions on which they do. There is, then, good prudential reason for politicians to play down the importance of politics and its impact on citizens' lives, except insofar as it services their electorally expressed wants.

That politicians have a vested interest in marginalising politics is not only due to limits on democratic participation. It also articulates a wider fear of disempowerment, which results from the opacity of much modern social life and citizens' well-founded belief that they are increasingly subject to forces – economic, technological, political – lying beyond their control. The managerial style characteristic of instrumentalist politics meets these fears by projecting itself as efficient – itself a form of technical expertise – but also as limited. Since part of the fear is of the power of politics itself, politicians have to steer carefully between over- and underemphasising their own instrumental effectiveness. The characteristic rhetoric of modern politics is thus of security, consolidation, and indemnity against radical change. The upshot, unsurprisingly, is a political culture prioritising Berlin's 'negative' liberties[21] over other objects of political action.

Despite appearances, it is consistent with this to observe that widespread scepticism prevails about the power of politicians to effect real change, at least for the better. This is not confined to radical scepticism about the 'parliamentary' route to effective political action. Partly it rests also on the well-founded belief that economic and technological forces lie largely beyond political control. Though they sometimes expound a rhetoric of control, politicians generally understand this well. They are nevertheless caught in bad faith, where part of their professional rationale is thought to be that they can control forces to which they are in fact largely subservient.

Here, as with other objects of social explanation, it is mistaken to proceed as if politics were some empirical raw material, innocent of thought, on which philosophical reflection then set to work.[22] The cognitive content of politics as an activity will, moreover, include thought of a normative kind. Since any adequate (judged by the explanatory standards set by any conception of social theory which is itself adequate) understanding of politics as an activity will attend to this normative content, it is at least not surprising that the conception of the political to which theoreticians think that their work should be true is one reflecting prevalent normative (less optimistically, ideological) assumptions. The filters may operate quite subtly: theory comes to reflect, or share, the assumptions characteristic of liberal democratic thinking. I have argued that, at the most general level, instrumentalist thinking about politics has its counterpart in anti-political political philosophy. These wider assumptions may license an unduly straitened view of what counts as a 'political' conception (of justice, say) while, from the other end, preconceptions about the nature of the phenomena waiting to be discovered are reflected in the conditions which, it is thought, must be satisfied by any philosophical theory aspiring to account for them.

There are then complementary narrowings, of the phenomena on the one side, and the modes of theoretical treatment deemed appropriate to them on the other. A good example is the debate about 'pluralism' discussed in the previous section. Because moral disagreement is often politically important, there is a temptation to run together a descriptive account of the phenomenon with a philosophical position which apparently explains it. This is encouraged by certain assumptions about agency. Philosophical theories are expected to provide theoretical explanations of actors' behaviour. Since philosophers take themselves to be purveyors of theory, it is tempting to fasten onto a theoretical explanation – metaethical pluralism – to explain the phenomena.

It is not merely that this move becomes more compelling if the disagreement is already taken as a manifestation of pluralism. The assumed nature of the protagonists themselves (as with the debate over essential contestability) helps to shape the philosophical conception of the considerations relevant to explaining their disagreement. The descriptive enterprise will however be beside the point if it succeeds merely in generating accounts of the protagonists' reasons which, though capable of *rationalising* their actions, nonetheless fail to explain them. As Korsgaard has argued,[23] there is a non-trivial gap, even on an 'internal' view, between agents' reasons for action, and the motivations on which agents who accept these statements of their reasons act.[24] To the extent that the enterprise is purely explanatory, an error theory may be more fitting. But that enterprise looks non-philosophical, treating of empirical psychological questions.

It may now be objected that the thesis I am advancing is self-defeating. For I have argued that one explanation for the anti-political cast of contemporary political philosophy is a wider political culture of instrumentalism, which appears to make the reductivist project plausible. However, if instrumentalist thinking dominates politics, then political philosophy as currently practised is only doing what I say it should – reflecting political realities. A political philosophy which seeks to do this reflects the instrumentalism which is to the fore in contemporary political practice.

This objection, however, moves too briskly. I have not argued that political philosophy should confine itself to the bland replication of dominant habits of thinking in politics. To say that political philosophy should address the nature of political practice is not to condemn the discipline to unambitious descriptivism. It is, however, to engage more fully with the phenomena of politics as they are. One role for political philosophy is precisely to expose tacit thinking about the nature and limits of the political, and understand how these habits of thought pervade both academic and lay thinking about the subject.

There is a further reason for the popularity of anti-political attitudes both inside and outside the academy, which expresses the defeated hopes of instrumentalist thinking about politics. In one form it is to be found in the thought that politics is too maladapted an instrument to achieve the political objectives they favour. Certainly recent decades have worsted hopes of radical social engineering – at least in the direction of greater equality or social justice, rather than of their opposites. It is tempting then to reject the political processes which negated these hopes. The developments which I have described in political philosophy parallel the withdrawal from national politics of those whose opposition to the status quo is channelled into activism perceived by its practitioners as non-, or even anti-political. The recent popularity of single-issue activism in the service of causes such as environmentalism and animal welfare, embracing hitherto politically antagonistic social groups, clearly illustrates the process.

That activism also represents the rejection of power as power.[25] This is a more radical rejectionism than mere dissatisfaction with the dominant political order. The rejection is not just of politics as it is, but of the very idea of politics, and in particular of power. It is not hard to see how the conditions for the first form of rejectionism may give rise to those of the second, by adaptive preference formation. For if the hopes that politics would deliver the instrumental goods have been disappointed, it is tempting to think of oneself as having at least remained unsullied by power, and by the moral compromises which power may bring with it. But belief that the world should, let alone that it could, be structured without power is a fantasy of omnipotence. That fantasy – which is in many ways *the* fantasy – consists in its idea of eliminating power, by exercising power.

This, again, is illustrated by attitudes prevalent among single-issue campaigners, such as those already mentioned: whatever may be said on behalf of, or against, animal welfare campaigners, the intended beneficiaries of this activism are unlikely to face what might be called (after the *Animal Farm* character) *Napoleon's Dilemma*: how to seize and wield power on behalf of the dispossessed, without repeating the corruption of the old order. The beneficiaries are also (unlike the classical proletariat) unlikely to turn on their tribunes to charge them with incompetence or class betrayal. Moreover, the fantasy of renouncing power can be preserved, given that its use is unaccountable to its constituency.

To this extent instrumentalism about politics tends to its own annihilation. For politics is usually seen as inefficient in promoting even the narrowly drawn instrumental goods, and then the urge among those who desire them to dispel cognitive dissonance is strong. It makes itself felt in the conclusion that there is something imperfect about politics as it is, and that an ideal world would dispense with it. The temptation then is to reject the very idea of political instrumentality, and imagine a world in which it is unnecessary. But this again is fantasy: no such world could exist. The reason why not is both more fundamental and in some respects less plangent than some writers have supposed. It follows not from supposed truths about the nature of value, but very basic facts about conflicts between ends.

It is also undeniable that political activity is not merely ugly when in progress, but often brutal in its effects. As Camus famously said, the great crimes of the twentieth century have been political crimes. This does little for the standing of the profession. Political crimes are more vivid and memorable than the humdrum benefits which may accrue from political action when it goes well. The best that can usually be hoped for from it is deliverance from tyrannies and injustices which have themselves been produced by politics. On the other hand, the evils delivered by political action are seldom seen as merely undoing the goods for which, after all, we have politics to thank. When we consider how to improve on reality it is easy to think that an ideal state of the world would dispense with politics, and that it is tainted even as an instrument of improvement.[26]

Thus an unselfconscious normativity often prevails in modern political philosophy. This seems to be based on a parallel fantasy to the one just noted in practical political activism. The thought of omnipotence readily coexists alongside a confirmed distaste for the real-world exercise of political power. That the moral, or the simply practical life are tainted by bad faith, obliquity and imperfection is no reason to recoil from philosophical engagement with them. Even – indeed especially – an avowedly normative contribution to theory has to explain how the changes it favours (for example, its preferred conception of distributive justice) would survive to implementation in a world where many, often most, side against rather than with it. If they would survive only in modified form, it seems pressing to state how far, and in what ways, the proposals of theory may be acceptably modified during negotiation.

It may be said that the rather local historical explanations for the recrudescence of normative theory presented above must be irrelevant, given that this style of political philosophy has a much longer pedigree than recent anglophone political philosophy. But the return of grand normative theory is a historically specific phenomenon, as noted at the start – one with wider historical origins, as well as local academic ones.

But the objection also seems to assume the truth of a methodological position already criticised, concerning the relation of contemporary political philosophy to its history. That position assumes the cross-historical applicability of texts in the history of political philosophy; but since current political conditions differ widely from those in which many of these texts were written, it is plausible to assume that their applicability to present-day political questions lies somewhere other than in their political content. This, as I have suggested, is their normative content: it is because the normative truths in these texts are timeless that they can be so applied. It then seems plausible to argue that purveying this content is the real business of political philosophy, and the more descriptive type of enterprise is correspondingly marginal.

It is anyway far from clear, particularly on currently fashionable assumptions about the methodology appropriate to the semantic recovery of historical texts, that there is anything with sufficient integrity to constitute a history of thought – not, at least, if that means that its notable practitioners have addressed a more or less fixed, trans-historical agenda of concerns. To the extent that contextualists are justified in rejecting the claim that there is such an agenda, the discipline as currently practised is less beholden to its past than the 'fixed agenda' view requires.

There can be cognitive gain in redescription.[27] Much debate in other areas of philosophy consists precisely in evaluating claims about appropriate redescriptions, such as whether minds are brains, or beliefs functional states, or moral judgements facts. There can also be cognitive gain in a greater degree of methodological reflectiveness than has been shown by most recent political philosophy. But a more far-reaching and valuable product of the descriptive turn is criticism of the major methodological assumptions informing current practice. Politics can be the instrument through which a certain normative conception, of the ideal society, is to be brought into being. It is hard to deny that normative theory does make such an assumption, for unless the assumption is true, normative theory is engaged in a pointless enterprise. Diversity extends to conceptions of the *political* good. A corollary of increased self-reflectiveness might be an awareness of how assumptions concerning the possibility of implementing a certain political order need to be made explicit or challenged, and may reflect unacknowledged beliefs about the nature of politics. If it is to do the job which it sets out to do, normative theory has to scrutinise the conditions of its own possibility. That means examining not only local assumptions informing ideal theory, but also the circumstances in which its prescriptions would be implemented.

Post-politics and beyond

If political philosophy is both to preserve its disciplinary autonomy and to make good the lacunae I have identified, it has to maintain some sense that politics as an activity is special. On investigation, this may prove not to be the case; it may be that there is nothing to be said about politics which is true only of it and of no other field of human endeavour. But if that is not true, there is a point in the philosophical analysis of politics, rather than regarding real-life political activity as the remediable imperfection of a pre-ideal world.

At the minimum this incurs an obligation to explain how the post-political order is implemented. It is obvious, after all, that no theory of justice will command universal assent. This already poses political problems. As Machiavelli said, those who pursue virtue quickly come to grief among so many who are not virtuous.[28] It may even prove, after all, that the goals of a given normative theory are better promoted by pursuing some alternative prescriptions to those which the theory itself enjoins.

As I have already argued, much contemporary theory fails to pay due regard to the autonomy of the political. A major source of this is tacit belief in instrumentalism – according to which politics exists purely to serve external goals. But if we reconstitute politics as a field of ethical agency, the way is open to reconstrue it as manifesting (not just instrumentally producing) certain goods of agency. This is not to say that a philosophical account of political virtue will simply replicate the structures appropriate to describing the virtuous individual: it is, after all, a central tenet of Machiavelli's theory of political virtue or *virtù* that it will not do so.

What would such an account look like? According to a reductivist view, virtue is exhaustively analysed as a disposition, or set of dispositions, to perform those actions for which the most defensible meta-ethical theory calls. There are certain theory-given actions, themselves intrinsically or instrumentally valued, such that virtue is analysed as the disposition to perform them – maximising expected utility, or acting solely from regard for duty, for example. There is however good reason to doubt that focusing exclusively on the structural features of actions fully captures the nature of virtue. This is suggested by Aristotle's remark, that virtue cannot be exhaustively constituted by dispositions to act, since what is required is not just that the agent performs an act of which a given virtue-term is independently predicable (for example, a habitually mendacious person who tells the truth from fear) but that the act is done *as* a virtuous person does it[29]- which in this case means, presumably, that its motivational ground is most perspicuously understood as regard for truthfulness for its own sake. Of course it is possible to reconstrue the dispositions precisely in terms of the theory's own approved account of conduct. But there is no reason to think that these are, or can be, dispositions of character. Not for the first time, we confront the issue of psychological realism in political philosophy. The alternative is a theory which is empty because inapplicable, and inapplicable because not tailored to human agency; it is an apt target for Marx's stricture on theorists who, losing themselves ever further in abstraction from the world, fancy that they are penetrating ever closer to its core.

The characteristic move of the theories of morality and practical reasoning most influential since the Enlightenment is to offer a reductivist analysis. A given moral theory offers its preferred conception of the true or primordial moral concept(s) – usually, a 'thin' concept such as that of the good, or the right – and duly issues a set of theory-approved prescriptions for understanding moral agency; the latter may be construed in terms of states of the agent in acting, or states of affairs aimed at by moral action, or some hybrid of the two. Since the theory-approved prescriptions are usually couched in terms of its preferred thin property, the following reductivist analysis becomes attractive: virtue is to be understood as characterisable exhaustively in terms of dispositions to act so as to conform to the theory-approved prescriptions, the justification for doing so being framed in terms of the thin property (more sophisticated versions, such as Parfit's and Hare's utilitarianism,[30] allow that a theory-approved agent may however not act under a description making essential reference to the property in question).

It should be clear why a programme of research into political virtue is an appropriate response to the criticisms voiced above. Some work in this direction has been done recently by Honig and Shklar,[31] among others, but it is very doubtful that an account of specifically political virtue can be brought within the recently revived interest in 'virtue ethics' in the work of ethical theorists such as Slote and McDowell.[32] Since virtue-concepts prove on the above analysis irreducible to the theoretical apparatus of instrumentalist views of the ethical, they provide a basis for a non-instrumentalist view of politics. This is, to repeat, not to claim that political virtue can simply be read off from the patterns of ethical evaluation appropriate to individual or private virtue. The forms of agency of which political virtue is predicable may differ radically from virtuous action in private life. One quite general reason for this lies in the Aristotelian remark already mentioned: if part of the *differentiae* of virtuous conduct lies in the way in which actions are done, it may simply be that there is insufficient resemblance between the forms of agency practicable in the private and public sphere for wholesale transposition (which, again, questions a defining thesis of instrumentalism).

It is not my aim to sketch here a more specific account of political virtue. It is unlikely, however, that a satisfactory account will be simply a sub-station of a wider moral theory, or that it will be separate from psychological and ethical (in the sense now of character-based) considerations, or that it will license procedural and decisionistic accounts of practical reasoning. There is room for significant debate between political philosophers both at a descriptive level and at a meta-ethical level as well.

My suggestions about the direction which future research in the discipline should take inevitably reflect my own theoretical commitments. But this does not mean that the research programme proposed must take a neo-Aristotelian form. Below I set out suggestions as to the direction which future research in the discipline might take. I do not deny of course that some interesting work has already been done in the areas listed – indeed, some of it is cited in the annotations. Nor is it intended that the list be exhaustive. The belief which drives the argument of this book is that the conception of the discipline implicit in current work is unduly narrow and has a constricted sense of its possibilities.

Further topics might include: the nature of political corruption, and the loss of political virtue; consideration of general questions of legitimation, not necessarily with reference to the notion of political obligation; the problem of 'dirty hands' and general questions concerning the relation between ethics in politics and elsewhere; non-idealised conceptions of public discourse, its form and content; the nature of public deliberation and of political argument; the imaginative structures created by political participation, and their modification in action; issues of public rationality, with regard (for example) to the design and functioning of political institutions and other corporate bodies; the form and possible justification of political lying, and its relation to mendacity in other areas of life; the nature of political rhetoric, and the role of the emotions in public decision-making, and the political relevance of particular emotions, such as fear, anger, pride, shame, and so on; the nature of political judgement, and its role in generating political action; general issues as to the nature of the political, its scope and limits, whether or not it admits of naturalistic or realistic definition, and to what extent a citizen's implicit understanding of the political can be rendered explicit, and more generally the significance of implicit understanding in political life; consideration of the constraints within which political action is conducted, for example, in democratic polities; the nature of public reason, for example, in relation to debates within ethical theory and the philosophy of action concerning 'internal' and 'external' reasons and the nature of individual rationality; the distinction between 'public' and 'private' realms, and more generally the nature of the 'public'; the nature of political failure; political epistemology, including reflection on the possible forms of public cognition, and the distinction (if any) between public and individual knowledge-acquisition; the nature of political power, particularly as regards its impact on public rationality; the nature of political myth, and its significance for political thought and action; the nature and justification of political violence; political ontology, and philosophical investigation into the kinds of object to which an understanding of politics is necessarily committed. One important question in this area concerns the nature of the sovereign state.

As might be gathered from several of the research topics suggested above, there is room in my view for more philosophical discussion of bad politics. At the end of his book *Liberalism and the Limits of Justice*, Michael Sandel remarks that when politics goes well, we can know a good which we cannot know alone.[33] This may be true. But equally, when politics goes badly, we can know a good which we cannot know alone. That may, moreover, be the best that can be hoped for. This political imperfectionism is not very current in contemporary political philosophy, with some notable exceptions.[34]

In one way my argument suggests that the ambitions of philosophy in its approach to politics should be curbed. But in another, that the problems in the discipline which I have examined require not less, but more (or at least better) philosophy. I certainly believe that the arguments given above should give pause for thought to those who think that philosophy can pre-empt, or replace, political engagement. I suspect – though without claiming to have established as much – that there are sharper limits on the scope for fruitful general theorising about politics than many of those who currently take themselves to be purveying 'political theory' suppose. But the positive programme outlined above requires a greater amount of philosophical reflectiveness, and in more ways than one. In one respect this demands more of what is known, in the currently fashionable misnomer, as 'meta-philosophy': that is, reflections, of the kind presented above, on what political philosophers are doing. That is not of course to demand that they concur with my own observations. In a second respect, as noted already it calls for checks – delivered by theoretical reflection – on the aspirations of theory itself. But what is needed above all is more politics.

2
Philosophy, Politics and Contestability

Introduction

Recent essays in political philosophy have embraced certain kinds of reflectiveness, while largely ignoring others. One example of the latter comes to the fore when we ask whether the answer to the question just posed is the same as the answer to the question, 'What makes political philosophy political?' In post-Rawlsian mode the core project has been taken to be the application of normative arguments to politics – for example, working up intuitions about justice into general distributive principles, while failing to ask how that project itself stands in relation to politics. The issue, roughly, is whether the nature of the *philosophical* project, as currently conceived within liberalism, is such as to make it no longer recognisably 'political'.

The overriding concern is with the attempts made within recent liberalism to circumscribe politics philosophically. The initial discussion is of essential contestability and its role in explaining political disagreement. The general thesis also raises the possibility, of course, that the term 'politics' itself may be essentially contested. I argue however that the thesis in its general form is threatened with incoherence. It violates plausible constraints on concept-possession, and in effect relies on an esoteric doctrine which short-circuits the thesis's original explanatory rationale, or else an error theory. Hence what sets out to provide a theoretical account of a pervasive political phenomenon turns away from the world of politics, towards an explanatorily redundant ideal theory.

By contrast I shall suggest that a more worthwhile enterprise may be to *reverse* the direction of explanation. Rather than its being the case that the political disputes (as Gallie and other proponents[1] of the thesis believed) are explicable by facts about conceptual structure, it may be part of what makes these matters of practical concern political that they occasion dispute. This is not meant to constitute an *ultimate* explanation. Maybe these disputes also take their rise from some quite other quarter, such as fundamental conflicts of value, or ideology.

These criticisms of the essential contestability thesis are not however intended to defend the possibility of either rational or *de facto* convergence in political judgements. What is political may itself be an irreducibly *political* matter. This may explain the unconvincingness of attempts to provide definitions of the political, and in particular a common infirmity of attempted definitions – the tendency of the *definiendum* to crop up in the would-be *definiens*. I shall suggest towards the end that reflection on this fact provides the basis for a transcendental argument questioning the liberal philosophical project of political design itself.

The project of political design

Modern liberalism engages in a rather specific kind of philosophical project. That is to arrive by philosophical argument a specification of the political procedures and institutions governing an ideal (liberal) society, in accordance with an independently derived conception of ethical requirements – one based, for example, on attention to the requirements of justice as 'the first virtue'[2] of society. The project, thus glossed, is to turn philosophical reflection to political account. It relies on philosophical argument to design politics. So on this view philosophy operates *prior* to politics, providing a framework within which the political is played out. The most popular current version of this approach is liberal *neutrality*, but it also extends to liberal *perfectionism*. I shall say a little about each of these in turn.

This is perhaps seen most clearly in the most philosophically prominent version of modern liberalism, namely neutrality. I take it that the most widely canvassed form of argument for liberal neutrality is an *insufficient-reason* argument.[3] This runs as follows. First, it is said: no attempt to justify political design succeeds which rests on insufficient reasons. Then follows a claim about the nature of value, knowledge about value, or conceptions of the good; the claim may be for example epistemic scepticism about value, a version of value-pluralism, or the claim that no conception of the good is such that it cannot be reasonably rejected, or a direct claim to the effect that there is insufficient reason to prefer certain conceptions of the good over certain others in cases where the values or conceptions of the good conflict (for example, about the nature of political design). It is then said that this entails that attempts to justify conclusions which rest on such values or conceptions of the good rest on insufficient reasons – including, in particular, attempts to justify political design which are controversial between the values or conceptions. Therefore these attempts fail. What we are left with, *faute de mieux*, is a justification of political design which rests on no claim which is controversial between the competing values or conceptions of the good; which is a version of the neutrality doctrine. Versions of the argument appear in the work of Rawls, Larmore, Barry, Scanlon and Habermas.[4]

Much has been written by political scientists and others about the concept of the political. It is not really my aim to provide another analysis of the concept, which experience suggests is a hazardous enterprise. Just to provide a brief illustration of the problems which this analysis encounters, we might consider the title of Adrian Leftwich's book *Redefining Politics*.[5] The main proposition advanced in the book is that western political science needs to broaden its understanding of politics by comparative anthropological studies. The issue here is not the value of such studies, but whether they can contribute to a project called 'redefining' politics. If we wish we can redefine 'politics' to mean whatever we like. But that would be a matter of purely lexicographic interest – in particular, it would tell us nothing of interest about politics. That the comparative anthropological studies by contrast may tell us something of interest about it testifies to the fact that the book is working *within* the 'definition' (whatever that may be) of 'politics' which we already have.

Similarly, it is sometimes said that 'politics' is an inherently normative concept, so that 'political' is construed as meaning something like 'ought to be political' .The problems here are obvious: we get the *definiendum* cropping up regressively in the would-be *definiens*. More saliently, though, if what is being offered here purports to be a definitive analysis of the concept – one which provides analytical truths about it – it seems that it fails. To say 'This is political, but it oughtn't to be', for example, doesn't seem to be incoherent in the way that, it *does* seem incoherent on its face to say, for example, 'You're justified in doing [or saying] that, but you ought not to be.' We then need to know why the *endoxa* (to use an Aristotelian term)[6] of the political fail to bear on the analysis, and what in their absence could do so.

One possible response to this is to suggest that the *political* is a prime instance of Gallie's 'essentially contested' concepts, endorsed by numerous other prominent political theorists – Alasdair MacIntyre, Christine Swanton, David Miller, William Connolly, Andrew Mason and John Gray among them.[7] The thesis offers an explanatory claim about real-world political activity. William Connolly has remarked that it is among the thesis's merits that it restores the autonomy of politics in the face of the reductivist tendencies of recent theory.[8] Connolly's reason for saying this (and the rationale for the thesis itself) is that the thesis explains how those involved in political arguments can disagree, as a consequence of certain features of the concepts figuring in their votaries' characteristic assertions. This should be distinguished from the claim that the thesis explains how the disputants may *reasonably* disagree, as we will see. I will, nonetheless, argue that the thesis is self-defeating, insofar as it aims to provide an *explanatory* claim about political disagreement. The alleged contestability of the *political* itself, I will suggest afterwards, can be given a different explanation.

I will take the *essential contestability thesis* as the following claim:

ECT: There are certain key concepts in political argument, which are essentially such that they both (a) admit of a variety of interpretations, and (b) are disputable.

This is Swanton's definition.[9] The thesis was first advanced by Gallie and has latterly been endorsed, albeit in modified forms, by Swanton, Connolly and Mason.[10] According to both Connolly[11] and Mason,[12] the essential contestability of politically significant concepts like those referred to above consists not merely (as Gallie's account had emphasised) in the fact that such concepts are intrinsically appraisive and internally complex in ways that enable disputants to assign different weightings to their constituent elements, but also in the fact they may also *interpret* the concepts differently. One consequence of this is taken (by Mason) to be that the disputants may hold mutually incompatible views of what counts (within a given set of practical options) as best expressing, or promoting, the concept and its associated value(s).

The interpretative claim advanced by ECT may be reinforced by the following *reasonable disagreement thesis*:

RDT: the concepts' interpretations may be (a) mutually inconsistent (b) individually reasonable, and (c) such that there is none which is justifiably regarded as superior to its rivals.[13]

We should contrast ECT and RDT with a rival claim, which simply provides a *descriptive* account of *political disagreement*, as follows:

DPD: Certain key concepts in political argument often, as a matter of brute fact, give rise to irresolvable disagreement, for example, over their extension.

It is important to distinguish the conceptual claims from DPD, which simply describes a set of political phenomena. The fullest and most recent account of the political significance of ECT and RDT has been given by Mason in his book *Explaining Political Disagreement.* Mason asserts that:

> According to essential contestability theses, there is a non-trivial sense in which disputes over the application of political terms such as 'democracy', 'freedom', and 'social justice' are *political* disputes.[14]

Thus the thesis promises to restore the *political* as an irreducible explanatory notion.[15] I shall endorse Mason's claim that these disputes are political, but shall argue that essential contestability provides no explanation as to *why* these disputes exist, nor why they are political (nor does DPD, which simply describes the phenomena of disagreement rather than explaining them). By contrast, a minimal and therefore minimally contentious characterisation of the political can offer a rival functional explanation of the phenomena of disagreement, as I shall argue at the end of the chapter.

Problems with the thesis

In this section I shall present two lines of argument. The first will conclude that RDT, the reasonable disagreement thesis, demands an untenable account of the conditions of concept-possession for contested concepts themselves. Second, I shall argue that the defender of the thesis is faced with a fork: either the thesis leads to contradiction, or it results in explanatory redundancy. I shall reinforce these conclusions, first by adverting to specific problems which arise when we press the modal claim made about contested concepts by the reasonable disagreement thesis, and then by considering a suggestion by Swanton which is designed to salvage the thesis. In both cases, I shall argue, the thesis's explanatory power is vitiated.

Possession-conditions

A plausible account of the conditions to be satisfied by anyone possessing a given concept *C* must, I suggest, include the following:

P: It is a necessary condition of the distinctness of any given concept *C* that it is individuated by its possession-condition(s).

In effect *P* says that the distinctness of any given concept *C* entails that any individual possessing *C* does so by meeting possession-conditions unique to it. To show the plausibility of *P*, suppose, contrary to hypothesis, that there are distinct concepts sharing their possession-condition(s). Then there is some single set of possession-conditions, in virtue of which a concept-user can be said to have mastered both of the concepts (it should be noted that this makes no commitments as between realist and anti-realist accounts of possession-conditions). If, however, they are distinct, their distinctness must manifest itself, at least in principle, in certain in-principle possible circumstances: the distinctness might surface in differential truth-value-assignments by competent concept-users to pairs of propositions differing only in that the term(s) referring to *C* is or are uniformly replaced by one(s) referring to another concept *C′*, or vice versa. But if so, the possession-conditions fail to provide a full account of concept-mastery, since these apply indifferently to both concepts, and so cannot furnish, even in principle, an account of differential recognition by concept-users of those conditions in which one concept, but not the other, applies.

The point can be brought out by considering the following possibility: suppose there are two really distinct concepts which, at the level of resolution available to human concept-users, admit only of a single set of possession-conditions – perhaps as humans we are incapable of formulating the distinctions which individuate the concepts in question, though the distinctions really exist. This would therefore be a counter-example to *P*, since in the imagined situation we have two really distinct concepts which are nonetheless not individuated by their possession-conditions. How, then, could the possession-conditions met by any human concept-user be thought of as individuating the one concept, rather than the other? By hypothesis, human concept-users are incapable of distinguishing them; nonetheless, again by hypothesis, the concepts are distinct. But then it seems that an insufficient-reason argument applies: there is insufficient reason in each case to regard the possession-conditions as being those of one concept, rather than the other. So it is true of each concept, taken by itself, that there is insufficient reason to identify the possession-conditions as the possession-conditions of *that* concept. Therefore they cannot be of either concept, but (at best) of some third one. So this possibility is not a counter-example to *P*, after all.

The possession-conditions set out by *P* cannot be satisfied by the concepts, because the individuation of concepts by their possession-conditions is inconsistent with ECT. Suppose that parties to a dispute about the concept both meet the same set of possession-conditions of the concept. They will, nevertheless, differ in linguistic and other dispositions, such as patterns of assent to sample propositions referring to the concept under dispute, or the referent of the concept. But then for each disputant we can extrude a distinct concept, so defined that *its* possession-conditions are such as to duplicate exactly those of the concept to which the disputant refers – the concept in question simply being *defined* as that whose possession-conditions give rise to the differential patterns of assent and dissent. But these will be distinct from each other. Then the (unitary) concept which, according to ECT, is under dispute, will not, contrary to *P*, be individuated by its possession-conditions.

It should not be surprising that the concepts fail this test. For only if the possession-conditions consisted in grasping some unitary set of properties – such as those properties because of which the concepts are essentially contestable – could they satisfy *P*. But then, because they would be working with the *same* concept, there would be no basis for disagreement, as we have already seen.

Explanatory redundancy

Suppose two parties disagree about an issue involving justice. What warrants saying that the two parties are disagreeing about a single concept *justice*, rather than talking past each other? There may be some common conceptual core to justice, in virtue of which both can be said to have provided a theory of justice – for example, 'the procedures which should govern the methods for determining the holdings of scarce goods in society', or something similar. It seems that we at least need something which characterises justice essentially, in order that the dispute be one about a single concept *justice*. But it would not follow that the concept was essentially contestable from the claims that there existed this common core, and that there were other aspects of the concept on which the parties disagreed. The possibility of such disagreement would have, as it were, to be *built in* to the concept *justice*, as part of its essence. But in that case, the thesis holds that the parties would have to *agree*, on pain of changing the subject, that the other interpretation was possible, and in this case the concept would no longer be contestable; the only way in which they could fail to do this is by making a mistake, or being in ignorance about the nature of the concept. If *justice* is essentially contestable, it has properties which make it such a concept, and these entail the possibility of disagreement. So to deny this possibility means denying that it has properties which are essential properties of the concept *justice*, as exposited by theorists of essential contestability, and so the concept of which the parties' conceptions *are* conceptions cannot be identical with that which those theorists have in view.

There are, in addition, specific problems with the modal claim made by RDT. On its most obvious interpretation, it imputes to the concepts the *de re* essential property of being contestable. A *de re* is a property of the concepts themselves, rather than of the way in which they are referred to: so being the square of 2 is a *de re* property of the number 4. If the thesis is true, then it is an essential property of the concepts that they are contestable, and this means that it is an essential property of any given concept that it gives rise to two or more incompatible interpretations. There are, however, problems in construing the properties imputed to the concepts by the thesis as *de re* modal properties. Suppose that the concepts give rise to logically inconsistent pairs of judgements. If each of these judgements is reasonable, and is generated by those features of a concept *C* in respect of which it is essentially contestable, each is reasonably derived from *C* via divergent interpretations of it, each of which interpretations is itself reasonable. Since the possibility of reasonable disagreement, and hence of the concept's being essentially contestable, depends on the reasonableness of these interpretations, we can say that unless these interpretations of *C* are reasonable, *C* will not in fact be essentially contested. But whatever is of the essence *de re* of a concept *C*, is that without which *C* would not be the concept that in fact it is.

Contestability is of the *de re* essence of *C*, and a consequence of its contestability is that *C* warrants different and reasonable, but inconsistent interpretations. So unless the interpretations of it which issue in the practical judgements p and $\neg p$ are reasonable, *C* will not be the concept it in fact is. However, each party to the disagreement will characteristically deny that the rival practical judgement, and the interpretation associated with it, is reasonable. But then each party to the disagreement must be working with different concepts – different, that is, both from each other and in *each* case from the original concept as construed by the thesis. For in the case of each party the interpretation of *C* is such that, according to that interpretation, it lacks that property (or those properties) which makes the other's interpretation reasonable – but in that case the concepts which the parties are working with must be different from each other, since each party denies that a property which according to the thesis is essential to the concept, is in fact one of its properties. There is then a question about whether either succeeds in securing reference to the concept in question. But if they do, the disputants' claims are erroneous, and the thesis cannot explain why one or both go wrong.

What if the essential property ascribed to essentially contestable concepts were interpreted as a *de dicto*, rather than *de re*, modal property? A *de dicto* property of an object is a property not of the object itself but of the way in which the object is referred to – so a bachelor, *as thus referred to*, has the *de dicto* property of being unmarried. The advantage of this proposal would be that it is consistent with a purely referential occurrence of the concept in the utterances of those contesting it. In particular, it would not be a necessary condition of a speaker's securing reference that he use an expression mentioning the essential property itself. The question then is whether or not the *de dicto* interpretation is defensible, and whether it preserves the explanatory force of the thesis.

There is good reason to doubt both of these. First, it is not very clear what the *dictum* or *dicta* in question would be. Of course there are familiar textbook examples of propositions ascribing *de dicto* essential properties, but that hardly shows that the relevant descriptions are to hand. The most obvious candidate is a proposition which wears the logical form of analyticity on its sleeve, analogous with familiar examples like, 'Necessarily, if *A* is a bachelor, then *A* is an unmarried male.' But it is not easy to think of an analogue for the most frequently mooted candidates for essential contestability. Certainly something along the lines of, 'Necessarily, *democracy* is contestable', does not make an obviously true statement. The danger is that *content-giving* candidates for the *dicta* in question will be precisely those which, so far from being analytical, are the subject of dispute.

There is however a more far-reaching problem with this line of response, which is that on this showing the reasonable disagreement thesis again loses its explanatory force. If what is in view is a *de dicto* modal property, then the property itself is coherently deniable of the concept under an alternative description, just as it *makes sense* to say

'Basil is married' even if, in fact, Basil is a bachelor. This is hardly surprising, since there is no obvious incoherence in a proposition which denies, of any given concept, that it is contestable. Moreover, since certain *descriptions* of the concepts are what are now held to be the bearers of the essential property, whether or not a given concept gives rise to disagreement will depend on the contingent fact of what descriptions are used about it. Thus it will not be the case that it necessarily gives rise to disagreement, that is, that it is necessarily contestable, since its contestability will depend only on how it is referred to.

Thus this interpretation shows only that reference *can* be secured by means of the relevant descriptions, not that it *must* be. As a result, reference can be secured by the protagonists by means of descriptions of which it is not true that they (the descriptions) are essentially contestable. The parties may disagree nonetheless about the extension of the concept. But if so, then the conclusion reached earlier is corroborated: the claim that the concept is *essentially* contestable does no explanatory work.[16]

The explanation might also bring in institutional factors – such as the fact that the disputants often belong to political parties competing with each other for power – which may accentuate disagreement. One alternative explanation is simply that people only disagree about what they *can*. Another is to say that political agents, like others, are sometimes irrational. No doubt it is an occupational infirmity of philosophers, as professional purveyors of theory, to aim at over-theorised explanations of the phenonema on which they reflect. It is however a curious procedure, which insists on political actors' rationality, and a role for philosophy, at the cost of incoherence.

This suggests that essential contestability leaves us without a satisfactory explanation of political disagreement, and in particular without a satisfactory explanation of political disagreement over politics itself. If my argument regarding the explanatory deficiency of the thesis is right, it must rely on an esoteric doctrine. This is true *regardless* of whether the thesis is construed as ECT or the stronger RDT. If it is RDT, then its licensing a plurality of interpretation will fail to explain why the parties think of themselves as disagreeing, rather than reaching a difference without disagreement. If it is ECT, and (as Mason conjectures) there is some interpretation more reasonable than the others, there will not even be a difference of that sort, since with best play the parties should converge on that: if they don't, an error theory will be required, and this will then necessarily *not* use the explanatory thesis itself. The explanatoriness of the thesis can only be sustained by an esoteric doctrine. That doctrine is a philosophical claim about conceptual structure of the contested concepts as set out by Gallie in his seminal article: that they are intrinsically evaluative, may be used aggressively and defensively, have multiple criteria of application, the relative weightings of which are vague or disputable, and so on. In its efforts to understand the political, the thesis in fact succeeds in moving the locus of explanation out of the political and into the philosophical realm.

Essential contestability has ramifications not only for our understanding of disagreements within politics, but of philosophical engagement with its normative content. After all, the thesis (or at least RDT) makes it doubtful whether conceptual analysis can reach normative conclusions regarding the concepts concerned.

The thesis also raises the question whether philosophy can in fact assume an olympian stance above the mêlée. In his book *The Conquest of Politics* Benjamin Barber calls on the essential contestability thesis to contravert neutrality, the thought being that if key concepts like that of justice turn out to be contestable, no form of political design can be substantively neutral.[17] There will simply be plural understandings of justice between which the project of political design must choose. The conclusion indicated by the discussion here, however, is that the thesis can countenance neutrality precisely because it supposes that political disagreement (including, for example, disagreement over the extension of 'politics' itself) masks underlying agreement, on the conceptual structures which Gallie hoped to lay bare. What makes neutrality sustainable is abstracting from the thoughts of political agents themselves. Its precondition is a sharp line between arguments justifiable politically and what is held to be philosophically justifiable.

Swanton

An attempt to defend the claim might be made on the following basis. Christine Swanton argues[18] that for certain concepts, such as that of *distributive justice*, there is no specifiable common core shared by different interpretations of it: '[o]ne may sensibly speak of contested conceptions referring to the same ideal without assuming that there is a core concept common to those conceptions'.[19] She arrives at this conclusion via the claim that 'the fact that terms lack a common meaning does not entail that they lack a common referent'.[20] In the case of the concept *freedom*, for example, there may be certain *endoxa* or 'common conceptions' shared by the 'many or the wise' (such as that free agency entails non-coercion), but uncertainty may reign over how this conception of freedom should be squared with other claims about it (such as that whatever an agent *can* do, he is free to do). Swanton goes on to argue that 'there is little reason to believe that ... there will be a "core concept" of freedom common to all', despite 'a high level of agreement on what is to count as the *endoxa*'.[21]

However, this only puts off the problem. Either the incorporation of the *endoxa* originally mentioned in the final resolutions is essential to their being conceptions of *freedom*, or else it is not. If it is, then it seems, contrary to hypothesis, that there is indeed a core concept, which includes at least the *endoxa* mentioned. But if not, as Swanton claims in the passage cited, it is far from clear on what basis it can be claimed that the conceptions are of a unitary concept. General assent to a proposition (the criterion she cites for determining the existence of *endoxa*) is not sufficient for the terms used in expressing it to share a referent – nor does it show that, despite the putative shared referent, those endorsing the *endoxa* assign to it different 'meanings' (presumably to be understood as distinct Fregean senses of a common referent).

Swanton's claim that the terms may share a referent rests on the assumption that this referent is provided by the *endoxa*. But the bare fact of assent to the *endoxa* is hardly sufficient to demonstrate that there really is a unitary referent. In the light of this, it is hard to see what content there is in her claim that different 'conceptions' may refer to the same 'ideal' – a notion whose status in relation, on the one hand, to the 'conceptions', and on the other, to the concepts themselves, remains obscure.[22] Swanton's argument anyway mislocates the explanation of the disagreement. Either the occurrences of the contested concepts – that is, in sample propositions contested politically – are purely referential or they are not. If they are not, Swanton's argument plainly fails to apply. But if they are, then the principle of substitutability *salva veritate* must hold, since the occurrences of the term are purely referential, and the fact that the parties attach different 'meanings', *qua* Fregean senses, to the term(s) in question is simply irrelevant.

The disagreement is then blankly over truth-conditions – that is, the sort of disagreement which is reducible to the assertion of contradictory propositions – irrespective of whether the parties attach different 'meanings' to the term(s). That means both cannot be true. But then there is no real disagreement: if all that is in play are different Fregean senses, the parties' claims can simply be conjoined. If on the other hand the fact that the parties may engage in different resolutions of the apparently conflicting *endoxa* is held to show that there is a real disagreement, it must be one over truth-conditions, in which case at most one party is right, and conceptual structure fails to explain the disagreement.

Moreover, if the reconstruction of the thesis offered by Swanton has this consequence, it cannot be by adverting to conceptual 'truths' that the dispute is explicable; what is needed instead is some form of error theory. Once again, we are left with an explanatory deficit.

A Wittgensteinian objection

It may be said against this that the argument rests on controversial assumptions about language. For example, it may be said that the neo-Wittgensteinian position from which a number of essential contestability theorists take their bearings simply rejects the linguistic starting-point of the argument I have set out. Detailed discussion of this issue would take us too far afield, but I take it that the main line of objection would run as follows.

The meanings of terms are to be understood as 'family resemblances', or in other words as being based on multiple criteria, whose individual content, and whose weightings with respect to one another, may be indeterminate. There may be a definite or indefinite set of such criteria, but if we examine the linguistic dispositions of native speakers, only a proper subset of them may figure in any individual's semantic mastery. Moreover, the criteria themselves may be indeterminate. This is the *poly-criterial* view of language, of which Gallie's own account of essentially contested terms is a clear counterpart, and contestable concepts' ability to create disagreement arises not from the fact that certain normative properties are given different valuations,[23] but that the standing of the criteria involved is indeterminate in the ways just specified. This neo-Wittgensteinian semantic theory, it may be said, undermines the arguments just advanced.

Take a term like 'justice'. Among the criteria underlying the use of the term might be taken to be the relation of justice to desert, or equality. So, it may be said, it is indeterminate, or subjectively variable, what relative weightings are to be assigned to desert or equality; or what these criteria themselves require (for example, how equality is to be applied in assessing the justice of a procedure, institution or distribution) or what its field of application is (for example, whether it includes our relation to animals, or to future human generations). These considerations are sufficiently elastic to permit subjective variation in applications of the term, while it remains the case that those who evaluate the criteria differently can think of themselves as participating in a shared discourse.

There are however good reasons for doubting whether the essential contestability thesis can be incorporated so smoothly. First, indeterminacy at the level of 'forms of life'[24] does not preclude intersubjective consensus about the way in which a term is to be understood or applied. Wittgenstein indeed sometimes seems to indicate that intersubjective consensus is part of what it is for a term to have a public meaning – that is to say, a meaning.[25] If so, a Wittgensteinian view of language seems not to support an essential contestability view, but to preclude it. In the case of a term like 'justice', the consensus may be pitched at a different level from that of agreement about first-order criteria: it may for example be a disjunction of criteria (or, more probably, a disjunction of conjunctions of criteria). That seems to be the thought underlying Wittgenstein's claim that concept-use relies, in his famous phrase, on 'agreement in judgements'.[26] Whatever the scope for disagreement, this agreement (in the case of justice) will consist in whatever it is that warrants us in recognising an utterance as being about justice.

Second, more importantly, Wittgenstein's view of semantic mastery seems to rule out the idea that meaning can be boiled down to underlying criteria of this sort. Either no such set of guidelines exists, or else the guidelines are insufficient to determine how the term is applied. What secures the meaningfulness of terms is our determination to use them in a certain way, but this natural fact rests on no further, ground-up justification – its sanction is just the brute fact of agreement in judgements. This seems to be the upshot of his well-known sceptical argument against rule-following as a model of semantic mastery. When we attempt to justify a particular way of applying concepts, we quickly find that reasons give out: 'If I have exhausted the justifications, then I have reached bedrock, and my spade is turned. Then I am inclined to say: "This is simply what I do."'[27]

It is not the main point here to engage in Wittgensteinian exegesis. But to the extent that concepts leave room for the indeterminacies just mentioned, the disagreement to which they allegedly give rise vanishes. No coherent account can be given of the truth-conditions of conflicting propositions in which the concepts figure. If it could, the concept itself would prove incoherent, or else there would be a truth-value which would show that one side or the other had made a mistake. If, on the other hand, the difference between the disputants is one of connotation, rather than denotation, there is no reason to regard them as *disagreeing* – any more than there is any necessary disagreement between persons who use 'Aristotle' and 'the Stagyrite tutor of Alexander the Great' to refer to the same individual. The relevant claims can simply be conjoined.

The elusiveness of the political

I want to suggest a more modest explanation for the phenomena which the essential contestability thesis attempts to explain. This will lead, via consideration of a constitutive problem which besets attempts to circumscribe politics by normative philosophical theory, to an argument which relies on a minimal, and I hope minimally controversial, characterisation of the political. And the aim is to show that this characterisation shows both the real source of the phenomena which essential contestability addresses, and why attempts to circumscribe politics are, in a sense, bound to fail. These attempts, as I shall suggest, perpetrate a form of category-mistake.

Politics as an activity admits of a wide variety of different characterisations. Roberto Alejandro,[28] for instance, lists the following, among others:

> a system of rules to realise the good of justice ... the quest for, and institutionalization of, common goods; a practice that defines and encourages the quest for an understanding of the human good; the pursuit of glory (Machiavelli); the pursuit of order (Hobbes); the teaching of the virtues for the sake of the individual's character; the teaching of the virtues for the sake of the public structure; participation to realize the good of the community; participation for its own sake; the creation of state power; a system of principles to address and, if possible, to solve public conflicts; a system of principles to *avoid* conflicts.

I shall not comment on these or other characterisations of the political in detail. Their heterogeneity is apparent. I shall proceed, however, from a different angle – from the *inescapability* of politics. Gregory Kavka plausibly argued that even a world of morally perfect beings would have to contain political actors.[29] One of the more obvious reasons why this is so is that public action requires an agenda – in other words, a set of practical concerns deemed urgent enough for the public to address – and that agenda will not write itself. The possibility of politics lies within the nature of public practical reason itself. But whether or not Kavka is right, any society in which politics exists at all, is one in which the possibility of disagreement exists.

This makes problematic the idealisations which aim to resolve political conflict by generic devices, such as discursive principles.[30] In situations of conflict, the *given* dispositions of the political actors are what made for the political conflict in the first place. The world's being different enough from how it in fact is to make the counterfactual true also tends to deprive it of its original point. As with the essential contestability thesis, what is removed is the motivational states which first created a political conflict. There is then this question about how we get from the no doubt aberrant motivations of the real-world political actors, to comply with the rigorism of theory. One way would be if the actors involved were better or cleverer than they are. But they are not. A political philosophy which aspires to normative prescription would then seem to have to address this, rather than hypothesising a state of the world in which politics has departed from the scene.

I give one example to illustrate the difficulties in this area. Suppose someone – a liberal, perhaps – was interested in toleration, as a distinct political value. This person might then aim to produce a justification of that value. In confronting the *political* circumstances in which toleration might be thought as warranted, however, we run into the following problem. The circumstances where the exercise of toleration is called for politically are precisely those where it does not exist: there is some action, say, which one group of people hope to stop another from doing. If either group were prepared to put up with the preventive action of the other, there would be no political problem. As it is, neither is prepared to do this.[31] The political circumstances of toleration arise where toleration itself has become impracticable. The authorities may nourish preventive ambitions of their own – such as preventing a riot. It looks as if their actions will only count as tolerant if they are motivated in the right way – as the permitting of that of which they disapprove. A desire to keep the peace, for instance, will not in itself constitute a motive to act tolerantly. The theoretical danger is then of substituting the existing motivational states of the protagonists – the ones which create the political problem – for motivations which are more tractable.

Those involved might have chosen to tolerate the disapproved-of activity, and what generates the political issue is the fact that they have failed to do so. It might be thought that these circumstances were peculiar to toleration, but in fact it identifies a pervasive condition of political action. The situation can be characterised functionally: whatever practical issues are not filtered out by other social agencies (for example, commercial, corporate-bureaucratic, or private and other civil society agencies) simply *are* the residuum which politics has to address. Practical decision-making in the public sphere requires the implementation of public policy backed up, if necessary, by the use of power, and this form of action arises from practical indeterminacy, of which one source is the fact that action is imperfectly guided by values such as liberty or equality. The indeterminacy which underlies disputes over liberty, justice, and so on, is the ultimate reason for the ineliminability of politics.

One possibility is that the phenomena of the political life addressed by the essential contestability thesis admit of a different explanation. This would not depend on *specific* characteristics of politics as a concept. The question might be framed by asking how philosophical argument could show how philosophical argument itself is limited, in relation to political phenomena. This seems to leave open a form of transcendental argument, that is, an argument from the limits of a certain form of knowledge to the necessary conditions of that knowledge. In this case the knowledge in question is of what can be justified politically by philosophical argument itself. The conclusion would call into question whether the internal position *can* be justified via a philosophical argument, since what is at issue is precisely *what* philosophical argument as such can justify. The question is how it could be argued philosophically that conclusions established by philosophical argument are prior to and determine the shape of political argument. What is at issue is the standing of one sort of argument with respect to the other, and so we can ask, given that this is the issue, what headway could be made in resolving it by relying on an argument which is itself of one or other sort.

Suppose we adopt this *partial* characterisation of politics: that it is a concept, disputes about whose extension themselves fall within its extension.[32] Put more informally, politics is a concept disputes about which are political.[33] This informal characterisation does indeed include the *definiendum* in the *definiens*. But that may be unavoidable. Note that in this case the 'talking past one another' objection lapses: we cannot say in this case that one party or other may be simply mistaken, or that the two are talking about different subjects, since once the dispute has been identified in this way, it concerns a concept which is, to this extent, shared.

Note that this definition does not claim that *all* disputes are political, only that disputes over what the extension of 'political' is are political. Nor does it identify the meaning of 'political' with that term's extension. All it maintains is that the meaning of the term is such that disputes about its extension are themselves political disputes. The partial definition is not empty, either, since it excludes those concepts disputes about whose extension do not fall within that extension (as is notoriously the case, for example, with 'humorous').

One advantage of this characterisation is that the *deniability* of claims about the scope of the political becomes intelligible. We saw earlier that an explicitly normative characterisation can be met by a denial that a given practical concern (such as sport) *ought* to be political. But the present account makes this denial intelligible, while also not ruling out *a priori* the opposite claim. Even if it is the case that sporting contacts should not be politicised, this claim is itself a political one. The fact of public disagreement over policy is enough to make *this* dispute political, but it does not follow that the claim that sporting relations should not themselves be politicised is unintelligible. What does follow is the plausible conclusion that in these circumstances someone who makes such a claim is liable to find themselves in a pragmatic contradiction.

From the minimal account we can see that the project of circumscribing the political is chimerical. For that requires the prioritising of philosophy over politics, whereas the very attempt to circumscribe politics in this way is itself a political one. The prioritising cannot achieve its aim, since the attempt to do so is in its nature a political act. Of course, it is possible to endorse the claim that the scope of politics should be limited by philosophy; the problem is that that is a judgement subject to political disagreement. Thus the project commits a category-mistake, the mistake of thinking that politics can be purged of disagreement, whereas politics just is the public forum within which disagreement plays itself out, including disagreement about what *counts* as political.

This leaves the possibility that politics is a sphere in which decisions lie beyond justification, or in relation to which the status of justification is indeterminate. This does not mean that there could be no philosophical explanation of why this situation obtains. It would be possible to argue, for example, that the explanation was due to this fact: the concept of politics is such that it itself enters ineliminably into the criteria for applying it. In other words, the suggestion would be that what 'politics' applies to is itself ineliminably dependent on politics itself. This is perhaps the truth in the abortive proposals criticised earlier, as well as helping to explain why they *are* abortive. On this proposal, we would have both an explanation of why attempts of this kind to 'define' politics misfire – the tendency for the *definiendum* to crop up again naggingly in the *definiens*, for example, or the indeterminate status of normativity in relation to attempted definitions of the political – and of the refractoriness to philosophical analysis of the concept of the political itself. It is plausible to think that the question of the relation which normative claims bear to particular tracts of political concern is itself an irreducibly political one.

This would suggest an obvious reason why the essential contestability thesis, which I take to be a *philosophical* thesis designed to explain certain political phenomena, fails to do its explanatory job. What makes a dispute over for example the extension of a concept like *justice* a political one may partly be that people are engaged in disagreements which defy, not necessarily rational, but *actual* resolution – whether or not this is due to some blunder of theirs. Perhaps politics just is the sphere in which these disputes are played out. This is quite consistent with there being a platonic form *justice*, which provides an objective standard against which particular utterances on the subject of justice might ideally be judged. As we saw with the conceptual structures appealed to by the essential contestability thesis, however, the existence of these structures will not be enough to explain why political disagreements are what they are. All they will do is to indicate some normative mark, which for some reason political actors are failing to meet.

Conclusion

The implications of this argument are that the locus of ideological conflict is displaced from the conceptual to the political arena. It is not merely that key terms in the normative vocabulary of politics, such as *liberty*, *democracy*, *justice*, and so on, are semantically indeterminate; rather, it is only when this indeterminacy is engaged politically that it becomes manifest. Behind this lies a neo-Wittgensteinian point: the meanings of the concepts should not be seen as latent but nonetheless always *there*. Instead we should deprivatise meaning, and regard it as displayed in political practice. A characteristic procedure of modern liberalism attempts the foreclosing of politics through the foreclosing of meaning, and this is effected through the privatisation of meaning.[34]

The discussion also suggests something problematic about the project of political design, as it is conceived of in contemporary liberal philosophy. For this is an attempt to circumscribe the political philosophically; but according to the analysis just given, this involves a category-mistake. The clearest example of this is neutralist liberalism. To whatever extent the conceptions of the good can play a role in the project of political design, that segment of the conceptions, or values, which is *political* has to be filtered out. For it is plain that where competing conceptions espouse rivalrous conceptions of the *political* good, the resultant political dispensation must rest on neither of them. If it did, the argument purporting to justify it would rest on insufficient reasons. The upshot is that no segment of any conception of the good is eligible for the project of political design, which includes a conception of the *political* good.

Essential contestability has ramifications not only for our understanding of disagreements within politics, but of philosophical engagement with its normative content. After all, the thesis (or at least RDT) makes it doubtful whether conceptual analysis can reach normative conclusions regarding the concepts concerned. The thesis also raises the question whether philosophy can in fact assume an olympian stance above the mêlée. In his book *The Conquest of Politics* Benjamin Barber calls on the essential contestability thesis to contravert neutrality, the thought being that if key concepts like that of justice turn out to be contestable, no form of political design can be substantively neutral.[35] There will simply be plural understandings of justice between which the project of political design must choose. The conclusion indicated by the discussion here, however, is that the thesis can countenance neutrality precisely because it supposes that political disagreement (including, for example, disagreement over the extension of 'politics' itself) masks underlying agreement, on the conceptual structures which Gallie hoped to lay bare. What makes neutrality sustainable is abstracting from the thoughts of political agents themselves. Its precondition is a sharp line between arguments currently politically and what is held to be philosophically justifiable.

Recognising the special status of the political need not issue in a fundamental reorientation of concerns or argumentative methods. It does however call for a revised understanding of the relation philosophising bears to politics. Most obviously this involves rethinking political philosophy as a *contribution* to political argument, rather than providing a limit to it. What would then probably also follow is more practical engagement with questions of implementation (broadly construed) which seek to address a world in which, as Machiavelli said, 'so many are not virtuous'.[36] This ignores what I take to be certain truths, indeed truisms. Though talk in contemporary liberalism is so often about conceptions of the good, the remit of much of politics is in fact the bad.

One fairly obvious reason for that is that conceptions of the good are often conceptions also of the bad – for example, conceptions of the badness of other people's conceptions of the good. By trying to deal with the bad, politics does itself no favours, as life is apt to give politics a bad name. In modern democracies, politics itself is apt to deny this, its apparent aim now being to take the politics out of politics. Symptom and cause are confounded in much current political philosophy, where the hope often seems to be that we might purge the badness of life by purging life of politics. That begins to assume the appearance of a pre-emptive strike on politics, rather than an attempt to understand politics philosophically. But if we see judgements, for example, about the extension of *justice*, as simply being under-determined (because of either judgemental error, or an indeterminacy in the concept itself), we may need other, real-world explanations of why a particular interpretation holds sway. In doing so we can make room for such uncomfortable phenomena as power.

3
'Political Obligation'

Introduction

What *is* 'the problem of political obligation'? One reason for the problem's philosophical longevity lies, perhaps, in its own elusiveness. It is possible to question the problem's formulation from a number of angles, and there may well be no canonical version of it. On some views, there is not even a *prima facie* problem to solve; on others, the problem is one of *legal* rather than political obligation; and it is questionable whether the justificatory task, which the formulation seemingly invites, is really best understood by reference to the notion of *obligation*.

The singularity of the 'problem' is, perhaps, obscured by its familiarity. By contrast, debate in ethical theory is not usually held to collect around 'the problem of moral obligation'. One reason why not, presumably, is that formulating matters in this way already concedes too much to ethical theorists of a certain stripe – namely those inclined, like some Kantians, to regard morality as a structure of obligations. For this reason, describing the problem as one of moral obligation either assumes that the more fundamental question 'Why act morally?' has already been answered, or at least that the question's only possible answer must rely on the notion of obligation. To cite an obligation can be to give a justification for action, but in relation to *this* problem only invites a demand for reasons supporting the obligation itself: obligation becomes a Janus-faced notion, looking before and after. This has generated confusion in attempts to justify *political* obligation.

In outline my argument in this chapter will be as follows. I shall contend that, if the object of justification is taken to be individual citizens' obligations to their state, the best formulation of the 'problem' is: *What reasons, if any, justify my thinking that I am under an obligation to obey the state?* However, liberalism requires that a satisfactory theory must provide reasons justifying political obligation which are also reasons justifying each citizen, acting on the obligations, in thinking that they are so obligated. The obligation-justifying reasons must be capable *in principle* of performing a motivating role – regardless of whether the reasons in question are currently reasons on which citizens are motivated to act. But, in general, obligations apply irrespective of (even hypothetical) agent-motivation; and where an agent has reasons for action, they need not entail any obligation, and will motivate only to the extent that they pre-empt first-person deliberation concerning obligation. Moreover, theories of obligation seeking to articulate reasons of the sort demanded above must take an 'internal' or 'external' view[1] of the reasons in question. Neither approach succeeds; nor do attempts to combine them. But these approaches are collectively exhaustive, so it is doubtful whether there are any reasons of the kind demanded. If liberalism is committed to satisfying these demands, its best prospects of justifying the state may be to consider justifications which make no essential reference to citizens' obligations. A *raison d'état* justification of state action, making no mention of citizens' obligations, may be all that is justifiable.

The 'problem' problem

It is not my aim here to provide a general formulation of the 'problem'. Rather I shall try to arrive at a formulation of it, and the conditions on solving it, which meet the following demand: that there are reasons justifying citizens' obligations, on which reasons the citizens could in relevant circumstances act. I shall explain later how this demand imposes conditions on acceptable *liberal* solutions to the problem. This is not the same as the question, *What justifies the state?* I shall however argue that, since there is no solution to the problem which meets the demand just mentioned, there is little point in construing the latter question as one about obligation.

As a first attempt, it might be suggested that obligation theorists try to answer this question:

(1) Why should I obey the state?

But this can hardly be the question – not, at any rate, if the answer *has* to be framed in terms of the notion of obligation. Question (1) can clearly be answered by saying, 'Because it will be worse for me if I don't.' So reasons which can be invoked in a true answer to (1) need not have anything to do with obligations, short of reaching for the device of 'obligations to oneself'. One trouble with this is that it locates obligations in the wrong place, directing them back towards the agent rather than towards the state. More fundamentally wrong is the fact that it gives the agent one thought too many:[2] faced with question (1) any number of self-interested reasons for obedience are possible, but it is conceptually otiose to have the agent think that there are these reasons, *and* that he is anyway obligated to obey the state.

One response to this is to deny that the fact that (1) can be answered without relying on notions of obligation means that no answer which does is possible: for example, if I am under an obligation to obey the state, this gives a reason – on one view, an *all-in* reason – to obey it. This is fair enough as far as it goes. But it is clearly fruitless to reply in these terms if the question asks what justification there is for the obligation itself, as in:

(2) Why am I under an obligation to obey the state?,

where for the possibly prudential 'should' of (1) is substituted the more aspiring notion of obligation. Is this then the real 'problem of political obligation'? If it were, we might go on to ground the supposed obligation in some other notion, such as that of promising, or some foundational deontology from which *political* obligations are derived. But if this is the ulterior aim, there seems little point in starting with (2) – not, at least, if the goal of theories of political obligation is to refute the philosophical anarchist, who will simply reply that (2) is based on a false premise. Accordingly, we might try deleting this premiss, and reframe the question along the following lines:

(3) Am I under an obligation to obey the state?

But this invites a flat 'Yes'/'No' disagreement between the statist and anarchist respectively, so it presumably needs supplementing with something like this:

(4) What reason, if any, have I for thinking that I am under an obligation to obey the state?

Again, however, the question will hardly do in this form. For one thing, there are possible answers to the question set in (4) which in no sense *justify* the state – those in which the notion of 'having a reason' to ϕ is (as it might be termed) *purely explanatory*. This relatively weak sense of 'having a reason' for an action is that consistent with saying that an agent had a reason for ϕ-ing, even though (it turned out) the reason was not very good: perhaps I was brainwashed, or otherwise deluded, in thinking I had *good* reason for ϕ-ing. Nonetheless, the reason I had for ϕ-ing, bad as it was, does *explain* my having ϕ-ed.

So once again we find a gap opening up between a purely explanatory report of the reasons I have or had for acting, and a more normatively aspiring view of those reasons. Perhaps a way to step across the gap is by moving from the agent-relative reason of (4) to a more impersonal formulation, such as:

(5) What reason, if any, is there for thinking that I am under an obligation to obey the state?

But this is ambiguous in a way which could still lead (5) to be read as equivalent in meaning to (4); we still need a *justifying*, and not merely explanatory reason or reasons. There is, in addition, an indisputable *legal* obligation to do what the state says, whose existence is not brought out clearly by the formulations so far. So, taking this into account, we might try:

(6) What moral reasons, if any, justify my thinking that I am under an obligation to obey the state?

This puts the sought-after reasons firmly in the realm of justification. It is, however, unwarranted at this stage to rule in only *moral* justifications of the state – it rules out, for example, purely *de facto* theories, but also a range of others where the reasons make no pretence of being moral ones. So in this respect it makes the requirements on justification too stringent. It seems better, then, to ask:

(7) What reasons, if any, justify my thinking that I am under an obligation to obey the state?,

which de-relativises reasons by bringing in the non-relative notion of justification, keeps hold of the fact that what is justified are obligations, and makes a suitably agnostic demand for non-specific justificatory reasons.

Still, this formulation is not beyond dispute. It might be thought that (7) was better formulated along these lines:

(8) What reasons, if any, justify my legal obligation to obey the state?,

which assumes there is an obligation which I am in fact under. It might also be thought that (8) avoids some of the problems facing (7) to be set out below – most obviously, that it locates obligation exclusively in the legal relation of citizens to their state. I shall argue at the end that (8) does indeed enjoy some significant advantages over other formulations of the problem – certainly citizens as such *are* under legal obligations, as (8) assumes. But the real advantage of (8) over (7) is that it displaces the locus of justification from individual citizens' reasons for action, and to this extent its demand for reasons is better understood impersonally. Liberals have usually sought to tie justification to individuals' reasons for action, and herein, I shall argue, lies their problem.

Obligations are a *sui generis* category of reasons for action, marked off by applying categorically. But this has caused problems for theorists seeking to build obligations into the problem's solution. Liberal theorists have tried to leave room, within a general account of the obligatoriness of law, for exceptions justifying civil disobedience, for example. Since this demands that law-breaking is sometimes justifiable, the obligatoriness of law became provisional – a so-called *prima facie* obligation.[3] But once obligations are softened in this way, it is unclear that we are dealing with a distinct class (let alone a categorical one) of reasons for action: what distinguishes such *obligations* from mere defeasible *reasons*? If the obligatoriness of the law is purely procedurally based, law will remain obligatory, even if it is unjust. The view that legal obligations are '*prima facie*' ones is then supported not by procedural considerations about the law itself, but the defeasibility of our reasons for obeying it.

Version (7) is prompted by the consideration that, in order for there to be more than a verbal difference between (4) and (5), there must be a defensible notion of non-agent-relative reasons for action – if I think I am under such an obligation, I acquire reasons for acting. It might simply be denied that any such non-agent-relative reasons-statement is true, unless there is a true corresponding first-person statement – that is, that the truth of the non-relative statement entails that of a corresponding purely explanatory first-person reasons-statement of the sort mentioned above; if this is right, it looks as though all bets are off, since in this case the talk of justification in (7) is either false, or after all reducible to the agent-relativised reasons of (4).

What if we reject this view? We should beware of exaggerating the exclusiveness of the options here: even if there are reasons for action which really are agent-impersonal in this sense, we still need some account of how they can – if only in principle – be reasons for *me*.

Transparency and distributivity

At its most general level, the demand for *transparency* is the demand that the fundamental principles on which society is run are themselves in the public realm – both that the public has access to them, and that these are open to public scrutiny. As such, the demand is recognisably Kantian, and has of course been restated by Rawls,[4] among others. It is not difficult to see why the demand for transparency should be thought to form an indispensable component of a liberal political order. For it seems that only if the latter is transparent is it possible for liberals to do justice to substantive ideals they hold, such as equal respect for persons, or autonomy: both of these are dubiously consistent with a political order whose *fundamental* rationale (rather than isolated, and agreed exceptions such as official secrecy) remains obscure to most of its members.

There may be local situations in which liberalism can allow that this is true. But it is less clear how it can accept this at the most fundamental level of justification for the political association (including for those exceptions which it allows). Then, assuming that a theory of political obligation aims to give the best statement of the reasons for acting on obligations, it is not the case that the reasons given by the theory must be those on which citizens act when acting on political obligations. If so, there can be no more than extensional equivalence between the reasons justifying obligation, and those on which citizens act; it is hard to see how even extensional equivalence could be sustained without resort to a form of *de facto* theory uncongenial to most liberals. It is also difficult to avoid the threat of manipulation posed by the asymmetries of knowledge or rationale which this permits. And it is unclear how a justificatory theory could claim to be action-guiding, if the best reasons cited in its support could be held to be distinct from those on which citizens had reason to act.

Though the non-commitment of the neutralist strand of liberalism may seem to avoid this problem, the justificatory basis for neutrality very often itself requires transparency – for example, those justifications, like Larmore's,[5] which justify neutrality from a shared commitment to rational and equal dialogue. There are also more purely political demands with which liberals have sought to associate themselves, such as that of democratic accountability, which are hard to square with non-transparency.

There is also, of course, the problem that such an order might run afoul of substantive liberal policy positions, such as opposition to censorship. I do not however mean to suggest that liberalism as such demands transparency: it might be that the liberal *summum bonum* (such as, say, the maximal promotion of personal liberty) was thought to be best promoted by political arrangements whose ultimate rationale remained to a greater or lesser degree unknown to the citizens. A well-known variant on this theme is the proposition that moral knowledge can destroy virtue,[6] and it is possible to formulate a political version of this claim. So there may be political orders which are non-transparent. Nonetheless, it seems to me that most liberals nowadays do demand transparency in some form:

(T) There must be reasons justifying political obligation, which justify the citizens in thinking that he is so obligated.[7]

This is a weak version of transparency: it does not demand the best possible reasons for political obligation, and leaves it open that the reasons justifying citizens in thinking that they are obligated are less than best. This demand is often coupled, or conflated, by liberal theories of political obligation with one of *distributivity*. Most often the way in which this is built in is through generalisation from the circumstances of the individual agent, or appeal to propositions about human nature, as in traditional state-of-nature theory; and it seems to fit the demand for a form of justification, like contractarian and other voluntarist theories, which take as their starting-point the motivations of individual agents. The distributivity requirement states that:

(D) There must be reasons justifying political obligation, which justify *each* of the citizens acting on the obligation.

We can then combine (T) and (D)[8] as follows.

(TD) There must be reasons justifying political obligation which justify each of the citizens, acting on the obligation, in thinking that he is so obligated.[9]

(TD) remains non-committal between 'internal' and 'external' reasons theories, that is, between theories which respectively do, and do not, link agents' reasons for action essentially to their current set of motivations:[10] in particular, it leaves room for the view that there are only internal reasons for acting, since if that view is right, the best statement of agents' reasons for acting will be statements about internal reasons. But equally, the reasons concerned could be held to be the best possible regardless of whether they were currently, or even foreseeably, reasons on which the relevant agents were in fact disposed to act. Not all moral or political theories, of course, see the need to satisfy (TD). Notable exceptions are so-called 'Government House' utilitarianism, or a republic of Platonic guardians. But these are both patently non-transparent regimes.

I shall take (TD) to mean that the reasons it mentions are capable *in principle* of motivating agents to act. As I underline later, this does not mean, even on the external view of reasons, that coming to believe a reasons-statement is to acquire a motivation. (TD) only states that any defensible theory of political obligation must be capable in principle of explaining how its reasons motivate agents to act. At its most basic the demand is the same as that on any acceptable meta-ethical theory – that it explain how obligations can be action-guiding.

Accepting (TD) does not mean abandoning ideal theory. (TD) is consistent with the view that many, or most (even all) citizens will not in fact act on those reasons on which the best statement of their reasons for acting says are the best reasons for so acting. But, to repeat, my aim is not to provide an independent argument for accepting (TD), nor to show that liberals *must* accept (TD), but to note that many liberals do so, and to argue that this causes problems for them in justifying political obligation; so that they must either abandon this justificatory project, or abandon this version of transparency.[11]

Obligations, reasons, motivations

There are grounds for doubting whether there *can* be motivationally effective, obligation-grounding reasons for action, as sought by (7) when subject to condition (TD). As I shall argue here, obligations apply irrespective of agent-motivation, and there is no general ground for thinking that (true) reasons-statements support a corresponding claim about obligations of the agents concerned. Where an agent has reasons for action, these will motivate only to the extent that they pre-empt first-person deliberation concerning obligation. Each of these considerations makes it doubtful whether a theory of (political) obligation *can* provide motivationally effective obligation-grounding reasons. I shall consider an alternative possibility (the *short-cut* theory), which attempts to dispense with foundational reasons in justifying political obligations, but will argue that this is unsatisfactory.

To be effective, agents' reasons must figure in their practical deliberations (and resultant actions) in the right way. Here we can distinguish between action *on* an obligation, and action *consistent with* an obligation. If I am unaware of being under an obligation to ϕ, but I ϕ anyway, it is far from clear that I am *acting on* the obligation to ϕ: the link between action and obligation seems entirely adventitious, and clearly cannot be strengthened by invoking relevant intentions. The same applies to the relation between any independent reason I have for ϕ-ing and the reason(s) which support my obligation to ϕ. An acceptable answer to (7) must impute to me reasons for action which make essential reference to the idea of my being under an obligation: it is no good if the answer simply mentions a set of reasons, acting on which produces conduct of the sort demanded by the theory of political obligation – particularly in view of the fact that these obligations (supposing they exist) are apt to be confused with their morally less ambitious prudential shadows.

If so, it seems that acting *on* an obligation, if not being *under* one, requires that I have accepted the obligation itself as providing a reason for me to ϕ. Here the problems facing the theorist of political obligation become clearer: if it is to go beyond the blank answer to (1), the theory has both to explain how the obligations hold in terms of supposedly more basic sorts of reason for action, while the notion of obligation has also to figure as an essential part of the obligated agent's thought. But if the obligation-grounding reasons really do their job, it is hard to see why the thought of *obligation* need enter essentially into the agent's practical deliberations. Without them, though, it is hard to see how to forge the link between action and obligation demanded by (7).

It is important to see the nature of the problem. A reason is sought which supports an obligation. But it seems that the reason specified must itself identify an obligation, in which case, given the Janus-faced nature of obligations, the original search resumes. If, however, we start from the other end, with reasons which are motivationally effective, then it is hard to see what warrants introducing talk of obligation. The cost of deriving reasons (for example, prudential ones) for obeying the state, or accepting legal obligations, which satisfy (TD) is that the notion of obligation becomes marginalised.

This is all the harder, given that obligations apply irrespective of agent-motivation. Contrast the relation which citations of rights and obligations bear to reasons for action. To say that I have a right to ϕ is not obviously to cite a *reason* for my ϕ-ing. It is true that saying 'I had a right to' may be a valid response to someone who challenges my entitlement to ϕ; but this reply remains in the realm of third-party justification, not of my deliberated reasons for acting. So it is unclear that citing a right to ϕ is a satisfactory response to what might be called the open questioner, as opposed to the grand inquisitor, asking why I ϕ-ed. This is because rights, as Hobbes said, are liberties to do, or to forbear.[12] In this sense they underdetermine practical reasons: they concern not my reasons for acting, but the relation which my action (or its consequences) bears to others' powers of intervention. So here there is indeed an unproblematic gap between the (TD)-ratified *justification* for my ϕ-ing, and my deliberated reasons for doing so. Obligations, by contrast, *do* purport to furnish reasons for action: that is, to impute an obligation to someone is to impute to them a reason for acting. It is fair game, conversationally, to reply to the open questioner asking why I should ϕ, by citing my obligation to do so. This is because obligations, unlike rights, are *not* liberties to do or forbear, but a special kind of reason for action – namely a purportedly all-in reason applying independently of agent-motivation.

Moreover, not all reasons ground obligations. Given that there is no clear procedure to determine which kinds of reasons-statements may figure in claims about practical necessity, there is no clear conversational limit on which reasons can be cited as action-guiding instances of that necessity. I may enjoy swimming regularly. But it would be bizarre to say, for example, that whatever good reasons I may have for going bathing each day are satisfactorily ontologised as a distinct category of reasons for action, *natational obligations*, however close my subjective identification with my daily swimming routine. It would be still odder, leaning on the reason-givingness of obligations, then to cite the obligatoriness of the swimming as my reason for doing it. And this situation is clearly quite distinct from one in which I go swimming *just because* I am under an obligation to do so. In the latter situation, the 'conceptual' manoeuvre is indeed compelling. But it is compelling only because the obligation in question is then groundless: the obligation is purely reason-giving, and once we ask about the grounds of the obligation itself, the familiar dilemma reappears.

Citing a relevant obligation is certainly an answer to a question of the form, 'Why should I ...?' But it is mistaken to think that answering 'Why should I obey the state?' with 'Because I am under an obligation to', raises a further question about the *reasons* for my being under this very obligation. This need not be because the search for these obligation-grounding reasons is doomed from the start. But if any such reasons come to hand, they will be of a kind which is liable to leave it obscure why the obligations they allegedly ground were introduced at all. If, as (TD) demands, the reasons justifying the obligations are the best reasons for those acting on them to think that they are obligated, it is hard to see what point there is in talking of their being obligated.

We may compare the political obligation theorist's task with that facing someone trying to justify, say, obligations to members of one's family. Here the dialogue might go: 'Why should I obey my parents?' – 'Because I am under an obligation to.' When it is asked what grounds this obligation, there seems to be no satisfactory answer which both answers this question *and* provides a clue to reconstructing the obligated agent's thought in terms of obligation. The most perspicuous reconstruction of the thought – one capable both of entering into the agent's own thoughts about action, and, *mutatis mutandis*, into explanations by others of the agent's action – might just be 'I must obey my parents', a thought which, again, requires the notion of practical necessity, but not that of obligation. It would be odd to suppose that the person's thought could be adequately reconstructed as 'I must obey my parents', together with a teleological rationale justifying the obligation on the grounds (say) that people in this situation have reason to preserve traditional family structures. Someone might say that the obligatoriness just *consists in* this thought: *I must obey my parents* – even though the notion of an obligation does not enter essentially into its articulation. The challenge is to explain why such a thought, given the non-identity of obligation and practical necessity as categories of reasons for action, should be called a thought about obligation.[13]

But if obligations are like this, it becomes harder to see how they *can* do the job assigned to them by theorists of political obligation who also accept (TD) – purportedly giving the agent a reason for acting, but at the same time by definition unrelated to motivation. This is not because *de facto* citizens may be currently unmotivated to recognise that they are under relevant obligations; it is that the theory-given reasons for obligation, if they are to be deliberatively effective, will leave it obscure what reasons they will give agents for thinking of themselves as being *under an obligation*. In trying to move from obligation to its grounding reasons, theory seeks to reconstruct, in the reverse direction, the deliberative path which agents might follow; but then, if the reasons really do their job, a thought about obligation is one thought too many.

Perhaps one way to make the link between obligations and their justifying reasons more secure is to rethink the role of obligation in practical reasoning and action. Here the idea is that the obligatoriness of certain kinds of reason for action is not, or at least need not be, reflected in deliberation which makes essential use of the notion of obligation itself. Rather the force of obligations comes out in a special relation between deliberation and action, or in a special way of acting. Indeed, it might be argued that the mark of such obligatoriness was precisely that the operative reasons *failed* to feature in practical deliberation – or at least failed to do so in the way that other reasons do. That the agent is under an obligation, on this view, emerges in the fact that the reasons motivate to action without deliberation. It might be thought that some kinds of spontaneous and compulsive actions fit into this pattern. In such cases, the absence of reasons of the relevant kind from deliberation does not mean that they are inoperative; on the contrary, that they *do* operate is expressed in the very fact that the usual deliberative routes are bypassed. This is the *short-cut* theory.

This pattern is an important and relatively neglected feature of agency. It is however highly unclear that reasons for action within the pattern are best characterised – let alone that they must be – as obligations. To think otherwise is to confuse obligatoriness with other action-categories, such as practical necessity. The problem with the short-cut theory then becomes clear: there is no way to distinguish acting *on* an obligation from other sorts of short-cut agency, such as those involving some (non-obligation-based) form of practical necessity. On the short-cut view, it is also very hard to retain what seems an indispensable feature of obligation, namely its *reason-givingness*: if obligation is a mode of acting (or of translating reasons for action into action) we still need some explanation of why the agent acts at all. The most apposite way of describing an agent who does act (non-*akratically*) from reasons which are not mirrored in deliberation, is by invoking the notion of practical necessity. And, while the latter notion is certainly not without application to the familiar objects of citizens' political obligations, it is hard to see why any short-cut interpretation of *obligation*, distinguished from it, should be of much help in justifying the purported obligations. More obviously, it is hard to see how the short-cut theory can satisfy (TD). For if the putative obligation-grounding reasons can be bypassed, as the short-cut theory allows, it is unclear in what sense they justify citizens in thinking of themselves as *obligated*.

If this is right, the objects demanded by (7) and (TD) have the peculiarity that they are reasons which justify agents' thinking of themselves as acting on them, in discharging their political obligations, even though it is in the nature of obligations that they apply irrespective of agent-motivation, and in the nature of reasons that, if deliberatively effective, they seem to pre-empt, rather than support obligations. I shall argue below that these justifying reasons cannot be found, whether or not they are identified with agents' actual motivations.

Justifying obligations

Here I will outline a general model relating agents and reasons for action, offering two possible construals of the relationship between agents and reasons for acting (on political obligations), with a third, conceptually possible, hybrid approach. I shall argue that since these models are collectively exhaustive, and since none of them can provide an adequate account of citizens' reasons for acting on political obligations, there is no model capable of answering (7) when subject to (TD). Citizens' reasons are either (a) based on existing motivations, but incapable of grounding political obligations; or (b) formulated independently of actual motivations, but incapable of satisfying (TD). I shall also consider a hybrid theory attempting to combine (a) and (b), but conclude that this also fails.

We can here introduce the idea of a set of agents who under some description each have the same reason for performing some act (individually or collectively). One example of such a set is that of chess players for whom in a given game-situation it is possible to force mate *only* by playing *Qf6*. Another example is that of Kantian agents in the Kingdom of Ends. It is important to note, though, that the formulation remains neutral as between sets in which the relevant reasons are distributed among its members, and those in which the reasons apply to the set as such (it may be both). In these terms, Kantian agents in the Kingdom of Ends share a *distributed* reason. This distinction is of some importance in view of Pateman's argument that theories of political obligation which argue for distributed reasons – basically liberal ones – are doomed to fail, while Pateman herself defends an account of obligation for undistributed reasons.[14] It is however certainly true to say that the most prominent traditional theories have usually assumed distribution (Rousseau's political theory is interestingly hard to classify in this respect).[15]

Motivational assumptions of some kind are required if the set's extension is to be determined: this applies to the examples already given. There are, it seems, two ways of building these in. One is to make the reason(s) in question a *residual* item – in effect, to determine the reason by reference to a pre-defined set of agents and action-type or token. In this case, with agents and action fixed, the reason will be determined simply as whatever reason(s), if any, *this* group of agents happens to share in respect of a given action (since the reason is being resolved for *given* agents and action, there may very well be no such reason). I shall call this the *residual* approach. The other approach fixes reasons *in advance of* the associated set, that is, it collects members of the set according to whether the determined reason is or is not a reason *for them*: I shall call this the *fixed reason* approach.

It might seem that some of the examples above cut across this distinction, since the relevant set in the chess example is fixed as those playing White (say), *and* there is a non-residual reason with respect to which the set is formed, namely the desire to force mate, for the action *Qf6*. But the distinctions did not rule out the possibility that there might be situations where fixing a reason determines a certain set of agents, but *also* conversely: call this situation *convergence*. Some forms of hypothetical contractarianism, such as Rawls's, and traditional state-of-nature theory, make this sort of convergence claim. I shall return to this possibility later. For now it is enough to note the peculiarity of convergence, and that game-situations like chess exemplify it because the set of players can usually be taken as identical with those wishing to force mate.[16]

Can we regard the class of citizens as a set related by reason(s) in respect of acting on a political obligation? I have already cast doubt both on the assumption that there can be obligation-grounding reasons as required by (7), and specifically whether reasons capable of doing this job will also necessarily meet the (TD) requirement that the reasons can be reasons *for* the obligated agent. Unless the latter condition is met, we are back in the non-transparent world of Plato's guardian state. But if it is met, we lack adequate grounds for thinking that the resultant residual set will be coextensive with the class of citizens.

If we first (a) consider the possibility that the reason(s) can be seen as *residual* in the sense given, we can simply ask what reasons relate the specified set of agents, that is, the set of citizens. Then we just collect whatever (internal) reasons are in fact shared by this set of agents. But there are no grounds for thinking that any such reason or reasons exist, given that we are working with the reasons which the agents concerned in fact think that they have; only some, or none, of them may think that they have reason so to act. This also fails to provide an answer to anarchists, who refuse to acknowledge the force of the reasons relating the other citizens. Indeed, if the 'internal' conception means that the set includes only those for whom the reasons are motivationally *effective*, it will also exclude agents like the *akratic* and accidic.[17] Any theory of obligation will have some preferred conception of obligation-grounding reasons – that is what it *is* for it to be such a theory. But then it is gratuitous, given motivational heterogeneity, to suppose that this will be replicated in the internal reasons of the citizens.

Even if there are reasons relating all the members of the set, it may well be that these are not the reason(s) countenanced by the theory of obligation, coupled with (TD). For, as we saw earlier (pp. 66–7), we need some account of those reasons which ground obligations, compared with those which do not; it cannot be that *every* reason which is motivationally effective entails an obligation. And the problem remains that the putative obligation-grounding reasons, when they are motivationally effective, will simply bypass the notion of obligation.

Moreover, the residual approach is liable to subside into the alternative, fixed reason style of theory. Given the heterogeneity of actual agent-motivations, any plausible theory will have to distinguish good from bad reasons among these motivations. When it does so, it will already have moved away from taking motivation at face value – some actual motivations will be theory-approved, while others will not. But then it is hard to see what warrant there is for working with given motivations – certainly if there is to be any show of explaining why citizens *as such* are obligated. Within the residual approach, presumably, only a fraction of citizens will be. The alternative is to identify *right* (that is, justifying) reasons, and say they are reasons for the citizens irrespective of whether or not they are motivationally effective. This brings us (b) to the fixed reason approach, which is in some respects more propitious. But I shall argue that it still fails.

This approach aims to identify an obligation-grounding set of reasons conformable to (TD), but unrelated to actual motivations. One problem with this is that if the theory abandons the attempt, made by (a), to work with existing motivations, it is highly unclear in what sense, as demanded by (TD), the reason(s) laid out by the theory *justify* each citizen in thinking of him- or herself as being under a relevant obligation. A second problem is that this approach is unable to satisfy wider liberal, and indeed democratic, requirements; a third follows from the earlier argument (pp. 66–7) that there are no obligation-grounding reasons in the sense required, and *a fortiori* none which also conform to (TD).

My being *justified* in accepting a proposition is not the same as my simply accepting a true proposition. If I have accepted something analogous to a mathematical proof of the relevant reasons-statement, the reasons in question are no longer external; on the other hand, if I have not – or if the reasons-statement is so 'external' to me that I have not even grasped its *content* – I am no more justified in acting on the obligations which the reasons purport to ground than I am in acting on an arbitrarily produced or incomprehensible statement of my 'reasons' for acting. Whether or not the fixed reason approach can show that reasons for action are intrinsically motivating, it still has to explain how even the non-*akratic* or non-accidic citizen would be justified in accepting the reasons provided by the theorists of obligation, given that these reasons are external ones.[18]

This is a conceptual fact about the relationship between reasons and justification, rather than about obligations – so that it reinforces, rather than presupposing, the arguments of the previous section. For the same argument could be applied to the reasons supporting some non-obligatory action. If the only reasons which justify doing it are external to me, then I cannot be justified in thinking of them as reasons on which I can act – if they were, the reasons would then be internal ones. This is unaffected by Korsgaard's argument that internalism must claim, not that true reasons-statements entail actual (effective) motivations, but only that rational agents *would* be so motivated.[19] For it is the justifiability of the reasons-statements themselves required by (7) and (TD) that has been challenged, not their translation from 'intellectual' acceptance into motivational effectiveness.

In addition, the theory has difficulty in satisfying wider liberal aspirations – for example, that the state maximises, or at least respects, citizens' autonomy. If the reasons really are deliberatively inaccessible to a given individual, it is simply false to say that his or her autonomy is respected by acting as if they were not: there is no sense in which this person's action is genuinely self-originated or self-directed. Even if there are paternalistic arguments for so acting, these are necessarily not arguments from autonomy, regardless of whether there is some single set of universally applicable (external) reasons-statements and an authority to promulgate them. In these circumstances, some form of 'noble lie' may well be required to secure citizen-compliance. Kant may have been consistent in thinking that moral agents can be stupid but still good; it is much harder to see how the stupid agent could remain (in Kant's own terms) autonomous. There are also good reasons for doubting that an external view of citizens' reasons can meet some fundamental constraints on democratic accountability: briefly stated, the concern is that the rationale for many political decisions by the state will be opaque to those citizens to whom the reasons in question are external.[20]

This supports a more general conclusion: there is no reason to think that the two types of justification mentioned in (TD) will tie up. On the external reasons approach there must be a possible gap, for any given agent, between current and ideal motivation. Nonetheless, we can still talk of what the agent is currently justified in *thinking* of himself as having reason to do: the point is that even if externalism is defensible, this will still differ from what, according to the externalist account, he would be justified in doing. Given the lack of tie-up, the theory will have to distinguish between ideal reasons for action and what, *un*ideally, agents have good reason to do. I shall pursue this a little further at the end.

There are other grounds for rejecting the fixed reason approach. By the earlier argument (p. 67) correct deliberation would have to conclude in a thought about obligation. It is not enough for the citizen to think 'This is what I ought to do', or something of this sort, since 'I ought to do ϕ' does not entail 'I am obligated to ϕ', or vice versa.[21] But it is very unclear that any reasons which really did their job would in fact issue in any such thought; they would at best issue in a set of reasons justifying the legal obligation the citizen is under. It is hard to see why this should be thought of as demonstrating *political* obligation. They are also not reasons *for* the citizens, since the reasons for the legal obligation apply irrespective of the reasons for action (or indeed existence) of individual agents. We can ask a separate question. *Why should citizens do what they are under a legal obligation to do?*, but it certainly does not follow that the answer to this must provide *justifying* reasons of the kind originally sought.

The greater plausibility mentioned above of the fixed reason approach is not accidental: it derives from the fact that it fits the motivation-independence identified earlier (p. 66) as characteristic of obligation. As such, it should be noted, the present argument is free-standing and does not rest on the considerations about practical reason and obligation assembled earlier as noted – for the problem of justification would arise even if obligations were not subject to the deliberative occlusions already mentioned. To this extent, matters are also not improved by trying to revise (TD) so that obligation no longer features essentially in the citizens' practical thinking. Such a revision would of course still have somehow to bridge the gap between acting *on* an obligation and merely acting *in conformity* with it, as already noted, but would at least absolve the obligation-theorist of the need to construct that thinking in such a way as to conclude – as I have suggested there is in general no reason to think that it will conclude – in a thought about obligation. But even if the citizens need not arrive at a thought about obligation, they will still not get as far as the theory needs them to go unless the reasons imputed to them meet the conditions on justification.

What about the possibility that the relevant set displays *convergence*, in the sense already explained? Here the set is identical with the set of citizens because the relating reason is customised to pick out this very set: that is, the set of agents which have this special relation to their association. Then, if the earlier arguments concerning the relationship between obligations and reasons are accepted, it might be argued that obligations simply consist in these irreducible reasons. There would on this account be no violation of the transparency requirement, since the relevant statement of obligations would simply be an improved *redescription* of the relation between citizens and state. Because of this relation between statements of reasons and obligations, the foundational worries voiced earlier would be irrelevant. This move, then, seeks to combine residual and fixed reason approaches. We might call this the *special* model. However, I shall argue that insofar as the model avoids the problems faced by these approaches, it collapses either into a *de facto* theory or into vicious circularity.

The special model denies that the truth-conditions of statements about the agents' reasons are secured by relevant items within the agents' logically and informationally optimised motivational sets. This offers the prospect of bringing back together the residual and fixed reason approaches, since if we stipulate that all citizens are necessarily related by their political obligations, we can say that the class of these obligations will necessarily be a residual item relating the relevant set – much as, in the chess example earlier, the residual relating reason was necessarily also reason-specific because of the way the set's membership was picked out.

On this view it is mistaken to look for further reasons: the reason *consists in* the specialness of the relation between citizen and state. This is indeed a possibility worth exploring, and some recent work, such as Horton's,[22] aims to find the obligation-grounding reasons in considerations of this form. But what seems entirely gratuitous is the demand that the reason in question must consist in, or otherwise depend on, a thought about *obligation*. There is in addition the problem noted earlier in discussing the short-cut theory, that this form of justification has nothing to say about situations where obligations are challenged by strong reasons for disobedience – unsurprisingly, since the special model is the political version of the short-cut theory.

This might seem to be a possibility distinct from the purely *de facto* account; but it is doubtful whether it really is. If the requisite reasons-statements are not to come out as identical, there will have to be some account of the differences in their truth-conditions: but it is difficult to see what these could be. Apart from the familiar problems posed for both models by local limitations to state power and by resident aliens, both models work back from *given* relations of political power to generate their required reasons-claims. The two ostensibly distinct possibilities represent the same thought: that the reasons citizens have for obeying their state are not comprehensible in isolation from the fact that the state is what happens to them, the citizens. The theory's plausibility is bought by its silence about the nature of the reasons supposedly justifying the state; once we probe the reasons involved, it seems that we have a bare *de facto* theory – since otherwise the reasons themselves would be doing the justificatory work, and we would be forced back onto either the residual or fixed reason approach. Failing this, since we can coherently deny that the state is justified in circumstances where the special relationship obtains, our conception of the justification-conditions must be independent of the special relationship. The only way round this seems to be to redefine the specialness of the relationship so that only the *Rechtsstaat* qualifies as special. But then we no longer have a non-circular criterion of state legitimacy, and once the internal-motivational condition is jettisoned, (TD) is no longer met either.

Since approaches (a) and (b) are defined as logical complements of each other (either based, or not based, on existing motivations), they are collectively exhaustive. I conclude that the attempt to find a general obligation-grounding set of reasons, of the kind sought by (7) and subject to (TD), fails. Below I shall briefly consider approaches to justifying the state which dispense with the notion of obligation.

Conclusion

Such plausibility as the special model enjoys arises from its similarity to another approach to the problem, which in effect bypasses the conditions on justification laid down earlier, and indeed the whole distributive approach to reason-giving. Nonetheless, it goes beyond the mere denial of distributivity, since there could be a true (relevant) reasons-statement relating the set as such, even though for some members of the set, or all, there was no true *individual* reasons-statement, and the truth-conditions of the relating statement were such as to satisfy the conditions on justification. The present proposal goes beyond this, by denying that the conditions on state justification require distributivity. However, if the tie-in required by (TD) cannot be achieved, we are faced with a potential gap between the reasons justifying state action, and those justifying citizens in obeying the state. This need not prevent certain justificatory targets being achieved: we can perhaps still have a justification of state action, and a theory explaining why citizens sometimes have good reason to obey the state. We could consider a question of the following form:

(9) What justification is there for the exercise of political authority?

As I argued earlier, (9) should be distinguished from:

(10) What reasons do I (*qua* representative individual citizen) have for obeying the state?

Neither (9) nor (10) makes any demands about the obligation-mentioningness of its answer, as there is no reason to think that they must rely essentially on citizens' (or anyone else's) obligations.[23] It also permits a form of transparency, since with obligation out of the picture, the best reasons grounding the justification can be those that the citizens themselves regard as best – at least in some cases. There may also be non-obligation-grounding reasons conformable to (TD) which justify obedience to the state, without themselves justifying the state. This becomes more obvious when we consider ways of justifying certain sorts of state violence, such as (non-civil) warfare. If, as non-pacifists think, this is sometimes justified, it is implausible to think that acts of violence by one state against citizens of another are *justified* by the latter's (that is, the citizens') obligations.

Nor is this surprising, when we recall that justification concerns *entitlements*, rather than obligations, and its conceptual fit with the latter is correspondingly poor. One way an entitlement can arise is through a countervailing obligation, as in contractual cases. But even there the fundamental consideration is of a contractually generated *right* to a good or service. Whether such a model is even intelligible as an account of political obligations depends on whether there is a prepolitical framework for contracting in the first place. Maybe this could be done by reviving natural-law contractarianism, providing a pre-existing framework for making and keeping promises. In some ways this offers the best justificatory prospects, since to make a promise is certainly to incur an obligation; but this only postpones the problem of justification. For if what secures obligation is the fact of having promised (rather than some independent consideration which imposes the obligation anyway), we need to know what *reasons* the pre-political agents would have for promising. They may have some. But it would be odd to think – even endorsing Hobbes's view that promises extracted by force still oblige – that the reason for promising, rather than the fact of having promised, is what imposes the obligation; if the reason for keeping the promise rests on coercion, that fact falls away as irrelevant anyway. Similar remarks apply to the versions of the claim which claim to find the reasons for promising in non-coercive considerations, where the sanction for keeping faith, if any, lies in the original motivating reasons themselves, not their promissory shadow. Seen like this, contractarianism pays the same homage as the earlier theories to an ideal of obligation, while placing the reasons for obedience firmly elsewhere.

I shall not discuss the conditions on state justification, in this sense, beyond noting that if the justification derives from the state's merely not being obligated *not* to act in certain ways, this is quite compatible with its citizens' being under no obligations towards it. In Hohfeldian terms, the state exercises a liberty-right in respect of its citizens, rather than an (obligation-entailing) claim-right. [24]

The more traditional type of theory also aims to justify the state's claim-rights against its citizens, and as a result, the justification will depend on the extent to which the latter can be said to be obligated: but this just leads back into the problems discussed earlier, of explaining how attempted justifications which begin with the individual agent net all and only those it intends to, and in the right way, by relying on obligation as its chief explanatory tool. This seems to me to exemplify a wider oddity in the discipline as currently practised, as was remarked in the introduction to this book – the attempt to reduce political theory to a more or less formal apparatus of ethical concepts.

If my argument has been right, we are left with a gap between the state's justification-conditions and citizens' reasons for action. But those seeking to solve 'the problem of political obligation' can perhaps still have much of what they want – reasons justifying some state action, plus a distinct set of considerations giving citizens' reasons (not necessarily purely prudential ones) for obedience. This is not to deny, of course, that anarchism remains very much a live option – particularly if the alternative to it is taken to be the justification of individual citizens' *obligations*. I have argued that the latter notion is unhelpful in framing the problem of justifying the state, and in some ways actively hinders its solution. In concluding this chapter, I shall indicate briefly the relevance of this conclusion to the wider argument I am advancing in this book.

My argument has sought to challenge political philosophers who believe that *obligation* is the paradigmatic notion in terms of which the justification of citizens' relation to the state has to be cast. These theorists have usually looked for types of obligation-grounding reason in explaining why the citizen is legitimately compelled to obey the state: a natural duty to conform to the decisions of just institutions, for example, or some direct form of contractarianism. As I have argued, since there is a difference between acting on an obligation and merely acting in conformity with it, it needs to be explained why (and how) the reasons offered by these theories are obligation-supporting. It is not enough to say that they are reasons on which an ideally rational, non-*akratic* agent *would* act, since we need an explanation of the reasons' deliberative effectiveness in supporting the peculiar category of reasons for action *obligation*. The thought may be that the situations which these theorists feel called upon to justify characteristically involve citizens' being obliged to do something, or to refrain from doing something else. But being obliged, or compelled, in these ways, or being legally obligated, is of course a different matter from being (morally) obligated.

The movement of the argument follows a pattern which (as I shall argue) recurs in the other topics investigated in this book. Philosophical reflection is prompted by a real-world political phenomenon – in this case, that citizens are indeed subjected to state power. The question might then be, what reasons they have to obey the state, and various answers could be given to this question, such as that they have no choice in the matter, that they are subject to *force majeure*, or that it will be worse for them if they fail to yield. But this is not in fact the question which most theorists of political obligation set out to answer. Perceiving that some of these reasons are morally unaspiring, these theorists have rather been concerned to ask what reasons citizens ideally *would* have, if the state were as they would wish it and the citizens were perfectly rational. What began as an exercise in *explanatory* theory becomes an exercise in hypothesising ideal conditions. The attraction of *obligation* as a category of reasons for action is then precisely its *dis*continuity with other reasons, as they figure in actual deliberation. That makes it peculiarly ill-suited to understanding citizens' relations to their state. This is the counterpart mistake in political philosophy to that identified long ago by H.A. Prichard – taking moral obligation as holding independently of the motivations of particular agents, then seeking a motivational basis for acting morally.[25] It is not surprising that this mistake should occur, since the notion of *obligation* has been imported from moral into political philosophy in discussing citizens' relation to their state, and liberalism has persistently sought a motivational basis for that relation. This is something to which we shall return.

4
Politics and the Limits of Pluralism

Introduction

In modern political philosophy, ethical claims are frequently regarded as being important for the design of political institutions and procedures. This is especially true of contemporary liberalism, whose exponents have often sought to derive institutional and procedural conclusions – or, as I shall refer to them, conclusions about *political design* – from claims of this nature. Such is the case, for example, with Rawls's insistence on the 'priority' of deontic concepts – specifically that of the *right* – over teleological ones.[1] Many other contemporary liberal theorists have thought that political design should be constrained or shaped by ethical and meta-ethical considerations. This chapter focuses on one ethical claim, *value-pluralism*, which has played a prominent role in recent liberal theory.

Liberal moral and political philosophers, including Berlin, Walzer, Williams, Hampshire, Gray, Larmore, Raz and others,[2] have held that value is plural, and that this has important consequences for political design. A representative recent view is that of John Gray:

> Agonistic liberalism is an application in political philosophy of the moral theory of *value-pluralism* – the theory that there is an irreducible diversity of ultimate values ... and that when these values come into conflict or competition with one another there is no overarching standard or principle, no common currency or measure, whereby such conflicts can be arbitrated or resolved. This anti-

> monistic, anti-reductionist position in ethical theory may appear innocuous ... but ... appearances are thoroughly deceptive.[3]

The part played by pluralism[4] in recent political philosophy is noteworthy in more ways than one. Those, like Gray, who talk of the 'fact' of value-pluralism assume the truth of a position which in meta-ethical theory remains the object of keen disagreement – namely, that value is a thing of a sort, about which it is correct – not merely intelligible – to think that there are facts. Sometimes, claims of this kind are held alongside a Humean, or at any rate non-cognitivist, position on the nature of value in general. The assumption that pluralists have only to prove their case against monists ignores the vulnerability of both protagonists to anti-realist positions in the philosophy of value. But more salient for my purposes is the assumption that these 'facts' about the structure of value have important consequences for political design.

I shall argue that there is reason to doubt whether pluralism, if true, really has these consequences. First, I shall consider a number of possible formulations of the doctrine of value-pluralism, with the justifications which might be offered in its defence – in particular, interpretations of the claim that pluralism is true because some values are 'incommensurable' with others. Gray and a number of other liberal writers[5] dismiss monism as a false theory of value. My aim, however, is not to show that monism is true, or even that pluralism is false, but to indicate that the monist's resources are greater than is often supposed. Though the arguments of pp. 81–92 are directed against certain well-known arguments for pluralism, the ulterior aim is not to promote monism in its stead, but to argue that since monism is consistent with (alleged) evaluative phenomena which are often thought to support pluralism, it is doubtful whether the issue between pluralism and monism is important to this project; or at least, if this issue is important, the case remains to be made. I then consider the consequences of pluralism for political design. The claim that there are diverse conceptions of the good in civil society should be distinguished from the claim, with which it has been conflated, that the diversity of the conceptions extends to the goods or values which they are conceptions of. The claim that there is this diversity is consistent with monism, as indeed is the claim that conceptions of the good have value *as such*. Moreover, commitment to democracy as *the* legitimate political decision-making procedure may involve metaphysical commitments, but there is little reason to think of these as 'pluralist': in important respects they favour monism. Liberals such as Rawls have been much concerned with the diversity of conceptions of the good in civil society, which is often taken both as evidence for the truth of pluralism, and as supporting a liberal political order. In conclusion I shall argue that, when taken as a claim about the nature of value, pluralism lacks – and on some popular versions of the thesis, *necessarily* lacks – positive consequences for political design.

Incommensurability and pluralism

Here I examine some possible justifications for pluralism, focusing on the claim that certain values are plural because they are incommensurable with one another. Gray writes that contemporary western society 'harbours conceptions of the good life and views of the world that, though they may overlap, are sometimes so different as to be incommensurable: they lack common standards whereby they could be assessed'.[6] Pluralism as a doctrine about the nature of value is often assumed rather than argued for, and the nature of the claim made by pluralism requires clarification. My ultimate interest, however, is not so much in the justifiability of pluralism, as in the consequences for political design of arguments purporting to justify it. In the discussion I shall speak of objects – goods or practical options – as *embodying* value. This is intended to carry minimal metaphysical commitments, and is meant only to countenance the possibility that a given value may be predicable of a number of objects. In particular, beyond this, it is meant to carry no commitments as to the metaphysical relation between value and the objects of which it is predicable. Following established usage, I shall also talk of *conceptions of the good*. I shall take it that a conception of the good necessarily regards some object (such as a form of life) as embodying value. However, the converse does not hold. Value-ascription only counts as a conception of the good if the object concerned is conceived of as good; someone might think that an object embodied the value of *humility*, but think that humility was self-abasement, or hypocrisy.

I shall not attempt a formal definition of *value-pluralism* at this stage. As a starting-point I shall use the definition given by Larmore,[7] who takes pluralism to be the claim that '[t]here are many viable conceptions of the good life that neither represent different versions of some single, homogeneous good nor fall into any discernible hierarchy'. However, important philosophical issues lurk beneath this definition. One point is that there is, as we shall see, a form of value-pluralism which regards the relevant values as incommensurable with one another, but also as falling into a hierarchy. A further issue, whose importance will become increasingly apparent during the course of the argument, concerns the status of Larmore's negative claim in the passage above. On the face of it, as this is purely a negative claim, it is consistent with scepticism, or nihilism, about value.

The problem then is that, though monism is indeed ruled out, it is hard to see why the mere absence of a single homogeneous good, of the kind proposed by monism, matters very much. It may seem to matter more if pluralism is held not merely to deny that monism makes a true (realistically construed) claim about the nature of value, but to offer in place of monism a rival realist claim of its own – that is, that the diversity of conceptions corresponds to a real plurality of values (or something similar) – a thought which underlies talk about the 'fact' of pluralism. I shall however argue towards the end that this impression is deceptive.

Non-linearity

What value-pluralism is committed to depends on what other claims justify it. One often-rehearsed justification is that values are plural because they are *incommensurable*;[8] but the latter claim requires clarification, and not just because the objects so related are values. For example, on one interpretation, the diagonal and side of a square of unit area are incommensurable, as the former is not expressible as a ratio of integers. It is true that $\sqrt{2}$ cannot be so expressed, but it is nonetheless possible to order this number in relation to any rational number. So this kind of incommensurability may show that we are dealing with distinct kinds of mathematical object, but as this does not preclude ordering, the implications for practical choice are unclear. Crucially, it does not entail that the objects concerned are *equal*. This has been a source of confusion in thinking about value, as we shall see.

One interpretation holds that the incommensurability between values consists in, or is expressed through, non-linear preference orderings. An example is provided by Raz,[9] who argues in *The Morality of Freedom* that the mark of incommensurability between values is as follows: the relation between two values, as embodied in two distinct goods (or practical options) *A* and *B*, is such that neither is better than the other, even though there is a third good *C* which, while better than one of the original goods, is not better than the other. So we apparently have a form of *non-linearity* (as I shall refer to non-linear incommensurability between values) for the relation between the relevant measures of value, since though *A* is not better than *B*, but *C* is better than *A*, *C* is still not better than *B*. Raz argues that where this is the case, the values embodied in *A* and *B* must be incommensurable and therefore distinct. Hence the existence of non-linearity is taken to establish value-pluralism.

However, this makes controversial assumptions about the nature of value. These assumptions surface when we ask whether the goods or practical options are conceived of as *themselves* being distinct values, or are conceived of as embodying measures of independently existing and distinct values. The realist claim made by pluralism only follows if it is true both that the ordinal measures of value expressed by the preference-rankings above correspond to real measures of value, and the non-transitivity (if such it be) of these measures is sufficient to establish that values which they are measures of are really distinct.

The monist can question each of these assumptions. All that the description mentions, after all, is comparative measures of *good*. But then it seems that the monist can concede non-linearity for this set of rankings, without abandoning the claim that there is a single value: a monistic system, such as that of ethical hedonism, is consistent with the rankings given. The hedonist may be a realist about the basis in value of divisibility, but simply deny that we can, at the margin, attain the epistemic resolution required for full linearity: the most we can hope for is a partial ordering. Nonetheless we can, as in Sorites-type comparisons, assert on purely procedural grounds that *C* is a tangible increment to *A* (for example, if *C* and *A* represent non-cardinal and distinct but homogeneous measures of a single good).

But monists need not say that the orderings reflect inaccuracy in the measurement of value. They can claim that the *way* in which *A* is good may differ incommensurably from the way in which *B* is. This is consistent with the claim that there may be a basis for certain ordinal rankings of the goods, or options – most obviously, if *C* and *A* are related as respectively larger and smaller measures of a single good. That may mean that the prospects for any comprehensive attempts to measure value are poor, but nothing in monism as such commits it to a fully transitive system of measurement.

Raz's exposition of non-linearity also assumes the truth of a dubious decision-theoretic principle, namely *the independence of irrelevant alternatives*. The principle requires that an individual's ranking of two alternatives *A* and *B* cannot be altered by the intervention of a third option *C*. The individual's preference for (say) *A* over *B* cannot be affected by the rankings of *A* and *B* with respect to *C* (of course, we notoriously get a cyclical ranking if *C* is preferred to *A* and *B* to *C*, whence it follows by transitivity that *B* is preferred to *A*). That Raz relies on the principle can be seen from the fact that his inference of non-linearity from the preference-orderings of *A*, *B* and *C*, assumes that the original ranking of *A* and *B* remains unaltered after *C* is introduced: only if this is so is it justifiable to infer non-linearity from the fact that, *ex ante*, neither *A* nor *B* is preferred to the other. For if the principle does not apply or is false, it is not inconsistent to claim that *C* is better than *A* but not better than *B*, while also saying that the *original* relation between *A* and *B* was one of equality.

It is, in any case, doubtful whether the account is coherent. Raz is at pains to stress that the non-ranking of *A* and *B* is not to be taken as indifference, but it seems that he has to rely not merely on indifference between, but the equal ranking of, the options concerned. In the situation Raz imagines, neither of the two options *A* and *B* is regarded as better than the other, while a third option *C* is regarded as better than one of the two original options, but not the other. Now the preference-relation between *A* and *B* cannot be that of equality, that is, it cannot be that they are regarded as equally good: their pairwise rankings with respect to *C* are expressly designed to rule that out. But then the fact that *C* is not preferred to one of the original options, and that that option is not preferred to *C*, cannot be taken to establish their equality either. But if we are not justified in assuming that they are equal in value, we cannot infer from the fact that *C* is preferred to *A* but not to *B*, that non-linearity applies, since we cannot assume that *A* and *B* are equal in value. The fact that *C* is preferred to *A* but not to *B* would only establish non-linearity if *A* and *B* had been taken to be of equal value – that *C* is *not* preferred to *B*, despite the preference relation of *A* and *B*, would only prove non-linearity (by the failure of transitivity) if *A* and *B* were equal. But that is what Raz rules out.

I conclude, therefore, that the argument from non-linearity fails to establish that the alleged incommensurability in preference-rankings is explicable only by value-pluralism.[10] Next I consider arguments which seek to establish pluralism from disputes involving value.

Rational interminability

Sometimes it is held that the existence of such disputes – for example, disputes about what courses of action, in a practical situation, values demand – provides grounds for believing in pluralism. The claim that disputes over value are 'rationally interminable' is more often made than explained or justified, and when the interminability is defined more closely and argued for, its apparent support for pluralism may prove illusory. If the grounds for asserting that the disputes are rationally interminable is that the parties to them are both reasonable and incapable of reaching agreement, then there are rationally interminable disputes about the practical requirements of a single value, such as that of justice, or loyalty. A person might be concerned only to be just, or loyal, but be uncertain as to which of a presented set of actions best promoted this. These can of course also be enacted inter- as well as intrapersonally. So the fact of rational interminability, thus interpreted, cannot be enough for pluralism.

In fact the informal definition just given is inadequate, since the parties' failure to reach agreement may be quite unrelated to any value-based consideration. What is needed, additionally, is a certain sort of *explanation* as to why they fail to agree: that explanation, roughly, will trace the disagreement to the nature of the values involved. Spelt out slightly more fully, then, the rational interminability claim asserts that the claims mounted by the disputants are such that none of the claims, even when supplemented with optimal empirical information, can be shown to be more reasonable than its rival(s), or that equally reasonable, optimally-informed persons may disagree about what the values require. Of course, the disputants will not see things like this, in the interpersonal case, but we can focus on the intrapersonal possibility. The optimally informed person may be represented as unable to decide, on the basis of reason, between the competing claims of these values, and this inability (the argument goes) is due to the fact that the values concerned are plural.

We can, however, note that this type of argument presupposes certain claims about the nature of value. The sentimentalist or emotivist non-cognitivist is apt to assert, as Hume put it, that morality is more properly felt than judged of. Given a broadly Humean conception of their nature, values will be such that propositions about them admit neither of rational demonstration, nor (where a conjunction of them yields logical inconsistency) of reduction to whatever proposition is most reasonable. If it is right to deny that talk about morality, including moral values, is guided by reason, this will explain why disputes about value are rationally interminable. Pluralism and monism are committed to rival forms of realist claim about the metaphysical structure of value. But since what is at issue between pluralism and monism is therefore not realism, the claim that pluralism is more successful than monism in explaining (at least some) disputes about value will not entail pluralism, even if it provides grounds for rejecting monism. There are, in any case, further reasons for doubting that the rational interminability of value-based disputes refutes monism. These follow from the objection to the argument from non-linearity to pluralism stated above, provided only that rational terminability entails truth-assessability.[11] It is, indeed, hard to see what rational terminus there could be to a dispute over value, unless the parties to it have a truthlike mode of assessment available to them. Given this, if it is neither true nor false that *A* is better than *B* (and it is not true that they are equally good), this entails that a dispute between two persons, one advocating *A* and the other *B*, is rationally interminable. For if the proposition *z* that '*A* is better than *B*' is neither true nor false, then it is not truth-assessable, and there is no rational terminus to the dispute between two persons, one of whom asserts, and the other of whom denies *z* – that is to say, disputes over *z* are rationally interminable. What about the proposition *z'*, namely that '*z* is neither true nor false'? Perhaps *z'* has a determinate truth-value: if non-linear incommensurability is true of the options named by *A* and *B*, then that value must be *true*. But that was the possibility which, we discovered earlier, was after all consistent with monism, as it was consistent with their being two distinct presentations of a unitary good *sub specie boni*. If *z'* is false, then it must be the case either that *z* is true, or else that *z* is false – in other words, it is the case either that *A* is better than *B*, or else that *A* is not. But neither of these propositions is inconsistent with monism, as we have seen. The remaining possibility is that *z'* itself is neither true nor false. But then, in particular, it is not the case that *z'* is true, that is, it is not the case that *z* is neither true nor false. So either *z* is true or *z* is false and, as before, neither possibility is inconsistent with monism. So if the grounds for asserting that a dispute over *z* is 'rationally interminable' are that *z* is neither true nor false, it does not follow that monism is false.

Conflicts of values

A further set of considerations held to support value-pluralism, which is sometimes thought to follow from the incommensurability of the values involved, is that values may come into conflict. Sometimes it is held that so-called 'tragic' conflicts provide illustrations of this. But it is not very plausible, if it is held that tragic conflicts provide reasons for believing in pluralism, to think that they are the *only* type of conflict which does so: it must rather be that the tragic conflicts enact in a pressing form value-based conflicts which often arise in more humdrum circumstances. The phenomenon of regret, often cited in this connection, extends from the 'tragic' cases to their workaday counterparts. On one view, tragic choices dramatise the conflicts present in precisely these day-to-day situations. The question, then, is whether there are practical conflicts involving values whose only or best explanation is that the values involved are plural.

To establish pluralism it is certainly not sufficient simply to point out that agents are often confronted with alternative actions, each of which is valuable, but not all of which the agent can, given the circumstances, perform. This may well constitute a rational basis for regret, both in tragic and non-tragic situations, as many commentators have argued.[12] But it is unwarranted to think that the existence of rational regret, in situations of conflict, is enough by itself to show that the elements of the conflict (distinct, and not co-attainable, actions, goods, and so on) embody distinct values. The rational basis for regret is that, given two or more severally possible but not compossible actions, I cannot perform all of them although each is valuable.

Thus the conflict may be between a number of incompossible practical options, each of which embodies the same value, such as different pleasurable ways of spending the evening. I may regret that, given that I am having dinner with a friend, I shall not be able to go to the theatre. But if what makes these options valuable is that each would be pleasurable, my regret at missing out on one of them cannot be due to its embodying a value distinct from that embodied in the option I choose. So the mere fact of rational regret is insufficient for pluralism. Differently, practical conflict may arise from uncertainty as to which of a presented set of options embodies, or best embodies, a given value, such as that of honour. This is something on which reasonable persons may disagree. If so, reasonable disagreement over practical options is consistent with monism, as argued previously.

What requires further investigation, then, is the *basis* for conflicts involving valuable options. If practical conflicts are to support pluralism, what needs to be shown is that the conflicts' basis lies in irreducibly distinct values. One line of thought would be that conflicts of value are conflicts between irreducibly distinct values when and only when their basis is non-contingent. I shall take the *basis* of practical conflict to be the condition of the incompossibility of the options it comprises. What then is the condition of the incompossibility of the objects (goods, options, and so on) involved in practical conflicts involving value? As we have already seen, it need not be that the objects embody distinct values. However, if the options can be so described that they are *logically* incompossible, it appears that there must be some single value, in terms of which the relevant descriptions are framed. It is not enough to rewrite the description of one object in such a way that it necessarily excludes the other(s), since we can make exactly the same move in cases where the practical conflict has a contingent basis, and indeed a contingent basis involving a single value. If it is a condition of certain kinds of practical conflict (not all, as we have seen) that there are plural values, then presumably those conflicts' basis lies in truths about the values concerned.

Suppose that an object embodies a value in virtue of something – say in virtue of its instantiating a set of naturalistic properties on which the value supervenes. Then, when it figures in conflicts of the kind envisaged by this argument, the conflict's basis is the condition(s) of incompossibility of the elements comprising it. Suppose these two elements are two objects *A* and *B*, related as above to distinct value. The condition must then amount to this: that *A* embodies a certain value *V*, in virtue of *A*'s instantiating a certain set of non-evaluative properties; that *B* embodies a distinct value *V'*, in virtue of *B*'s instantiating a certain set of non-evaluative properties; and in a sense to be determined, the members of these two sets are incompossible.

It may be that the properties are logically non-coinstantiable, that is, such that it would be logically impossible for an object to instantiate (members of) both sets. But this will not be enough to provide a non-contingent basis for the conflict if the relation is only that of supervenience, since a distinctive feature of this understanding of the relation of naturalistic and evaluative properties is the lack of *logical* entailment between the statement that an object has properties of the subvenience class, and the statement that it has the evaluative property: all that the supervenience account requires is that objects identical in respect of their subvenience properties must be identical also in respect of any properties of the supervenience class. So then there will be nothing to stop a monist denying that the conflict's basis is non-contingent. This denial could be based on either of two grounds. First, it could be said that it is not impossible that one or other of the objects could embody its value via a different set of subvenience properties, and that this other set could prove compossible with those instantiated by the other object, so the conflict's basis would be contingent. Or it could be denied that one or other object embodies the value it is held to embody. Furthermore, and as a consequence of this, the basis for the conflict between the *values* (as opposed to the subvenience properties) must be contingent, and the rational basis for regret may be precisely the wish that both values were attainable.

It will be noted that this argument trades on philosophical positions peculiar to the doctrine of supervenience/ resultance, and it may be said as a result that the argument, if it works, applies to this alone. But it is hard to see how *any* construal of the conditions required for an object to embody a value could establish a logically necessary basis for conflict.

The following seems an uncontroversial requirement: that if an object embodies a value, then the object has some property or properties, in virtue of which it embodies the value. Either the logical relation between statements predicating the evaluatively relevant properties of the object, and that predicating the value of the object, is that of entailment, or it is not. Suppose that it is. Then what is required for the conflict's basis to be non-contingent must be this: that the values, as embodied in their respective objects, non-contingently conflict, because the objects' evaluatively relevant properties are incompossible. It must also be the case that one object's embodiment of its value *entails* the instantiation of certain evaluatively relevant properties incompossible with some of those entailed by the other. If not, an objector could simply say that the basis of the conflict in the objects' evaluatively relevant properties was contingent. But then what we are apparently left with is a conjunction of entailments, the consequents of which, taken together, yield a contradiction. Truth-functional analysis then yields a consistent proposition – that is, yielding the overall value *true* under some, but not all, truth-value assignments. More saliently, all those assignments on which the proposition is true are inconsistent with the truth of the conjunction of the value-predicating propositions. So the overall proposition is true only if one or other value-predicating components is false.

Perhaps what is involved here is some relation other than that of entailment. But if so, it is hard to see how it can be shown that the conflict does not have a contingent basis. The problem for the pluralist is to show that a monistic explanation of the conflict *cannot* be right. For an argument to show that the basis of a given practical conflict is non-contingent, it seems that what it has to show is that the relevant sets of evaluatively relevant properties cannot be coinstantiated. In view of this, it is hard to see what demonstrative argument there could be, from the fact that there are practical conflicts involving values, to the conclusion that value is plural. Some arguments for pluralism are based on contingent conflicts of value. Stocker[13] argues that there are rational practical conflicts (he accepts that there are also irrational ones). It is a condition of the *rationality* of practical conflicts that there is no single, homogeneous good, measures of which each option embodies: for then there must be some object(s) embodying the greatest (or equal-greatest) measure of value. But, he continues, if that is so, then any agent believing that there is a *conflict* between the objects must be irrational, since there is one object which, measured in terms of the single value, surpasses all its rivals, and it is irrational, given this, to believe that a conflict exists. So if there are rational practical conflicts, there must be plural values (Stocker explicitly denies that all cases where plural values conflict must give rise to rational conflict).

One response to this is simply to deny the first premiss on the familiar Humean grounds that the considerations, in respect of which value is imputed to objects, are in their nature not susceptible of rational appraisal. I shall however not take this further, focusing instead on the second premiss. Stocker's thought seems to be this: since it is irrational to prefer the lesser to the greater good (where they can be measured on a homogeneous scale), it must be irrational to experience conflict when this is true. He remarks that 'what is obviously giving us plural values is my requirement that each of the conflicting options has something good about it not also had by the other'.[14] However, the phrase 'has something good about it ...' is ambiguous. It cannot mean simply that each object embodies a distinct volume of good, since that is true regardless of whether the values involved are plural; but it is not clear that any claim beyond this is justifiable. So the conflict cannot be explained by the fact that, given that each option available is valuable, the agent would be better off having all of them, rather than just one – for that is true when only one value is involved. Nor is it enough, as Stocker acknowledges, for the values simply to be distinct, since in some cases the value of one object clearly surpasses the (distinct) value of another. But then it seems that the argument assumes the equality, or rough equality, or (rough) epistemic equality, of the options involved. Stocker might try to press the claim that there can be no rational conflict where only a single value is involved. But if the grounds for saying that there are rational conflicts involving value is that there are plural values, it is unclear what response Stocker makes to a monist who denies that there are such conflicts.Here the risk of circularity clearly looms. At the methodological level, this raises the question whether the phenomena (that is, here of regret) would be discredited if it turned out that monism was true, rather than suggesting that the phenomena themselves give grounds for doubting that monism is inconsistent with rational regret.[15] But in any case, as we will see later, intractable arguments arise for pluralistically based political design if his argument is right.

This is not to deny that there are practical conflicts. Moreover, nothing I have said prevents a pluralist from arguing that distinct, conflicting values may simply present themselves as an irreducible feature of certain situations. Nor does this mean that there cannot be contingent practical conflicts involving irreducibly distinct values. What I have objected to is that means of *demonstrating* the values' distinctness which locates the conflicts' basis in non-contingent conditions of their elements' incompossibility. What follows from this, I think, is not that there can never be practical conflicts involving plural values, but that it is doubtful whether there could be a satisfactory philosophical argument to establish this. If that is right, it is doubtful whether these features of practical conflict could provide conclusive reasons for belief in pluralism.

But, regardless of the issue between pluralism and monism, if saving the phenomena of practical conflict is what political philosophy must do, the fact of conflict is more important than the theoretical explanation of it. I have suggested that monists can save these phenomena. But even if that is wrong, to provide a correct explanation of the phenomena of conflict is still not to explain how to deal with it politically. Whether or not value-pluralism is the reason for (some) practical conflicts, what is *politically* important is how the conflicts are dealt with. But – to anticipate the argument at the end of this chapter – if Stocker *does* succeed in showing that pluralism gives rise to rational conflicts, then *ex hypothesi* pluralism will not be available to solve them. Next, however, I consider a form of value-incommensurability which expressly rejects the claim that pluralistic values cannot stand in a hierarchical relation.

Lexical rankings

A clear-cut form of incommensurability consists in the possibility of *lexical* rankings of values.[16] Rawls famously ranked the two principles of justice lexically in *A Theory of Justice*.[17] This was held to be required by the absolute priority of certain kinds of consideration (such as freedom of conscience) over others. The relation between the values can then be mapped as a vertical or horizontal indifference curve. As I remarked earlier, what value-pluralism is committed to depends on what considerations (if any) justify it. If it follows from lexical incommensurability, it will be committed to rejecting, for example, Larmore's definition of value-pluralism as the claim that there are values which both do not constitute versions of a single homogeneous good, *and* do not form a hierarchy. For a hierarchy is what a lexical ordering is. It is weaker than incomparability – at least to the extent that the latter entails the falsity of something which lexical incommensurability, as applied to a given pair of goods, entails, namely the judgement that one good is better than the other.

This relation between goods is held to be represented by the fact that an infinite increment of one good would be required to compensate a finite loss of the other. It is not clear here that the relation between these goods is one of incommensurability, since the goods may be regarded as subject to trade-off at a transfinite level of cardinality, and the idea of commensuration is not obviously inconsistent with such trades. The claim can be strengthened, to say that *no* increment to the one good compensates *any* loss of the other. It is often said, for example, that no amount of a trivial good like ice-cream would suffice to compensate a loss of a limb. Space does not permit extended consideration of the thesis that this relation holds between certain values, or the goods embodying them. We should, however, bear in mind the following points. First, as Griffin points out,[18] it may be that trivial goods are characterisable as subject to sharply diminishing marginal utility, and this may yield a finite number when summed over infinite amounts of the good. Further, it may be that the 'incommensurability' concerns the terms of the comparison, not the goods compared. Loss of a (whole) limb is an all-or-nothing matter. But loss of the *use* of a limb is not: it can be graduated. Then it seems less bizarre to think that a small loss of use might be offset by a sufficiently large volume of ice-cream: the indifference curve may be rectilinear only along a certain portion of its length, or asymptotic to a line parallel to the relevant axis. Similarly with comparisons where trivial goods are measured against loss of life. Individuals often engage in trade-offs involving the gain of relatively trivial goods for the (reasonable expectation that) a certain *amount* of life will be lost as a result: being dead, like being bereft of a limb, is an all-or-nothing matter, but that does not mean that the comparative judgements on the basis of which decisions are made in situations of practical choice involving such goods, must also be all-or-nothing.

My argument need not, however, reject the possibility of lexical incommensurability. The question is rather what follows for liberalism if it is true of certain values, or the goods embodying them. The possibility of lexical incommensurability between goods does not falsify monism, since there is nothing incoherent in the thought that one good's embodiment of a value may be incommensurably greater than another good's embodiment of the same value: this is sometimes entailed by comparative aesthetic judgements, for example. Alternatively, it may be said that there can be finite and transfinite measures of a single good. One possible form of lexical incommensurability – a version of which, as already noted, Rawls endorses – applies to the relations between the meta-ethical concepts themselves.

Meta-ethical incommensurability

A further possible interpretation of 'pluralism' applies to alleged structural relations between the meta-ethical concepts themselves. On this interpretation, what is plural is not value, but the relation between 'thin' concepts such as 'right' and 'good'; that there are different philosophical accounts of the relation between deontic and evaluative 'thin' concepts is, on this view, a form of ethical pluralism. To use Dancy's metaphor, our conceptualisation of the ethical structure of a practical situation, and the possible courses of action which we can take in it, may be *shaped* differently, when viewed from the perspective of one 'thin' concept, rather than that of another.[19] These different shapes, notoriously, may yield divergent conclusions about what, in the circumstances, is the thing to do.

We can formulate the possibilities in meta-ethical parallel to the ethical pluralisms already distinguished. Thus it may be held that one class of 'thin' (that is, deontic) ethical properties is lexically prior to another (for example, evaluative) class. Or it may be held that differences of ethical 'shape' are such that *no* ordering is possible. Or (to anticipate a further form of pluralism distinguished below) they are distinct, but equal, ways of conceptualising ethical properties. Not all these possibilities need be of much significance for political design. It is far from clear that they are aptly described as instances of *value*-pluralism, since what is at issue in a situation of practical choice, or act-assessment, is how far value-based considerations (rather than other kinds of axiological ones, such as virtue-concepts, or deontic ones) are appropriate to its ethical conceptualisation. If the 'thin' properties are held to be non-lexically incommensurable, or commensurable but equal, it is hard to see what *general* consequences this has for political design – not least because, at this level of generality, a wide variety of first-order normative commitments is compatible with any given view of the meta-ethical relation. If that relation is one of non-ordering or equality, reference to that fact alone must underdetermine political design.

It is moreover clear that meta-ethical forms of pluralism must be distinct from those considered hitherto, since on one view of the relation between the 'thin' concepts, pluralism between values may not matter much precisely because deontic concepts enjoy priority over the evaluative ones. Rawls's neo-Kantianism is accordingly designed to contain the conflicts to which pluralism gives rise. Given Rawls's priority ordering, the fact that different values existed could be held to operate only at a level below that at which decisions about political design should be taken. Below I shall suggest that the belief that value-pluralism is important for political design is often supported by implicit appeal to this form of priority ordering.

Of course, the reverse priority ordering might be argued for. Then 'thin' evaluative concepts would have priority over deontic ones. If in addition the concepts thus prioritised comprised plural *values*, a form of value-pluralism would have been reinstated. I shall however argue below that theorists who, in taking value-pluralism to support liberalism, have sought an ethical structuring for political design, have mistaken its significance: either they fail to recognise how inimical this form of meta-ethical structuring for value-pluralism is to the project of political design, or they rely on non-pluralistic considerations in carrying this project through.

Pluralism in political design

I have now distinguished several varieties of pluralism, and questioned some incommensurability-based arguments for them. Here I consider their role in political design. It is important to note that the differences in the philosophical *content* of positions to which the term 'pluralism' is commonly applied correspond to differences in the role which these positions may be thought to play in political design.

Given that form of meta-ethical pluralism which subordinates evaluative to deontic considerations, for example, the claim made by *value*-pluralism is of secondary significance; what matters is the meta-ethical ordering itself. On another view, 'pluralism' simply names a sociological fact of life in modern societies, that is, that they in fact contain persons or groups professing distinct (and perhaps conflicting) conceptions of the good. Accordingly, a second conception of pluralism's argumentative role is that it justifies liberalism by providing the only set of political principles on which the partisans of different values, or conceptions of the good, can agree; a version of this is Rawls's 'overlapping consensus' idea. I take this up below; in brief, my conclusion will be that the argument relies not on pluralism, but on *agreement* about normative principles; and that where the political problem, which liberalism is held to solve, consists in the existence of diverse conceptions of the good, this already involves a fundamental normative commitment to the political significance of this very fact – where, usually, the commitment derives from the fact that those conceiving of the good are *persons*. This is not to deny the urgency of the political problem which this sort of pluralism may pose. It is however to suggest that the conditions for recognising the problem in the first place, and for solving it, are unlikely to involve a commitment to *value*-pluralism.

Most modern political philosophers accept that democracy is the only, or the most, justifiable form of political decision-making procedure. To be sure, this countenances quite wide disagreements about how best to embody democracy in political design. It is, however, hard to see how the claim that democracy enjoys this primacy can be justified without making certain kinds of value-based commitment (in addition, that is, to the value of democracy itself). As has often been observed, if the *only* reason for favouring democracy is that it promotes instrumental goals more effectively than rival procedures, there is no reason not to abandon it in favour of some other decision-procedure, if that proves more instrumentally effective. The alternative to this view need not be taken to be that there are intrinsic goods (such as that of participation in public life, or civic education) which a democratic polity necessarily promotes – *intrinsically instrumental* goods, as they might be called. It may be instead that democracy is the only way to respect the legitimate moral claims of the citizens, such as their entitlement to equality of respect, or to autonomy. A commitment to democracy not based purely on instrumental effectiveness typically rests on judgements concerning the moral status of those whom it seeks to enfranchise. One version of this is the contention that persons are equal as self-originating sources of valid claims on public resources.

It is not my aim to show that a non-instrumental commitment to democracy *necessarily* makes moral commitments of this kind. Rather I wish to elucidate the relation between them and the claims made by those who identify plural conceptions of the good life in civil society. I shall take it as an uncontroversial observation of social life in western societies like the US and Britain that they do, as a matter of fact, contain a diverse range of cultures, and that one of the ways in which those cultures are differentiated is that their members profess and enact different conceptions of the good life. It is hardly more controversial that there is an indefinite variety of further conceptions of the good life which are not in fact enacted within these societies. The question, however, is what significance the prevalence of these diverse conceptions of the good life has for political design.

The *de facto* existence in civil society of diverse conceptions of the good life does not show that there is a no less diverse range of values to which these conceptions correspond, or which provide truth-conditions for relevant propositions concerning value which might be asserted by those holding the conceptions. Some of these conceptions, or all of them, may simply be false (as a realist would put it), or inappropriate (as a non-cognitivist might say). Gray argues that value-pluralism cannot entail, or ground, liberalism in any general, still less universal way.

> The historical fact of a diversity of conceptions of the good ... may be a good reason for the adoption of liberal institutions in that society; but if value-pluralism is true, the range of forms of genuine human flourishing is considerably larger than can be accommodated within liberal forms of life. As a matter of logic alone, it is safe to say that value-pluralism cannot mandate liberalism.[20]

As I shall now argue, the fact that there are diverse conceptions of the good has significance for public policy only if the conceptions themselves, directly or derivatively, have value; and the *way* in which the conceptions have value (if they do) makes a difference to the theoretical response appropriate to them.

Value-pluralism need not concede that conceptions of the good *as such* have value. But in the passage cited above, Gray moves from the historical-factual observation that there is a diversity of conceptions of value to the conclusion that the conceptions are, directly or derivatively, of value themselves. It could then be said that the conceptions, *qua* conceptions, have direct value, or that they have value derivatively, to the extent that they correctly represent the independent truth about the values which they are conceptions of. The latter approach has, however, to acknowledge that it is likely to yield only an attenuated list of conceptions which have value. Conceptions of the good are, after all, often also conceptions of the bad, and not infrequently impute badness to other conceptions of the good. So the derivative approach will have, at least in principle, to sort out which conceptions have value, when there are internal conflicts of this kind. This does not of course mean that this approach is mistaken. But it does, as I shall argue in a moment, present problems of political justification within liberalism.

The alternative approach which I have identified takes the conceptions themselves to have value *as* conceptions. It might be argued that a form of transcendental argument applied here – that it is a condition of identifying the conceptions in question *as* conceptions of the good that they are seen as independently valuable. Perhaps that argument can survive obvious objections to it.[21] The question, however, is whether it provides a *pluralist* justification for liberalism. On the direct view, what matters is that the conceptions are bearers of value in their own right. But then it is of secondary importance at best, whether or not the conceptions are held to represent the *truth* about value. So the justificatory efficacy of the direct view does not depend on whether or not the diversity of conceptions represents a real diversity of value, as reported by value-pluralism. Then it seems that what will be important in political design is something akin to the pre-commitments characteristic of non-instrumental justifications of democracy. But those commitments were not *per se* pluralistic. They were commitments to a certain conception of what is of overriding importance for political design – equality of respect, personhood, and so on. This is consistent with denying that value-pluralism is true, and in many accounts (such as Rawls's) will follow from a meta-ethical model in which deontic considerations have priority over evaluative ones – a version of the meta-ethical pluralism considered earlier. If conflicts can arise from plural values, the latter will pose political problems, but it is unwarranted to assume that they must also determine or limit acceptable resolutions of these problems.

In contrast with the direct view, the derivative view holds that the conceptions' value derives from what they are conceptions of. We noted above, in discussing Raz's case for non-linearity, that his argument equivocated over whether allegedly incommensurable goods are equal in value. But the non-linear or lexical pluralist is surely *not* asserting that these conceptions are all equally good – that there is a single currency of value, equal measures of which each conception realises. That leads back to the rejection of pluralism, or at least away from a pluralistically based liberalism, as I shall now argue. The former alternative clearly applies if pluralism entails that the relation between the values concerned manifests non-linearity or lexical ordering. For equality of values is compatible with linear orderings of goods embodying them (for example, if one object embodies a larger volume of one value than another object does of a second value). Similarly, lexical ordering precludes equality. It is important to stress this, because arguments for certain forms of political design, or policy, often implicitly rely on the assumption that if values are plural, then they must be equal. If the values are plural because of non-linearity, no very clear practical implications follow. In particular, it does not follow that a policy, or aspect of political design, favouring one value over another is irrational, or unjustifiable. This obviously applies *a fortiori* with lexical pluralism.

Raz claims that values are plural to establish autonomy-based perfectionism. His argument is that it is a condition of acting autonomously that the agent has a number of valuable options from which to choose; therefore political design should secure the availability of these valuable options. This is a version of the derivative approach, since it relies on the claim that the options have independent value. It is possible to object to this argument on a number of grounds. For example, it is implausible to represent the options as susceptible of the choice regarded by Raz as necessary to autonomy – in which case the latter notion is incoherent. The pre-eminent status accorded to autonomy is also questionable, since presumably many of the valuable options will not themselves value autonomy, or not to this degree. It is doubtful, moreover, whether the argument needs to claim more than that there are a number of incompatible forms of life, and it is possible to conceive of each of them as having value; or, for a significant number of people so to conceive them. This makes no realist commitments. As argued earlier, even within these commitments, a monistic picture remains possible.

It may, however, be argued that values are plural but not incommensurable – that, indeed, goods embodying them can be equal in value. This would, then, purport to be a new, incommensurability-free, form of pluralism. Whether it counts *as* a form of pluralism depends on whether pluralism is committed to the following claim: *For all values* A, B, *if* A *and* B *are plural, there is no uniform scale, in terms of which goods embodying* A *and* B *can be measured.* Thus it might be said that different goods could be equally good, while realising different kinds of value, just as different kinds of noise may be equally loud. I shall call this *equality-pluralism.*

One response to this is to say that in this situation there *is* a single homogeneous good, of which the presented options are versions insofar as they have value. This is however insufficient for pluralism, since the fact that the goods differ from each other is consistent with their embodying the same value. I shall not discuss the broader metaphysical thesis which this pluralism demands. As noted above, it will require an argument establishing both that a value has properties beyond those determining the ranking, in relation to other goods, of a good embodying it, and that this rankability excludes monism. For our purposes, the question is what role equality-pluralism plays in justifying liberalism. On this form of pluralism, there are a number of values, these values are equal, and they are distinct despite being equal. Then, on the derivative view, the conceptions of the good presumably have equal value because what they are conceptions of – that is, distinct values, presented to the holders of the conceptions *sub specie boni* – have equal value. It is, of course, on this view indeterminate how many such derivatively value-bearing conceptions there will be, but political problems will only arise if these conceptions give rise to competing claims on public resources. It may then be said that certain characteristic meta-political[22] and substantive positions follow – for example, that political procedures should be neutral between the conceptions, or that policies of non-censorship or toleration should be implemented in respect of them. I have elsewhere criticised pluralistic arguments for neutrality – specifically, where the fact that the values are plural is held, via an insufficient-reason argument, to support neutrality.[23] Where the values are equal, the fact that it is impossible to choose both is no reason for choosing neither. Value-pluralism may operate at a relatively low justificatory level, below that at which major questions of political design are decided.

This is not to say that the equal value (understood derivatively or directly) of conceptions of the good would have no consequences for political design or policy. But where equality-pluralism does real justificatory work, it is hard not to conclude that the important consideration is the claim that the values are equal, rather than that they are plural. This can be illustrated, again, by considering the justification this form of pluralism would give for toleration. On one view, the circumstances of toleration are such that a given value, as embodied in certain practices, is only eligible for toleration if it is regarded as inferior. Even if it is coherent to regard the tolerated value as not inferior, a policy of toleration only follows from pluralism because it is regarded as equal: the fact that there are other value-properties besides that in virtue of which the value is equal is irrelevant. But, as we have seen, the fact of equality by itself is at least consistent with monism. Even if for some independent reason equality-pluralism is true, we still need a reason for thinking that it is the plurality of value, rather than its equality, which supports the policy.

The derivative approach claims that the value of conceptions of the good is derivative from the values themselves. But we can ask what relation this argument bears to false conceptions of value. On many liberal views, the fact that the conceptions of value may be false need not debar their holders from entitlement to neutral treatment or toleration; Mill's arguments in Chapter 2 of *On Liberty* are a case in point. Insofar as certain propositional judgements in which the conceptions ensue are inconsistent with judgements made by the votaries of rival conceptions, one or other must (at least, on realist assumptions) be false. But on many liberal views, the fact that two individuals or groups assert propositions which are collectively inconsistent is not a reason for favouring one over the other. If not, the relation of these propositions to 'facts' about value cannot be what determines public policy towards them. Suppose a form of life espoused by a considerable number of people arose from a false conception of value. The political question would remain: what is to be done about these people with their false beliefs? The relation between conceptions of value in different conceptions of the good life, whatever it is, matters only insofar as the conceptions form the grounds of possible conflict. That means that they must be enacted in the lives of citizens. But then issues about the metaphysical structure of value become irrelevant, irrespective of whether (as in Larmore's definition) the conceptions form a hierarchy. Even if the value represented by one conception is discernibly better than another, it need not be the case that the first is preferred to its rival when they conflict. As already noted, where there is held to be no such hierarchy, non-neutrality remains a possibility. It is possible to justify preferring one conception to another on grounds distinct from the conceptions' relative worth; and neutrality may only apply at a certain level, the motivation for a neutral policy being a commitment to some non-neutral value such as that of autonomy.

Thus it is hard to believe that the derivative approach provides pluralist support for characteristic liberal positions. It may still appear that this form of pluralism is likelier to have consequences for political design than its rivals do, but it is doubtful whether those liberal theorists who have taken pluralism to be important for political design have had this version of it in mind: this is ruled out by incommensurability-based pluralisms. It seems that those theorists who have taken value-pluralism to be important for political design have had in view something closer to the direct approach. This is consistent with some of the conceptions' being false, and on this view the indeterminacy of pluralism for policy is less important.

We have now distinguished forms of pluralist claims – equality, lexical and non-linear pluralism – which, respectively hold that pluralism entails that the values to which it applies are equal, unequal, and neither equal nor unequal. Many discussions, however, either fail to distinguish these version of pluralism, or more frequently confuse them with the observation that a number of conceptions of the good exist in society. Often it is this last claim theorists have in mind when they contend that pluralism supports their conception of political design. To reach this conclusion, however, they have to rely on a normative claim about those conceptions of the good, usually the non-pluralist thesis that conceptions of the good have value, or equal value, as conceptions. But by itself it is consistent with monism, since this view requires only that value is ascribed to a single kind of thing – namely, conceptions of the good. A variant of the form of argument criticised has recently been advanced by Barry, who argues that 'no conception of the good provides a basis for agreement on terms that nobody could reasonably reject. Neutrality ... [is] the solution.'[24] But the absence of a basis for reasonable agreement only matters if it matters that some people hold a conception of the good at variance with that basis; and judgements about what matters are normative judgments. This comes to the surface when we ask whether there might not be conceptions of the good featuring a view of politics which rejects this reasonableness criterion. Then, whatever else may be said, the solution will not be neutral with respect to these latter conceptions; moreover, the normative judgement which holds that what matters politically is what conceptions of the good are held in society is quite independent of value-pluralism.

The best-known attempt to work out a political *rapprochement* with these issues is that of Rawls. In recent work,[25] Rawls has argued that the fundamental desideratum of a theory of justice, in circumstances of actual pluralism, is that it command reasonable assent from the partisans of different conceptions of the good. This 'overlapping consensus' is necessary to entrench stable principles of justice among the persons or groups subject to them. As such, this construction of the circumstances of justice is a version of the direct approach to justification: conceptions of the good are to be taken account of politically *as* conceptions. But then attention shifts to the normative grounds for regarding the conceptions as eligible for political consideration. It seems that they require that holders of the conceptions are, as such, entitled to equal respect, but this does not demand value-pluralism, as we have seen. This is equally true when attention shifts to Rawls's stability desideratum: if the principles are capable of commanding reasonable assent, this will be true *despite* the differences between conceptions of the good, not because of them. Gaus[26] has recently argued that Rawls's concern should not be with what the parties will in fact assent to, but what they would assent to insofar as they were reasonable. If, however, this demands that political principles should attend not to conceptions of the good but to whether they are reasonable, a value-pluralistic basis for liberal political design will need an argument to show that these principles, if reasonable, must be shaped by pluralism itself. But value-pluralism may well manifest itself in different conceptions of what is reasonable. If so, the implications of value-pluralism for political design are to this extent indeterminate.

Many conceptions of the good, some of them prevalent in Western societies, reject the conception of moral personhood, equality, or autonomy on which non-instrumental justifications of democracy are usually based. Thus, a pre-commitment to democracy founded on these kinds of moral claim will preclude regarding as equal those actual or possible conceptions of the good which reject the claim (and often, with it, the commitment to democracy). It is then hard to see how a liberal with such commitments could regard the objects of these conceptions as equal. The alternatives seem to be either to deny such conceptions' equality or to move to a different form of pluralism – most obviously, that offered by the direct approach. But then, as I have argued, it is no longer pluralism which is doing the work of justification.

Conclusion

Recent liberal theorists have argued or assumed that political philosophy should shape its ideal theory in accordance with pre-existing conceptions of (moral) value – ideals of moral personhood, justice, rights, autonomy and so on. At the same time, they have tried to respect value-pluralism. If political philosophers set out to shape theory in accordance with a pre-existing apparatus of moral concepts, it is tempting to think that 'truths' about the latter should bear upon the design of theory, particularly when pressing political issues – those posed by actually conflicting conceptions of the good life – seem to find their echo in them. Some of these conceptions certainly compete, though this is quite compatible with their differing, in some cases, only indexically.

I have argued that none of the forms of value-pluralism which I have distinguished has much significance for political design. Some of the most popular arguments for pluralism prove to be consistent with monism. Moreover, those versions of pluralism which take their cue from alleged incommensurabilities of value have to acknowledge that if values are commensurable, the implications for political design are ambiguous. Some characteristic liberal positions will then not be justified by pluralism. For example, the mere 'fact' of value-pluralism will not be enough to justify policies of toleration towards conceptions of the good in which the relevant values figure. In general, it will not be available to pluralists to invoke an insufficient-reason form of argument in justifying meta-political positions such as neutrality. For the fact, if it is one, that values are plural, does not show that there is insufficient reason to prefer one value to the other – even with equality-pluralism. The most that will follow is that the plurality of the values themselves will be insufficient to ground a preference for one value over the other(s).[27] But even this is a Trojan horse. I shall argue for this conclusion by means of a *reductio*. Its target will be the claim that value-pluralism is a thesis whose truth bears significantly on the project of political design. Either value-pluralism is true or it is not. If it is not, then it has no consequences for this project, though the fact that it is false may have. But if it is true, not much follows for political design either; the only way in which politics can take seriously the ethical claim made by incommensurabilitarian value-pluralists is by abandoning (to the extent that the values were plural) the project of structuring political design ethically.

I exclude from the argument the lexical form of pluralism; if Larmore's definition is accepted, this is not pluralism anyway. If, however, the values figuring in certain conceptions of the good are lexically ordered over those in others, then certain policy and meta-political positions popular in contemporary liberalism, such as (in some of its versions) neutrality, will be ruled out for the values concerned. Insofar as the relations between values figuring in conceptions of the good manifest lexical incommensurability, it favours, if anything, an older, non-neutral form of liberalism (for example, Millian perfectionism). Admittedly, if certain values, such as liberty, are lexically ordered over others, this may have consequences for public policy. But this is not the way value-pluralism is usually taken to support traditional liberal policy stances. Since lexical ordering is not a form of pluralism for which the existence of diverse conceptions of the good in society is plausibly regarded as evidence, there is little reason to think that it will support policies which seek to address that diversity; the justificatory paths diverge when extant conceptions favour the opposite of these policies.[28] As we have seen, that support is to be found in independent considerations about equal status, autonomy, or a negative-liberty conception of the person. Whatever else they are, these are liberal values – values which are politically contestable.

So I confine the argument to non-lexical pluralism. Suppose, contrary to the argument of pp. 86–94 above, we could show that the explanation for certain practical conflicts lay in irreducibly distinct values. These values must have the capacity to generate conflicts if they are to be of any importance for political design. If they could not do so, it is hard to see why any political questions should be raised by them. Unless the conflict is due to lexical pluralism, reference to the values themselves will fail to determine what, in the situation, is the best thing to do. Suppose value-pluralism is true. It may, as noted, operate at a fairly low level, and there may be other kinds of consideration which, in practical conflicts generated by pluralism, guide action by overcoming its practical indeterminacy. But to the extent that pluralism is true, action is imperfectly guided by the values concerned. There may or may not be an 'overlapping consensus' about values, and it may or may not be accommodated adequately to different conceptions of value. But if consensus exists despite these differences, it will attest not to the values' plurality, but to their similarity. If practical conflicts brought about by adherence to plural values pose political problems, then *ex hypothesi* reference to the values alone will not be sufficient to resolve them. This will apply also to argument basing pluralism on the alleged incomparability of values, where this is distinguished from their incommensurability. The fact that values are incomparable provides no guide to political design; all possibilities remain in play when we learn that certain values cannot be compared with others. How could that knowledge alone suffice to guide action?

This is not to say that there is no consideration by reference to which value-based conflicts might be resolved in political design. But wherever that consideration comes from – even if it comes from one of the conflicting values – it will necessarily not be the 'fact' that the values concerned are plural. This is why the insufficient-reason argument is a Trojan horse. For if plural values mean that reason is insufficient to guide action, it is insufficient to guide political design. This is true even if everyone is agreed that the values are plural (rather than the single-minded partisans of one value confronting those of another). To know that practical indecision arises from plural values is to frame the problem, not to solve it.[29]

If so, the justificatory power of value-pluralism, in its non-lexical form, is limited. This is good news for liberals, insofar as it relieves them from relying on controversial claims about the nature of value. But it also suggests that justification may be a more local enterprise than that aspired to by recent theory. This has been obscured by conflating under the label 'pluralism' the direct and descriptive valuations of conceptions of the good discussed at pp. 95–6. There are wider problems facing value-pluralism when it sets out to structure political design. This is most obvious on the direct approach, but is true also of many values countenanced by versions of the derivative approach as well. As the passage from Gray acknowledged, a liberal conception of politics and its demarcation from civil society will itself express a particular conception of the good – one to which many other such conceptions are inimical. It is hard to see why a non-liberal conception of politics cannot be part of a conception of the good which is pluralistically related to others. Indeed, there are conceptions of the good in which political design is not seen as derivable from claims about the structure of value. This is particularly awkward for pluralistic arguments to meta-political conclusions, such as procedural neutrality.

Liberals could, of course, narrow 'pluralism' to refer only to values or associated conceptions of the political which they endorse. This may offer a more theoretically stable position. But it also offers a more normatively limited version of the justificatory project than that to which many liberals have lately aspired.

5
Moral Theory and Political Philosophy

Introduction

What contribution can philosophy make to deciding what we have good reason politically to do? The question is not often posed as baldly as this, and when it is, there seems to be a number of possible answers.

However, discussion in political philosophy very often assumes that the question has a quite specific answer. That is that there is a certain class of reasons for action, namely moral ones, which play a fundamental role in determining the shape of political institutions and procedures. The philosophical task is then taken to be that of determining political design from theoretical reflection about the nature of fundamental moral requirements, with differences of opinion about the nature of those requirements and the fundamental values, or moral concerns, from which they are held to result. Thus in Rawls[1] and Barry[2] we find that the prime concern is with justice; in Raz, autonomy;[3] in Nozick[4] and Gewirth,[5] individual rights; in Dworkin[6] and Larmore,[7] equality of respect for persons, and so on. My concern is ultimately with the justifiability of this starting-point.

Most recent political philosophy has rested on two methodological assumptions: the sovereignty of morality, and cognitivist internalism. The first assumption is, roughly, that moral considerations take precedence over others, and therefore the task of political philosophy is to attempt the project of political design guided by what theory takes to be its fundamental moral commitment or value – justice, autonomy, rights, equality, and so on. The second assumption vindicates the project of prescribing conclusions about political design by means of theory. But, as I argue, these assumptions pull against one another. What emerges is an immanent critique of cognitivism, whereby the theory's presumptive *point* – that is, to provide an explanation of how theoretical reason can be practical – is undermined by externalism. A cognitivist view of the status of moral propositions is, I argue, quite consistent with the view that amoral agents are not as such irrational.

Hence the methods of political philosophy promote post-political theorising. The tendency is for theory to retreat from explaining political actors' real motives into an account of how they *would* behave if their motivations conformed to the prescriptions of ideal theory, while politics, most of the time, has to work with *given* motivations. This is my fundamental *theoretical* explanation for the currency of ideal normative theory in political philosophy.

The plan of this chapter is as follows. I shall set out and examine a number of forms of internalism – claims linking statements ascribing moral properties, or reasons, to agents and their prospective actions, with statements about their motivational states. I shall argue that there is reason to question each of the forms of internalism examined. I shall argue for the coherence, and persuasiveness, of externalism, and suggest that this is quite compatible with cognitivism. The main assumption, in general shared by both cognitivists and non-cognitivists, which I shall challenge is that it follows from the truth of cognitivism that the agent who fails to act morally is to that extent convicted of acting irrationally; this assumption is often shared by *non*-cognitivists, who in consequence reject cognitivism in order to show that the amoral agent is not as such irrational. My major concern in this chapter, however, is in the wider distortions in moral theory which the widespread adoption of internalism has brought about. In particular, and perhaps surprisingly, internalism has led to a neglect of motivations themselves: philosophical theory articulates a set of theory-approved actions, to which the moral agent's motivations are required to conform, rather than enjoying any independent status. Since, as I have argued so far in this book, much contemporary political philosophy consists in the application to politics of moral theory, it is unsurprising that internalist assumptions, which dominate the latter, surface in political theory also; if anything, a re-emphasis on the ethical content of agents' *given* motivations is more pressing, however, in political philosophy, since rational political action has to take into account, as Machiavelli said, a world in which so many are not virtuous.

Ethical inquiry

Below, I distinguish between two forms of philosophical approach to ethical inquiry. As I shall argue, they really are distinct, and only come together if complex and contentious assumptions are made, as I shall try to bring out.

The first of these approaches takes morality as a *found* phenomenon – as the sort of thing of which it would in principle be possible to write a natural history. On this approach, morality has as good a claim to existence as, say, Switzerland, or the collegiate method of aggregating votes in the US to determine who is elected president. Morality just does exist *qua* cultural-historical artefact; nothing philosophically controversial, for example between ethical realism and anti-realism, is presupposed by this. Philosophical inquiry within this approach then proceeds to analysis – for example, analysis of specimens of moral concepts and language, their semantics, usage and logical form. Thus it may be argued that we can distinguish (in Clifford Geertz's terminology) between 'thin' and 'thick' ethical concepts,[8] and theory may then set about deciding which is fundamental – on a strong view, identifying that concept to which the others are reducible.

The second approach tries to reconstruct moral thinking and agency, so to speak, from the inside – not, to be sure, by means of a phenomenological account, but by attempting to (re-)construct those good reasons on the basis of which moral agents act. This more agency-orientated approach seeks to understand morality, roughly, as a possible part of practical reason – to explain, in Kant's terminology, how theoretical reason can be practical. This need not be a normative task either – theory can address, for example, the possibility of *akrasia* as a given phenomenon of the moral life. But in practice, in setting out a theoretical analysis of the reasons on which (moral) agents *can* act, ethical and political philosophy has often sought to provide a prescriptive account of how they ideally *ought* to act.

I shall suggest that these are distinct philosophical inquiries, that it is an assumption, open to challenge, and that if they are to issue in a unified philosophical account of morality, there are specific theoretical obstacles to be overcome.

One theoretical procedure runs roughly as follows.[9] Meta-ethical theory argues, as already described, for a particular view of the primordial ethical concepts – say, a view of the deontic as being that to which other kinds of ethical concept are reducible, or in terms of which they are expressible. We could call these concepts *theory-preferred*. Thus for consequentialists, certain kinds of evaluative measure – hedonic, eudaimonistic, and so on – are theory-preferred, while in general for those favouring a deontic characterisation of ethical theory, concepts such as the *right*, or the *obligatory*, are likely to be preferred.

The prescriptive move is often as follows. Having first derived a theory-preferred account of morality in general, philosophical argument then aims to establish a set of prescriptions for theory-approved action, cast in terms of the theory-preferred concept(s). On the most straightforward construal of the relation, theory-approved action just consists in conduct sanctioned by the theory-preferred account of morality, though in some cases (for example, Parfit's utilitarianism)[10] the relation may be less direct. More esoteric construals of the relation will be considered later.

Thus the prescriptive part of the theory is often assumed to be derivable from a construal of morality in terms of the concepts which are theory-preferred. This seems to be a contingent assumption, since there is no obvious reason *a priori* why the found phenomena of the moral life, referred to above as constituting the subject-matter of the first approach, should not defy theoretical regimentation of this kind. However, this is not the main focus of the argument which follows. My aim is to show that the assumption is just that. My ultimate concern, naturally, is the relation of moral theory to political philosophy, but this embraces sub-arguments, which will be disposed of before addressing this concern directly. I shall argue that the sovereign status of morality is bought at the cost of its deliberative accessibility. The sovereignty doctrine itself is unconvincing, moreover, if it claims that failure to act morally is intrinsically irrational. Before that I examine forms of internalism, and argue that it is unconvincing particularly in its cognitivist form. The best way to secure the latter against non-cognitivist objections is to espouse externalism. Insofar as political philosophy seeks, by normative theorising, to enforce conclusions which must be followed on pain of irrationality, it fails; room should be made for other kinds of practical concern.

In what follows I shall consider highly general aspects of thinking about morality and agency. My approach is quite schematic, as my immediate expository aim is to tease out the implications of some influential styles of theoretical thinking about these questions. I shall only progress to consider the implications directly for political philosophy towards the end. I shall however take it as read that the methodology of political philosophy is strongly influenced by ethical theory. As will come out later on, the nature of the ethical theory in question is rather specific. My ultimate question, accordingly, concerns the impact on political philosophy of challenging the assumptions behind this theory. This will necessitate a lengthy divagation into moral theory, but I hope that the relevance of the discussion to political philosophy should be clear by the end – clearer than it has been in many recent contributions to the discipline.

Internalism and Smith's antinomy

The usual way in which linkage between the two approaches is effected is via some form of moral internalism, versions of which are defined below.

We can define different forms of internalism, depending on the nature of the proposed relation between the agent (A), relevant beliefs and motivations of A, and a prospective action of A (ϕ-ing). In what follows, p = 'A ought to ϕ.' It will do duty as an all-purpose ascription of moral obligation to a named agent. We can then use p to distinguish various internalist positions; in each case, the externalist alternative to them can be defined by simple negation. Since it is possible to desire an outcome as not having been brought about by one's own agency (as such), I shall take 'motivation', unlike 'desire' to be essentially agency-entailing.

The *assertoric* version of internalism has it that:

ASI: Necessarily, p is only sincerely asserted by A if A has a motivation to ϕ,

where 'asserted' is a quasi-technical term so interpreted that A asserts p only if A intends that the person to whom p is addressed should thereby come to believe that A believes that p.

On the other hand, *existence internalism* has it that

EXI: Necessarily, if p, then A has a motivation to ϕ.

A third possibility is *psychological internalism*, holding that

PSI: Necessarily, if A believes that p, then A has a motivation to ϕ.

It is important to note that PSI *is* an entailment. It is not, in particular, a mere claim that the relevant psychological states are, as a matter of brute fact, constantly conjoined, or that the belief is normally accompanied by the motivation. As such, it must stand or fall on the semantics of the propositions imputing the relevant psychological states to *A*. This is a strong requirement, in that it makes the externalist alternative (that is, 'It is not the case that if *A* believes that *p*, then *A* has a motivation to ϕ') strictly nonsensical. So it should not be confused with the perhaps plausible contention that the psychological states are constantly, if not invariably, conjoined.

I shall not discuss the assertoric version of internalism ASI in any detail. It has more than one possible interpretation, depending on whether the claim is taken to concern the semantics of terms occurring essentially in *p*, or the identification-conditions of a particular class of assertoric speech-act. Either way, however, it is not very convincing. For (as for example emotivist accounts of moral language rapidly discovered) it is unclear that *any* motivational state of the utterer enters into the criteria for determining the semantics of expressions in *p*, or for deciding, on the strength of a given token-utterance of it, whether or not it qualifies as a particular kind of speech-act – sincere or otherwise. A possible counter-example to it is that *A* utters *p*, believing wrongly that he has a motivation to ϕ. A more general question, which can be raised with the other forms of internalism, is what general account is given of the semantics of normative propositions in which no agent is identified.

Most current forms of internalism rather address the relation between motivations and the truth-conditions of propositions of the form of *p*. However, deciding between EXI and PSI poses problems for the internalist programme. Nagel states that '[i]nternalism is the view that the presence of a motivation for acting morally is guaranteed by the *truth* of ethical propositions themselves';[11] which is EXI. I shall return to this issue later.

In his *The Moral Problem*,[12] Smith argues that the following triad of propositions is apparently inconsistent, but that each proposition taken severally is commonsensically true.

(1) Beliefs and motivations are distinct existences.
(2) Morality, as embodied in propositions of the form '*A* ought to ϕ' involves beliefs about matters of fact, the fact in question being what it is the case that *A* ought to do.
(3) Moral internalism: that is, if an agent *A* believes that he ought to ϕ, then, with other things equal, he has a motivation to ϕ.

So we have psychological Humeanism, meta-ethical cognitivism, and a version of internalism (specifically EXI, accoutred with a *ceteris paribus* clause). One response is to deny that the triad (1)–(3) is formally inconsistent.The other is deny one of (1)–(3). Roughly, those who take an anti-Humean view of psychological faculty-divisions will deny (1); non-cognitivists will deny (2); and obviously moral externalists will deny (3).

Smith himself, on the other hand, seeks to prove the formal consistency of the ensemble (1)–(3). The basis for Smith's claiming this is that internalism, and in particular the *ceteris paribus* clause, should be interpreted so as to mean 'insofar as *A* is rational'.[13] This then makes way for Smith's rational agent advice model, whereby the motivations mentioned in (3) are understood to be those *A would* acquire were he to heed the advice of a perfectly rational *alter ego*. But if psychological Humeanism is true, then there can be no general entailment from beliefs (for example, the belief that *p*) to motivations. If there is a philosophical argument which shows that PSI is true, for example, it would show that Humeanism was false. If so it looks as though equivocation will be required to salvage consistency from (1) to (3).

I turn next to consider a major bone of contention between theorists of reasons for action. The notion of *reasons* seems to provide a possible linkage between cognition and motivation, the idea being that the acknowledgement (or perception, or some other quasi-cognitive apprehension) of the relevant reasons-proposition can, from one side or the other, bridge the divide with which psychological Humeanism faces us. Note that propositions (1)–(3) say nothing about the agent's *reasons* for acting in which there is a possibility that he ought to act morally. Williams[14] gives a neo-Humean account of reasons for action in 'Internal and External Reasons'. Purely informational adjustments aside, Williams characterises the difference between internal (RI) and external (RE) reasons theorists as whether or not they affirm the conditional

RI: A reason to ϕ is truly imputed to an agent, *A*,[15] only if *A* has a motivation (such as a desire), which will be satisfied by *A*'s ϕ-ing,

and RE can be defined as the negation of RI: the antecedent of RI may be satisfied even if *A* has no desire which will be satisfied by *A*'s ϕ-ing.

There is, then, this question about the relation between ascriptions of reasons for action and ascriptions of motivations. 'Internalism' is sometimes used indifferently for the cluster of positions represented by PSI, EXI and ASI above on the one hand, and for RI on the other, though these positions are mutually non-entailing. Armed with RI, the internalist cognitivist can, then, make the link between cognition and motivation via the notion of moral reasons. This in effect is Dancy's approach, for example, and entails the falsity of the Humean faculty-division represented by claim (1) above.

Those, like Williams, who are more sympathetic to non-cognitivism, will obviously reject (2). Though, as just noted, RI does not entail internalism of the kind expressed by (3), it does entail that unless an agent has a motivation to ϕ, he will not have a reason to do so. It is however plausible to say, as I shall discuss in more detail below, that moral propositions such as *p* are, *in some sense*, reason-entailing. That is,

MR: Necessarily, if *p*, then there is a reason for *A* to ϕ.

But if the reason in question is an *external* one, then Williams's position has the consequence that there are no true *p*-like propositions where the agent named by *A* lacks the motivation to ϕ; so the only true statements of the form of *p* are those where the agent has the relevant motivation, that is, where the agent has an internal reason to ϕ.

So we can construct the following argument. Given that

(4) it is the case that *A* ought to ϕ, [*p*]

we can infer that

(5) there is a reason for *A* to ϕ, [MR]

and thence infer that

(6) *A* has a motivation which will be satisfied by *A*'s ϕ-ing, [RI]

so that we can say that *p* entails the existence of the relevant item in *A*'s motivational set; which is tantamount to EXI. Contrapositively, then, the absence of the motivation falsifies the proposition expressed by *p*.

This indeed is what we find that Williams says, in another paper, '*Ought* and Moral Obligation':[16] 'if it [that is, *p*] just tells one a fact about the universe, one needs some further explanation of why *A* should take notice of that particular fact'.[17] What this asks for is a *reason* for *A* to take notice of the fact, and that requires a motivation, from Williams's position in 'Internal and External Reasons'. The above argument can then be used to infer the falsity, or inadequacy of cognitivism. So a consequence of accepting RI about reasons for action, coupled with MR, is that internalism provides a correct account of the truth-conditions of moral propositions, or at least those of the *p*-form, with a named agent and associated obligatory action.

We can now see that for this kind of internalist, the apparent inadequacy of EXI, as pointed up by Dancy in commenting on the passage quoted above from Nagel, rests on an envisaged counter-example which cannot in fact arise. For Dancy's worry was that EXI would fail in precisely those cases where an agent was subject to an obligation, as in *p*, but was unaware of the fact. But the above argument secures *p*'s truth-conditions on the existence of the motivational items themselves (the conditions of whose existence may on some models of action, such as psychoanalytical ones, simply bypass cognition anyway). It emerges from this that Dancy has in view, notwithstanding his own internalism, a different view of *p*'s truth-conditions – one on which it makes sense to deny that they are secured via beliefs on motivations, which amounts to PSI. But from an internalist perspective, it is far from clear what this might be. I shall return to this later.

It should be noted that Brink's[18] account identifies as 'reasons internalism' the claim that

BRI: If *p*, then *A* has a reason to ϕ,

which is consistent with Williams's view if 'having a reason' is tied in the way explained above to *A*'s motivational set. Sometimes however Brink seems to imply that reasons-externalism, *qua* the negation of this position, is inconsistent with MR. On the line of argument sketched out below, however, this does not follow. For MR is agnostic about the status of the reasons entailed by *p*. It therefore remains open that MR's truth depends on the reasons' remaining external to the agent. I shall suggest in due course that this means that the reason-entailingness of morality cannot be invoked to demonstrate the amoralist's irrationality.

We have seen that Williams denies that there are in his sense any external reasons for action. However, when we look at quite humdrum possibilities countenanced by institutionalised features of morality, this claim seems to be clearly refuted. Perhaps the most clear-cut case is that of promising. If it is the case that *A* has promised to ϕ, then it seems straightforwardly to follow that *A* ought to ϕ, and if it is the case that *A* ought to ϕ, there is a reason for *A* to ϕ. It may nonetheless be true that *A* has no motivation to ϕ, and never has had any (even at the time of promising). So the reason-claim is external to *A*'s motivational set: *A* is not there, and will not reach the claim through deliberation. This then provides a clear counter-example to RI.

It is no coincidence that the example of promising is also that cited by Searle[19] in arriving at his counter-example to the alleged non-entailment of normative by factual propositions. If it is true that *A* promised to ϕ, then it is true that *A* ought to ϕ, and for all agents *X*, if it is true that *X* ought to ϕ, then it is true that there is a reason for *X* to ϕ – that is just what it *means* to say that *X* ought to ϕ. So the normative conclusion which Searle validly derives from the fact of promising in his well-known article semantically entails, on grounds independent of the obligated agent's motivations, that there is a reason for that agent to ϕ. It may be a natural fact that I promised, but if it is, it simply does follow analytically that (at least *pro tanto*) I ought to ϕ, since promising is none other than the acceptance of an obligation where (usually) none existed before.

I shall not discuss how widely the net of external reasons might be cast. It is important to keep in view, however, the wider philosophical setting within which the discussion proceeds. Though nothing in definitions obviously requires this, the main candidates for external reasons – even the *sine qua non* for the proponent of RE – are *moral* reasons. The point of RI, as espoused by Williams, is to show in conjunction with internalism that cognitivism must be false. For if there are only internal reasons for action, so that reasons are motivation-entailing, then the existence of moral reasons for action entails that there are relevant items in the subjective motivational sets of those of whom the putative reasons are predicated. So since moral propositions of the form of *p* are held to be reason-entailing, their truth-conditions are tied to *A*'s motivations. Moreover, given Hume's psychological faculty-division, as we have already seen, beliefs and desires are taken to be 'distinct existences'. So, in a familiar non-cognitivist pattern of argument, Smith's antinomy is mobilised using RI to show cognitivism's inconsistency with the conjunction of Humeanism and the acknowledged capacity of morality to guide action.

If the above account of promising is right, neither the cognitivist nor the non-cognitivist (as represented by Williams) can have all of what they want. The cognitivist cannot have what (at least very often) seems to provide cognitivism with its *raison d'être* – that is, an account which reduces moral assessment to cognitive assessment. For in this case there is no purely cognitive failure; rather the agent's failure is to make the reasons provided by the fact of having promised into reasons *for* him, by their enjoying motivational force or in other words, by becoming *internal* reasons. On the other hand, promising seems to provide a clear counter-example to Williams's general position on reasons for action, namely RI. If RI fails, then the claim that the truth-conditions of propositions like *p* entail the existence of relevant items in *A*'s motivational set fails also.

Against this it may be said that if the agent has no motivation to ϕ, then *ipso facto* he has no reason to ϕ. It should however be noted that the foregoing remarks are simply a descriptive account of how reasons-talk works discursively. The status of morality as reason-giving is what underwrites its use to prescribe actions *irrespective* of agent-motivation. The proponent of RI may then ask what in turn underwrites the reason-givingness of morality; but it is mistaken to think that the appropriate response is then *either* to provide a further, morality-grounding set of reasons, *or* to abandon the view that moral reasons are a counter-example to RI (I enlarge on this in discussing Phillips's views below). G.E. Moore's well-known 'open question' argument refutes the first possibility, while (as I have argued) considerations of morality's discursive role provides an existential disproof of the latter. The remaining possibility is that morality can cite *external* reasons for action, but reasons which cannot be encompassed by a general theory of morality-supporting reasons.

Insofar as non-cognitivism aims to show that there is no basis for moral judgements other than reasons on which the relevant agents are in fact motivated to act, then, it fails. With this to hand, though, there is still no basis for thinking that one of the cognitivist's main objectives – to show the irrationality of the immoral or amoral agent – has been achieved here. If *A* has indeed promised to ϕ, then there is a reason for *A* to ϕ, regardless of whether *A* has any desire or motivation to do so, that is, an external reason of the sort countenanced by RE. This is however not necessarily a situation in which the RE-countenanced reason is somehow overborne in deliberation by other kinds of consideration: it may never get a look in. So we cannot use an 'outweighing' model of the sort available where a reason of a certain weight is nonetheless discounted in the face of other, weightier, reasons. Even so, this is not a situation where the agent's behaviour is simply unintelligible: but he acted as if something which in fact was a reason for him was not, because this consideration had *no* deliberative weight (of course, the fact that he promised may in other circumstances have some weight, although it is outweighed by other reasons). This does not mean however that the currency of moral assessment is that of cognitive evaluation. Presumably the agent knew that he promised, that promising creates obligations, that obligations are reasons for action, and so on; to paraphrase Aristotle, nobody not in the thrall of theory would think that the status of these beliefs *as* beliefs is somehow revoked by the consideration that in these circumstances the reason lacked motivational force. What is relevant to the moral assessment of this agent is not whether he (really) believed that he had this reason, but whether the existence of this reason held any motivational sway over him. If beliefs and desires really are distinct existences, then their constant conjunction is a contingent, and contingently rather than analytically defeasible, claim.

All this is quite consistent with the observation that agents are often motivated to act on their moral beliefs. D.Z. Phillips argues[20] that we act on moral beliefs, but beliefs we would not have unless we also had relevant concerns (by which Phillips means motivational items, such as moral sentiments). Once we naturalise morality *qua* cultural artefact, it becomes the sort of thing of which it makes sense to say that we can have beliefs about it, and that those beliefs can be true, as beliefs about the highway code, or about syntactic differences between the English and Latin languages, can be true. No doubt it would be odd to claim both that morality exists but that the concerns in question play no part in its natural history. The (none too happily labelled) 'Enlightenment project' of writers like Shaftesbury, Hutcheson, Hume and Smith was in large part an attempt to write (or at least describe the conditions of the possibility of) such a history.

This however establishes nothing so strong as the internalist claim PSI. Compare a term from the thick gastronomic vocabulary, such as 'succulent'. A conjectural etymology of this word which made no reference whatever to the normal causal properties of succulent objects in relation to human appetition would be strange. But this does not mean that someone with no liking for succulent things cannot assert or accept judgements like 'This is succulent' and their enquotational counterparts. When considering the merits of (3), it is important to avoid psychologistic confusion. We should, again, distinguish carefully between the project of providing a philosophical description of what morality is, and giving an account of the antecedents of moral agency, including whatever deliberation an agent may undertake when considering whether or how to act morally. There is extensive psychological literature, of relevance to the present discussion, on the empirical role which motivational factors can play in gerrymandering belief – cognitive dissonance being an obvious example. That motivational factors may have a bearing on belief-formation, however, is insufficient for the truth of (3). For (3) is an entailment, not a psychological generalisation.

Again, the promising example already discussed provides a refutation of motivation internalism in the form of EXI. For p, as we have seen, does validly follow from the fact that A has promised to ϕ; but it is clear that *A* may have no motivation to do so. What about PSI? It is an undeniable fact (amnesia, and so on, discounted) that *A* believes that he promised to ϕ at this earlier time. Presumably PSI internalists will maintain here that the truth-conditions of the belief-ascription in the antecedent of PSI must be kept distinct from those of *p* itself: *p* simply follows from the fact that *A* promised to ϕ, whereas unlike *p* the belief-ascription entails facts about *A*'s motivational state. But again, it seems only too obvious that *A* may believe this without having any motivation whatever to ϕ. There is accordingly a difficulty, particularly bothersome for cognitivist forms of internalism, in explaining how the beliefs in question are appropriately world-guided. By contrast, it seems entirely plausible to say that *A* may come to believe that *p* through believing that he promised to ϕ, it being a contingent psychological fact whether *A* is motivated to do what he promised to do.

PSI also seems to block one route to moral knowledge which many moral theorists, particularly cognitivists, have wished to keep open. This consists in reasoning from impersonal premisses to a first-personal conclusion about what one ought to do, but on the account of the truth-conditions just given, this need not be a valid form of inference: sustaining the inference may require that the agent rejects this form of internalism. If cognition and motivation are really distinct existences, then there is no reason to think that a motivation will be forthcoming once the agent has moved through the relevant inferential steps. Either the truth-conditions of the motivation-statement are tied in the way in which PSI claims to the truth-conditions of the corresponding statement of belief, or they are not. If not, PSI obviously fails. But if they do, they induce a double-mindedness about the grounds for belief themselves. An agent might think, for example, that the *ought*-proposition's capacity to motivate was precisely dependent on his seeing its truth-conditions as being distinct from his motivational states, and it was *this* which motivated him to act on it. Looked at in this light, internalism becomes an *esoteric* doctrine, one whose capacity to explain agents' action stands only if it is a theory which the agents themselves do not believe. It is, accordingly, very hard for the theory to provide a coherent acount of how the truth-conditions of *p*-like propositions are rationally related to the conditions under which the propositions are rationally believed (first-personally). This is obviously particularly problematic for cognitivist versions of the theory. For cognitivism purports to be a theory which explains how, or at least that, we have moral *knowledge*.

An objector might argue as follows. I have accepted MR, but argued that what this entails is that there is an *external* reason to act morally (though of course it should be noted that this does not mean that an agent could never arrive at an internal reason so to act by coming to believe a moral proposition). What about the situation where an agent acknowledges that he is morally required to perform a certain action, but nonetheless fails to do so? Surely in this case the agent is acting irrationally. Then it may be said that there is something wrong with the *general* position which holds that the reason-entailingness claim MR is consistent with denying that the amoralist stands convicted of irrationality: for (it may be said) surely an agent is irrational if he acknowledges the truth of the moral proposition but fails to act on it, and if so the general claim may be questioned.

I shall suggest below that the non-irrationality claim is consistent with the external-reasons reading of MR, and show how this follows from allowing that *A* may not be irrational in failing to ϕ where *p* is true – since the reason in question is internal, it is motivation-entailing, and on this view *A* does not act irrationally by failing to ϕ where he lacks the motivation to do so. The objection denies, however, that this concession applies when *A* believes that *p*. Very often when *A* has this belief, *A* is motivated to ϕ, and so has a reason to do so according to RI. Then failing to ϕ in the circumstances described by (8)–(10) below will indeed be irrational. But the internalist view of the matter, applied to many familiar samples of moral discourse, seems simply false.

But it follows according to PSI, since *Y* can only believe the relevant moral proposition (and therefore know it) if *Y* has a relevant motivation. I have chosen *lying* as an example of a term with (at least *prima facie*) 'thick' ethical properties. What is at stake in accounting for the agent's utterances (and behaviour, if they are acted on) is not the professed beliefs, but how much their content *matters* to the agent. It is strange to insist on cognitivism's view of moral ontology, while also insisting that the (moral) facts which this view countenances are such that one who becomes apprised of them is *ipso facto* motivated to act on them. This is where Mackie's well-known 'argument from queerness'[21] bites: it is, after all, the obverse of Williams's point against cognitivism cited earlier. Either the moral facts fail to motivate; or if they do, they must be 'facts' of a kind quite distinct from anything else in the world. Both arguments express, from opposite ends, the inconsistency of (1) with the conjunction of (2) and (3).

Morality and reasons

Much discussion in moral philosophy has addressed the alleged categorical status of morality, and what sort of reasons, if any, morality generates. In 'Morality as a System of Hypothetical Imperatives', Foot argues that the rules of morality cannot be distinguished by their applying categorically, because (say) the rules of etiquette, or club rules, also so apply.[22] Foot seems to conclude from this that morality must therefore be hypothetical, not categorical, imperatives – though the obvious inference from this would be that the gap should be closed from the opposite side, and certain classes or non-moral reasons, accordingly, corralled into the domain of the categorical. Nonetheless, D.Z. Phillips takes it as refuting Foot that club rules may, at an appropriate level of inquiry, be taken as hypothetical imperatives.[23] What rather seems to be at issue is whether or not morality generates motivation-independent *reasons*. This is only a warranted assumption if it follows from the claim that morality applies categorically that it generates such reasons; Phillips's point about clubs would then work against Foot by showing that since there is no such reason for belonging to a club, its rules cannot apply categorically (unlike morality). Phillips says later that,

> [i]f a person comes to appreciate that there are [reasons for action over and above non-moral *oughts*], he will not have come to do so by finding that he has relevant reasons for heeding moral considerations, but by coming to see the moral considerations as constitutive of relevant reasons.[24]

Foot's ulterior point is that to say that morality requires that A ϕ is not by itself to give a *reason* for A to ϕ. But this is not inconsistent with arguing that morality is categorical. Nor does the latter claim conflict with the observation that there are non-moral rules which also apply categorically – only with the claim that the latter is the distinguishing *mark* of morality. So we can accept that morality applies categorically, but also deny that this identifies a set of reasons for action. I have accepted for the purposes of argument the claim of MR that morality is such a set, but that does not follow from its applying categorically. That is what Foot's argument shows.

Morality may be held to constitute reasons of its own, as Phillips argues in the passage just quoted. But to note that morality applies categorically is certainly not by itself to provide a reason for acting morally. Indeed, Phillips's view of morality seems here to be that it is no different from, say, netball – I may see certain considerations as constitutive of relevant reasons if I have come to embrace the netballing way of life, but clearly, *ex ante*, as a non-netballer, that provides no reason for me to netball. Morality may be claimed to be reason-entailing as MR maintains, but that claim stands or falls independently of whether it applies categorically.

An objector may now say this. I have accepted the morality-reasons link proposed by MR. But if that holds, then a moral proposition such as *p* entails that there is a reason for *A* to ϕ, *irrespective* of *A*'s motivations. So then the cognitivist aim, as I have set it out, of proving the irrationality of *A*'s failing to recognise that this means that *A* has a reason to ϕ, will have been achieved. I shall refer to this as the claim that *A* is *weakly irrational*. The claim that an agent failing to recognise the truth of a moral proposition like *p* is *strongly irrational* follows in the same situation when the following position about the overridingness of morality is endorsed:

OM: Morality is that category of reasons for action which override all others.

Strong irrationality is then manifested when *A* fails to accept that he has a reason to ϕ when there is a moral reason to do so. Strong irrationality entails its weak counterpart, since from the claim that *A*'s failure in these circumstances to accept that he has a reason to ϕ is irrational it follows *a fortiori* that it is irrational for A to fail to accept that he has a moral reason to ϕ. I shall not discuss the problems faced by OM and its supporters (for example, Kantians), such as the possibility that some moral reasons may conflict with others, or – more awkwardly – that in some circumstances non-moral considerations can plausibly be thought to trump moral ones. The claim that the agent described above is strongly irrational follows from the fact that the truth of *p* is held to present an *overriding* reason to ϕ, irrespective of *A*'s other reasons for action.

I shall now suggest, however, that this does not follow. A very important aspect of reasons-ascriptions are that they are capable of explaining action.[25] External reasons cannot figure in a true explanation of why an agent in fact acted in a certain way: an explanation of why *A* ϕ-ed cannot be that *A* had no motivation to ϕ. If external reasons are explanatorily redundant in this way, they cannot be cited to show the irrationality of agents who fail to act on them. To explain an action is to provide an account which makes it rationally intelligible – one in the light of which we can understand what the agent was doing, or at least thought he was doing. But external reasons-ascriptions cannot do this, since it is in their nature that they are not reasons on which the agent can act. Of course, if the agent comes to believe them, they may acquire motivational force, but then the reasons are no longer external to him.

Foot considers[26] an objector who admits that the amoralist is as such not irrational, while nonetheless maintaining that the person has a reason to act morally. Foot argues that this position is inconsistent, as follows. The conclusion

(7) *A* is going to act irrationally

is validly entailed by the conjunction of

(8) *A* has an (internal) reason to ϕ,
(9) *A* has no reason not to ϕ,

and

(10) *A* is not going to ϕ;

whereas (7) is not entailed by the conjunction of

(11) *A* will act immorally unless *A* ϕs,

together with (9) and (10). It follows from this that (11) cannot entail (8): in particular, where (9), (10), (11) and the negation of (7) are all true, (8) is false. So the weak irrationality claim fails, since there is in this situation no true reasons-statement for the agent to accept. The consequence of this for the present position is that the entailment of (7) by (8)–(10) is consistent with its non-entailment by the reasons-statement obtained from *p* and MR:

(12) there is an (external) reason for *A* to ϕ,

since the conjunction of (12) with (9), (10), and not-(7) is consistent. So, by a parallel argument, (12) cannot in this situation entail (8). As I have argued, the mark of external-reasons claims is precisely that they cannot be invoked to demonstrate agent-irrationality in circumstances such as those just described. Accordingly, what distinguishes the reasons countenanced by Williams's RI is precisely that they, unlike those generated by MR (as such), support charges of irrationality against the agent in the circumstances described by (8)–(10). The irrationality claim (7) is only entailed by (8)–(10) if circumstances warrant the imputation to the agent of an internal reason to ϕ. What picks out moral reasons, *pace* OM, may be that they exist irrespective of agent-motivation, but their being in this sense external reasons cannot establish the strong irrationality claim, since they are consistent with the falsity of weak irrationality, and that entails the falsity of strong irrationality.

We can see this from another angle. Where there is a benefit to be had from ϕ-ing, we can ask whether the agent *ought* to ϕ. Some, like Dancy,[27] have argued that since evaluative properties result in deontic ones, in this situation ϕ-ing must be morally obligatory. But, as I have argued at greater length elsewhere,[28] where there is no *antecedent* obligation, it is implausible to pin one to a specified agent, in which case the ambiguous claim that

(13) somebody ought to ϕ,

when disambiguated, at best supports the wide-scope interpretation of the *ought*-operator: that is, as saying that there ought to be somebody who ϕ s, rather than there is a specific somebody of whom it is the case that he ought to ϕ. The former is merely the deontic translation of the relevant evaluative claim, and fails to tie an obligation to particular agents. The corollary of this conclusion, as regards the present discussion, is that the defensible interpretation of (13), when conjoined with a non-agent-specific version of MR, supports only the external-reason claim, that is, a claim most naturally rendered in English by a sentence such as

(14) there is a reason for someone to ϕ.

Does this then mean that the claim earlier described as plausible, namely the morality-reason link MR, has to be abandoned after all? Not necessarily. A proposition such as *p*, if true, does (at least in certain cases) entail an *external* reason for *A* to ϕ. That is simply the role which a *descriptive* account of the semantics of such propositions will construe propositions like *p* as playing, and it fails to save this aspect of the phenomena of the morality system not to acknowledge this. In such cases the function of morality talk simply *is* to postulate reasons for action where these cannot be tied to agent-motivation.[29] This is not a *theoretical* infirmity of the sort which RI was devised to expose. Insisting on the 'external' reason for action is precisely the response we get when agents' other, non-moral, motivations lead them to fail to acknowledge an overriding reason for acting morally.

There is a question, or rather a number of questions, about the reason-givingness of morality. One question is what *picks out* morality as an ostensible category of reasons for action, to which one answer is that it is that set which collects reasons which apply categorically. But, first, this does not differentiate reasons which we would independently identify as *moral* ones from others which so apply; and second, the mere fact of their applying categorically is no reason at all – let alone an overriding one – for acting on them. Nor should their applying categorically be identified with the claim that they apply universally. There can be categorical reasons which apply, for example, only to postmen. Nonetheless, a descriptive analysis of the occurrence of moral terms in propositions like *p* does indeed suggest that they apply categorically, if they apply at all. A second question is whether morality gives any reasons to act, as MR states; again, I have suggested that the phenomena of morality do indeed show it to be, in propositions like *p*, intrinsically reason-stating. A third question is whether the reasons just mentioned are overriding. I have argued that there is no good basis for thinking this, at least if it is held to entail that someone who fails to act on them is irrational. A fourth is what reasons can be given in response to someone who challenges the citation of a moral reason, as (according to MR) is entailed by *p*.

It is doubtful whether there is any general answer to this question. Often debate focuses on whether the moral considerations really apply, but that does not mean that an agent who replies to someone who cites these considerations by saying, 'Yes. But I don't care', is therefore irrational. The point however is that the more the categorical and RE-ratified status of the moral reason is insisted on, the less amenable will it be to support by genuinely independent reasons. Kant insisted on the *unconditioned* nature of the antecedents of moral agency as the precondition of keeping that agency free from heteronomy; but plainly, the more this is insisted on (as Kant clearly saw), the worse are the prospects for grounding moral reasons in other less peculiar and more deliberatively accessible reasons for action.[30] The insistence that, in addition to its applying categorically, morality also provides an *overriding* class of reasons for action is not one that readily lends itself to support by the heterogeneous considerations on which agents act – as, again, Kant was well aware. If the preceding argument is correct, there is a clear sense in which this is right: morality presents itself as a reasonless reason; or, as it might better be put, morality is that for which no reason can be given *because* its basis lies in that which makes practical reasons themselves intelligible. But neither the fact that (as I have acknowledged) morality is categorical, nor that it often instantiates external reasons for action, suffices to show that it is overriding.

Looked at in this way, cognitivist and non-cognitivist internalists can be seen as sharing an assumption which, I have suggested, there is no good reason to accept. This is that an agent would stand convicted of irrationality if it were the case that moral propositions like *p* prescribed reasons for action but, in spite of this, the agent still failed to be motivated in the right way to act morally. A non-cognitivist like Williams avoids this by allowing that the agent has reason to ϕ so long as the proposition expressed by *p* bears the right internal relation to the agent's motivations; and, since on this view the relation is such, as we saw earlier, that the proposition entails the existence of the motivation, irrationality is ruled out. The point of RI is precisely to show that the purported reason-givingness of morality cannot be mobilised to convict the amoralist, or the backslider, of irrationality even if MR is true.

A cognitivist internalist, on the other hand, will say that the belief does not exist unless it does its motivational job. Once again the possibility of irrationality is ruled out. The *akrates*, for example, in the work of a cognitivist internalist like McDowell, is one from whom the ascription of belief is withheld precisely on the grounds that the sought-after element in the agent's subjective motivational set is absent, or effectively absent. Thus we see in modern guise the ancient doctrine that the wrongdoer necessarily acts in ignorance. This of course fails to resolve the moral antinomy discussed earlier, since the conditions for desire- and belief-ascription are no longer such as to preserve their status as *distinct* existences.

There are two relevant explanations for the popularity of cognitivist internalism among political and moral theorists. The first, more cynical, explanation is that this is the theoretical position which is the most gratifying to philosophers' *amour-propre*. Morality is something about which theoretical truths exist, and can (in principle) be determined; these are, moreover, truths which the rational agent can not only recognise, but also thereby become motivated to act upon. The more theoretical explanation is that philosophers have aimed to arrive at conclusions which are resistible – in thought or action – only on pain of irrationality. Externalism denies that there are considerations based on the content of morality which compel this recognition; noncognitivism threatens to reduce the antecedents of moral agency to something brute, immune to reason, and is hard to run alongside externalism.

If the argument of the last section and those before it was right, there is a tension between the doctrine of the sovereignty of morality, as expressed by OM, and internalism. Morality appears as something unique, *sui generis*, but as something which internalists have sought to connect to motivation. That position then has to explain why human beings are often motivated to act badly, or to act well but for the wrong reasons – or simply lack the required motivations. In this situation, there is an inevitable pull towards the ideal – to preserve internalism by insisting that the theory-approved conduct is what the agent ideally *would* be motivated to act on, if fully rational. This is basically Smith's move, in the form of the advice-giver model. But the stronger the pull in this direction, the weaker internalism's hold becomes on its original rationale, namely the rooting of morality in motivation. This is the insight behind Kant's insistence that morality, in order to be what he thought it was, had to be immunised against 'heteronomy'. The more the *sui generis* character of the *moral* as a category of reasons for action is insisted upon (as in the passage quoted from Phillips above), the harder it is to support it philosophically by reasons figuring recognisably in real agents' deliberations. The alternative, as I have argued, is to abandon this insistence on the specialness of morality, and concentrate instead on those motivational patterns which have concrete existence for agents. A consequence of this is an appropriately enlarged sense of the significance, both for ethics and political philosophy, of *character* as expressed in deliberation.

Political philosophers could of course aim to show only that their preferred principles of justice, and so on, are such that agents should act on them *insofar as they are rational*. But, as I argued earlier, if moral propositions are reason-entailing, but lack motivational force, someone failing to act on them (or to be motivated to act on them) is not thereby convicted of irrationality. An externalist view is liable only to expose this fact. While internalism licenses the assertion that the content of the preferred principles (and so on) retain the desired semantic link to motivation, it has to address the fact that theory's prescriptions are not those on which agents are currently motivated to act (despite appearances, Hobbes's distinction between obligation *in foro interno* and *in foro externo* assumes that this link has already been made good). This is, it seems to me, the strongest single explanation for the popularity of ideal normative theory in contemporary political philosophy.

None of the foregoing remarks bears on the practicability of an 'applied' or extensional kind of philosophical project – such as that which aims to decide which sorts of distribution, or more abstractly which sorts of principle governing distributions, fall within the extension of the term 'just'. There are indeed independent grounds for scepticism about this, some of which have been articulated by Alasdair MacIntyre. But if the foregoing argument is right, the methodological issues start one step further back: they begin with the assumption that political design is to be structured by means of normative concepts, such as that of justice. Whether or not it is defensible to argue philosophically for certain kinds of claims about the extension of normative concepts, there is a prior question whether this is the way to structure political design – or indeed whether there is a coherent philosophical project which aims to arrive at such structuring.

I have argued that there is no failure of reason involved in failing to heed particular moral injunctions such as that expressed by *p*. To this extent non-cognitivism's case against cognitivism succeeds.[31] But it is fallacious to infer from this that morality must be what non-cognitivism says it is – that is, if non-cognitivism says that morality is intrinsically motivating, using Humean internalism to dispose of cognitivism. For the inconsistency of the triad (1)–(3) in fact masks the fact that (1) and (3) taken separately are inconsistent. This is required by psychological Humeanism. If motivations ('passions') are the sorts of entity Hume thought, they are not entailed by anything, least of all beliefs; 'passions' are not semantic objects. To think otherwise is from a Humean perspective to commit what old-style linguistic philosophy called a 'category mistake'.

It should be emphasised that irrational behaviour is *unintelligible* – which is not of course to say that it is impossible. But, as I have argued, the amoralist's behaviour *as such* is not unintelligible, so any claim which entails that it is is false. Even in the most favourable case, where the structure described by (8) in conjunction with (9) and (10) is a *moral* reason, the agent only acts irrationally if the reason in question is an internal one. Some internalists have sought to avoid the implausibility of the irrationality claim via PSI. The truth in internalism is that someone may acquire an internal reason by coming to believe a moral proposition such as *p*. But if moral reasons-internalism holds that the truth of *p*, or the agent's belief in it, entails an internal reason for the agent to ϕ, it is false. This is consistent with claiming that propositions like *p* may entail an external reasons-statement. But precisely because the reasons are external, they will not suffice to convict an agent failing to act on them of irrationality – regardless of whether they apply categorically, or whether as such reasons they are overriding. It is implausible to claim of moral reasons that they are invariably overriding, and equally implausible to think that there is some general procedure, discoverable by philosophical inquiry or otherwise, for assessing their relative weight compared with other kinds of reason for action.

The most favourable case for the irrationality thesis is where there are *no* other reasons for action. This, naturally, is seldom the case in real situations. Some of the least tractable cases are, moreover, liable to be political. The most clear-cut explanation for this is that disputes over matters of public concern – in other words, politics – may arise precisely over whether or how far morality applies to an issue of policy. I have suggested that there is no reason to think that those on the sceptical side of the question must be irrational; the purely political issue would remain, even if they were. A very familiar instance of this sort of problem is where (roughly) securing some external benefit by political action involves – either intrinsically or as a foreseeable consequence – action which is morally disagreeable.

Looked at more optimistically, these remarks make room for an expansion, as well as a contraction, of philosophical effort. Stocker's remarks about moral theory can be applied to political philosophy.[32] In the article referred to, Stocker's major point is that contemporary moral theory is largely blind to motivation, treating it at best as a theoretical adjunct – roughly, as what an agent will have who is disposed to perform theory-approved acts. This ignores the possibility of a more axiological account of political action, particularly as regards the dispositions and patterns of evaluation which have value in political agents. One – though only one – possibility worth considering is that the demands of moral theory, construed as generating a set of theory-approved actions, map imperfectly onto what proves to be valuable from the more agent-centred perspective.

Recent political philosophy has attempted to infer conclusions about political design from normative premisses – from justice as the 'first virtue' of social institutions, from engagement with the 'fact' of 'reasonable pluralism' and so on. Of course, it is possible to maintain that the programme only seeks to infer these conclusions *insofar as* we attend to normative considerations, but this qualification is rarely made. The objection does not rely on a form of global scepticism about morality, where scepticism consists in denying that the amoralist is irrational. Certainly political philosophising from the ground upwards will need to take that on, but problems remain even if the discussion starts at a later stage. These problems concern the place of normative considerations in practical rationality. There is, I have suggested in addition, a problem in making the prescriptions of ideal theory motivationally effective. Theories which too blithely dispense with the latter consideration are liable to run into problems of internal consistency – at least if those theories, like many in the liberal tradition, uphold the value of autonomy.[33] There is anyway room to ask how important those considerations are to a philosophical understanding of politics; we can ask why the philosophical project is almost universally taken to be the investigation of politics from the standpoint of morality.

Moral theory and political philosophy

The assumptions about morality which I have criticised so far have had a significant impact on political philosophy. In the first four chapters, I have examined several debates within contemporary political philosophy, arguing in each case that distortion has arisen from a questionable conception of politics itself, and of philosophical theory's relation to it. In the case of the essential contestability thesis, the protagonists have relied on over-theorised accounts of actual political behaviour, assuming that disagreement must admit of a *conceptual* explanation. I have argued that the thesis is incoherent, and that the best replies to the charge of incoherence sacrifice the thesis's explanatory power; but even if it were coherent, it would remain to be shown why different interpretations of a given concept *matter* politically. There is assumed to be a certain kind of linkage between theory (in particular, that which is held to deliver the thesis itself) and deliberation, as it occurs in the opinion-formation and arguments of political disputants. But the most it can show is not that the conceptual structures *in fact* explain the contrary opinions of these people, but that it would show how they might have arrived at a particular view of the contested concept's extension *if* they were being rational.

If we recall the arguments of Chapter 2, we can see a similarity between the role played by philosophy in political design, and in arguments over externalism. There I argued that philosophers sought to circumscribe politics by philosophical argument. If political realities failed to correspond to the prescription of theory, that in no way undermined the claim that *if* political agents were moral or rational, then they would do so. Here, in discussing internalism, we have seen (Smith's response to his antinomy being a case in point) that internalists rely on a similar conditional claim. It is now clear that this similarity is not coincidental. What was lacking in philosophical arguments for political design was a philosophical argument to justify the primacy of philosophical reasons themselves, and this could not be provided without begging the question. Similarly here we have seen that no argument is forthcoming from internalists to show why the relation between moral belief and motivation is something which requires philosophical treatment, given the possibility that the relation between them is a contingent one. Again we lack a non-question-begging philosophical argument for the primacy of philosophical explanations over others (in this case psychological ones). In each case, unsurprisingly, the upshot is a sharply revisionist account of human motivation – one in which the aberrant tendencies of political and moral agents are subjected to the bracing correction of theory.

Distortion has been particularly apparent in discussions of 'political obligation'.[34] There is in fact a number of distinct justificatory problems which are conflated under this head. The most plausible candidate for the application of *obligation* is that of justifying the legal requirement imposed on citizens to obey their state. But discussions of obligation have been confounded by the duality of obligation as a justificatory concept: on the one hand, citing obligations is itself purportedly reason-giving (cf. MR), while on the other, those who have seen themselves as addressing the problem have seen the obligations themselves as demanding supporting reasons. The difficulty then is that as long as the obligations are thought of as applying unconditionally, there is not much that will do the job of providing obligation-grounding reasons. In particular, the pull is towards providing reasons which will connect with agent-deliberation: but then it is to that extent less likely that the grounding reasons will retain the unconditionality of the obligation itself, and when this fails, theory is likely to take refuge in an externalised account of reasons – in other words, in hypothesising reasons on which an ideally rational agent *would* act. This is the version, in the case of political obligation, of the move which Smith makes in attempting to resolve the antinomy posed by propositions (1)–(3) above – where internalism is rescued by reconstruing motivation (where the latter proves refractory) as the reasons on which an ideally rational agent would advise his imperfectly rational real-world alter ego to act.

This is one reason for the attractiveness of contractarian solutions, which as I have already argued in the more general case provide a counter-example to Williams's reasons-internalism RI. This nonetheless merely postpones the problem, since then the question arises what reasons the putative contractors would have for signing, and these will then predictably lack the unconditionality of the obligations which they are invoked to justify. Once this is acknowledged the standard resource is a version of the externalising manoeuvre, which abstracts from real agents' reasons for action to those on which ideally rational agents (say, those negotiating under the veil of ignorance) *would* contract.

It is easy to say, in response to this, as Ronald Dworkin did[35] in criticising this aspect of Rawlsian contractarianism, that the obligatoriness of a hypothetical contract remains as hypothetical as the contract itself; only real contracts bind to performance. But, if the foregoing argument is right, the problems in fact begin one stage further back. The obligation-grounding reasons – in this case, the reasons which hypothetical contractors would have for signing – are already external ones, since the best to be hoped for is that theory might set out reasons on which agents *would* contract, insofar as they were rational. I have suggested, and argue in more detail elsewhere, that there are good grounds for doubting whether this optimum is attainable. But since the objector in the obligation theorist's sights is the supporter of RI who demands a rational link to agents' *actual* motivations, the move is effectively an *ignoratio elenchi* anyway. We can certainly doubt whether citizens are under specifically *political* (as opposed, for example, to legal) obligations. But if they are, they are paradigmatic external reasons. There will be nothing to provide an entirely general theoretical link to agent-motivation, and then the Smithian externalising manoeuvre is required to maintain coherence. But even this is likely to fail, since 'political obligation' just is the counterpart, in political philosophy, of the reasonlessly reason-giving 'ought' of MR delivered by a descriptive account of its use in everyday moral discourse.

With regard to pluralism, discussed in Chapter 4, there is a confusion between explanation and prescription. The meta-ethical thesis that the truth about value is that it is plural rather than singular, null, or unknowable, is confounded with a descriptive thesis, also going by the name 'pluralism', about cultural diversity in large modern cosmopolitan societies – and then it is the latter thesis which is taken to have normative political weight. One explanation for this conflation is that it may appear to reduce controversial theoretical commitments – in particular, those which pronounce certain conceptions of the good as superior, or truer, than others. There is however no reason in general to think that the values which those subscribing to the meta-ethical thesis regard as values must find their reflex in the conceptions of the good prevalent in society at large, either internally or *vis à vis* one another. Here, as with obligation and contestability, theorists begin from observations about modern political circumstances – in this case, the fact of diversity – then work out from there the normative implications, from the presumed meta-ethical 'facts' to which the fact of diversity corresponds. But it is far from clear how the protagonists are supposed to deliberate from their particular conceptions of the good to the desired conclusion. The most we could get is something like Rawls's 'overlapping consensus', but then it is what the different conceptions have *in common* that is doing the justificatory work, not the fact of diversity. What in fact underpins the normative response (such as a version of neutrality) to diversity, as I argued, is a unitary principle consistent with the rejection of meta-ethical pluralism, such as that of equal respect. But this may be a principle which the groups espousing conceptions of the good in society reject. There is then no deliberative path for members of these groups to the proposed normative resolution.

Thus a certain pattern emerges. In each case theory begins by considering certain political phenomena, such as political disagreement, state coercion, civil-society diversity, and so on. A philosophical model is then articulated, purporting to explain the phenomena under review – a model delivering (as it intends) theoretical truths about conceptual structure, obligation-grounding reasons, the metaphysics of value, and so on; as philosophical models, they essentially aim to provide theoretical *reasons* for the phenomena which provided the theory with its point of departure. Then – the crucial step – these reasons are made normative. That is, the reasons generated by what began as an *explanatory* project – that of accounting for the political phenomena in question – are taken to be prescriptive or normative for political action: the theory-generated reasons for disagreement, for political design, or for coercion, diversity, and so on, are taken to *rationalise* certain courses of action. These courses of action are not, however, simply the brute facts with which the explanatory project began. They are rather taken to be the basis for an essentially normative account of how ideally rational political agents *would* act: for example, the reasons on which ideally rational citizens obligated to obey a legitimate political authority would act, the reasons on the strength of which rational agents may espouse a certain view about the extension of a contestable concept, or the reasons on which suitably enlightened agents can, in the face of diversity, approve of political structures for coping with this diversity. Thus the explanatory project becomes a normative one, with an idealised account of reasons supplanting those on which real political agents act.

In the case of neutrality, things may at first appear to be different. In the first place, the aim of neutrality is avowedly prescriptive rather than merely explanatory: it offers a solution to a political problem which arises in most modern societies. The neutralist's starting-point is usually taken to be the the existence of different conceptions of the good, or moral values, which fact has the capacity to generate political conflict. This by itself perhaps entails no normative claim; the political question may simply be what should be done about this fact. Thus neutrality may seem to constitute an exception to the general strictures offered so far. But, as I argue in Chapter 6, when it comes to *justifying* neutrality, theorists face a quandary, which comes to the surface when we ask whether the argument offered for neutrality is itself one which respects neutrality (a merit of Larmore's *Patterns of Complexity* is its sensitivity to the problem which this question poses). On the one hand, they can espouse a form of insufficient-reason justification, but this fails to yield substantive conclusions about political design. On the other hand, neutralists may adopt forms of justification which rely on a normative conception of reasonableness, or rest the justification on a version of status neutrality. However, the latter all rely on normative premisses. In view of this, the justification of neutrality proves to involve normative commitments after all.

This does not mean that something along the lines of Rawls's 'overlapping consensus' idea is ruled out: it may indeed prove to be possible to accommodate the conceptions of the good by a 'political' conception of justice appealing to considerations internal to each of them. But this is often not the case in neutralist work, as we shall see in Chapters 6 and 7, and even in Rawls's case the argument appears not to be that the parties concerned will in fact find the political conception compelling, but only that they *should*. More generally, the neutralist position relies on a certain imputed relation between the parties' motivations and their attitude towards political solutions – that is, one which regards the motivations are subject to revision in the light of considerations of reasonableness, and so on. But, of course, it is precisely because such an attitude is lacking that there is a political problem to solve. Thus the absence of the sought-after motivations is an aspect of the political problem itself.[36]

My explanation for this normative turn, cast in terms of the argument of the introduction, is as follows. The shared pattern manifests a turning away from explanation of real-world political phenomena, even though the latter provide the starting-point for theory. This is not surprising, since it is not plausible to think that the presumably heterogeneous reasons on which real political agents act are those which would conform to any interesting normative specification of how they ideally *should* act, where the latter is not tied to given motivations. What is interesting and significant about the prevalence of moral internalism (particularly its PSI and EXI versions) is that, despite its apparent stress on the importance to morality of agent-motivations, the latter's theoretical role is habitually treated as adjunctive. Moral theory prioritises its preferred 'thin' ethical notion, such as the *right*, or the *good*; theory-approved action is then articulated in terms of this notion, as action falling under the extension of terms naming these notions; and motivation is simply treated as a dependent term, or in other words as that psychological state which impels the agent to perform theory-approved action. It is very doubtful whether substantive ethical motivations can be translated into these terms. In particular, it may be a condition of agents' having these motivations that they do *not* see the motivations' objects as merely instantiating the properties, axiological or deontic, favoured by moral theory. The result, paradoxically, of pressing the claims of internalism is a moral psychology impaired by its neglect of agents' motivations.

There is also, from the other end, good reason to doubt whether in general it *could* be the case that agents acted on motivations determined by theory. As I have argued in the case of each example cited, a form of incoherence is involved in imputing the reasons articulated by theory to the political agents involved. In the case of political obligation, the incoherence stems from the incompatibility between obligations and other categories of reason for action; with essential contestability, from the self-defeatingness of the explanation of disagreement; and with value-pluralism, from the incompatibility between the reasons for action furnished by an internal or 'ethical' view of a *particular* conception of the good, and the rationale for political arrangements dealing with diversity in society as a whole. In each case this incoherence arises from the discrete and competing perspectives of philosophical theory on the one hand, and the 'thick' reasons of embodied political agents.

Hence the theory is, in this way, anti-political. It turns away from actually deliberated reasons and, in the examples I have discussed, introduces theoretical apparatus unfitted to modelling real deliberation. Partly this can be ascribed, as I argued in the introduction, to a conveniently theory-friendly conception of the material on which philosophical reflection sets to work. But it also shows a devaluation of the real phenomena of politics, one which as I have argued is prevalent not only in academic political philosophy but also in contemporary attitudes towards politics and politicians, some of which politicians themselves have an interest in promoting.

It should now be clearer how the anti-political *methodology* of contemporary political philosophy supports its anti-political *aims* – the aims in question being a philosophical description of a state of the world in which political engagement over fundamental issues no longer exists – a world after politics. As we have seen, the methods of political philosophy are normative rather than descriptive and, even where theory begins with political phenomena, often shifts towards a normative style of theorising. This gap between normativity and explanation is particularly clear in the case of political obligation and essential contestability. But when theory attends exclusively to an idealised account of reasons for action, politics is liable to disappear from the picture.

This is not to say that the ideal account must be right, since a version of *Leviathan*'s distinction between reasons which oblige *in foro interno* and *in foro externo* – as it were, the Hobbesian equivalent of partial compliance theory – may still apply. But even apart from this, a very large part of politics just is the public exchange of (at least purported) reasons for action – deliberation over presented courses of action, the introduction and discussion of new options, with their attendant justifications, would-be refutations, and so forth; while the non-deliberative business of politics is apt, from this perspective, to appear at best as a distraction, and at worst a hindrance to right reasoning. So, given that *theory* takes as its business the determination not of operative, but of *right* reasoning, that is, a normative or prescriptive account of reasons for action, politics (at least when understood as just described) is liable to appear as a rival, and inferior, method of determining reasons for action: the best it could hope to do is to confirm the deliberations of theory, but given its characteristic *modus operandi*, including for example the use of power, political decision-making is liable to fall sadly short of this ideal. Consequently political philosophy is continually subject to a pull away from the mere determination of reasons (as they might figure, for example, in public).

It may be said that internalism is irrelevant to the practice of political philosophy, because normative theory does not proceed on the assumption that agents will in fact become motivated to act on the conclusions of theory, but only that they *should* do so, insofar as they are rational; it may be added that the temptation to theorise in a motivational vacuum will be as stronger – perhaps stronger – if externalism is true, and motivations are independent of moral beliefs. It is not, however, the aim of the argument presented in this chapter to show that because internalism is false, the arguments of political philosophers who produce normative conclusions lacking motivational force are thereby refuted. The argument concludes that political philosophers, like their colleagues in moral philosophy, have largely neglected actual motivations for the tidiness of theory, and it is *symptomatic* of this that internalism is current – since then motivation becomes parasitic on what we have good (moral) reason to do. This is not surprising, since most contemporary political philosophy consists in the application to political design of normative – and usually, more narrowly, moral – considerations, rather than working from the ground up, in the manner prescribed by Spinoza in the epigraph to this book. This obscures the possibility of relating normative theory more closely to given motivations, and begs the question whether political design should be structured by these considerations. The doctrine of neutrality, the subject of the next chapter, is the main way in which liberals have sought to head off this objection.

6
Neutralising Politics

Introduction

Neutrality, in one form or another, is sufficiently widely-held to be called the dominant version of modern liberalism.[1] Neutrality is a house of many mansions, and definition is hazardous. But as a first approximation, it holds that

N: those political structures or outcomes alone are justifiable, which as far as possible remain impartial between competing interest-groups, holders of conceptions of the good, and so on, in civil society.

The most common occasion for neutrality is the circumstances of modern political and social life, and in particular the fact that it seemingly contains a wide range of different, and potentially competing, conceptions of the good life. However, it is not obvious that the possible existence of diverse conceptions of the good life poses any political questions, unless these conceptions are the subject of actual, or at least potential, conflict within civil society. In practice that means that there must be individuals or groups which are the bearers of those conceptions, and a political authority available to adjudicate between them.

Neutrality may also be construed as the negative claim that no state which fails to aim for impartiality, in these circumstances, can be justified. The state is ideally a referee, holding the ring between vying particularisms, systems of beliefs, and so on, while itself remaining uncommitted to any substantive moral outlook – or at least any outlook controversial between the representative groups or individuals in society.

For these reasons, neutrality is sometimes referred to as the 'privatisation' of morality: the state no longer takes a position on matters of moral dispute – though everyone (except some anarchists, for whom the debate presumably lapses) believes that there ought to be state-sanctioned moral requirements on citizens, in the form of the criminal law and penalties annexed thereto. This already poses problems for neutrality, though perhaps no problems *distinct* from that facing the outcome version of neutrality in general.

The problem usually takes the form of rival, and often conflicting, claims on public resources. A large part of neutrality's attraction, accordingly, is that it offers the hope of rationally resolving political conflict in a manner agreeable to all, without having first to solve the theoretical problems posed by moral conflict. The neutralist argument places the *onus probandi* on those who would argue for a *non*-neutral political order. This is the *non-partiality advantage*: neutrality avoids deciding whose conception of the good is correct, cutting straight to the political resolution.

I shall distinguish between the two types of argumentative role for neutrality – on the one hand, neutrality as a *side-constraint* on justification, and on the other, as an *object* of justification. The side-constraint requires not merely that political outcomes be neutral, but that there is a neutral *justification* for these outcomes. I shall argue that side-constraint neutrality is presupposed by object neutrality: there is little point in trying to justify neutral political design unless the justification respects neutrality as a side-constraint on acceptable forms of argument. Neutrality seeks to secure the non-partiality advantage by respecting the neutralist side-constraint, and this means employing a form of insufficient-reason argument. I shall however suggest that this by itself is not enough to ground a neutralist political order. Attempts to amplify neutrality standardly appeal to a conception of the equal *status* of the protagonists. Neutralists are faced with a dilemma. Either they keep faith with neutrality as a side-constraint, but cannot justify a neutral form of political design; or they forgo the non-partiality advantage and justify neutral political design by values controversial between conceptions of the good, which is tantamount to abandoning neutrality itself. The idea that the method for deciding political design respects equal status often serves, as I shall suggest, to conceal this move. Prominent versions of neutrality vacillate between a pure insufficient-reason argument, and one based on substantive moral commitments; what began as an attempt to avoid disputed philosophical doctrines ends by resorting to them.

It is also possible that a neutralist justification will be rejected precisely *because* it justifies conclusions which the political actors reject. I shall suggest that any neutralist justification of political design would have first to eliminate from conceptions of the good a vital area of contention between them – their account of politics itself; they have to limit the content of the eligible conceptions of the good so as to exclude explicitly *political* conceptions of value.

Forms and functions of neutrality

To conceive of neutrality as a side-constraint is to hold that the political structures are only legitimate if their *justification* satisfies a certain conception of neutrality. This need not mean that the neutrality condition is sufficient as well as necessary, so the condition by itself does not justify a particular conception of political design – even *insofar as* it has to deal with the competing interest-groups. The second possibility, that neutrality is the object of justification, holds that it is the aim of the state to promote neutrality (which may be particular kinds of neutral outcome, or neutrality of status). Object neutrality aims to justify certain kinds of political arrangements, while side-constraint neutrality sets out to impose constraints on what can *count* as a possible justification. This is not to deny that each possibility may be embraced by individual theories. Indeed, some neutralists, such as Larmore,[2] explicitly commit themselves to both.

Clearly, in addition, object neutrality consists in certain normative conclusions about the nature of politics itself – about political institutions, procedures, policies, and so on. This is not merely because normativity might be held to consist in the fact that neutralists aim to establish prescriptive conclusions about what optimal political structures look like. The neutrality doctrine need not say, and usually is not taken to say, that morality can be entirely evacuated from politics. Neutrality may seek to exclude normative considerations but may seek to embody non-controversial normative doctrines in political design, whether in outcomes or procedures.

Very often, the political problem which neutrality sets out to resolve is taken to be determined by certain meta-ethical considerations. One prominent example is meta-ethical value-pluralism[3] – though this is often conflated with a descriptive thesis of the same name. As we shall see, however, other meta-ethical positions can also be held to require neutrality. This is perhaps clearest in contractualist models where the contracting parties are assumed to have interests, values, conceptions of the good life, and so on, which are (or are potentially) in conflict. Here the motive for neutrality, as an object of justification, is that it appears to provide a basis on which the contracting parties rationally can agree. One version of this is the 'overlapping consensus' idea lately favoured by Rawls[4] as a response to the fact of 'reasonable' pluralism. This will be dealt with in the next chapter. In the present chapter I shall consider other neutralist models instead, in particular those of Barry, Ackerman and Larmore.[5]

Object neutrality

The initial problem posed by neutrality is to understand how it should be interpreted – in terms of definition N given above, what the phrase 'political structures or outcomes' is taken to mean. One possibility is that the demand for neutrality is met by a given procedure or distributive mechanism only if the outcome is neutral between those whom it will affect (which can be taken to be either all citizens, or those who have an interest, moral or otherwise, in the policy at issue).

The obvious problem with outcome neutrality is that often no such outcome seems to exist – or at least not purely *qua* outcome. In some cases, indeed, it necessarily does not exist, as where the outcome favoured by each side necessarily precludes that favoured by the other. It is not simply a contingent matter that the political outcome favoured by pro-abortionists precludes that favoured by anti-abortionists, for example, and it is implausible to think that some better but as yet unattained state of the world would satisfy all parties to this dispute; it would certainly not be mere legislative silence. This is partly because legislation – or the lack of it – is taken in many cases to express society's stance on fundamental values. Thus it is not merely that the Supreme Court verdict in *Roe* v. *Wade*[6] happened to be non-neutral; given the distribution of opinion on the matter in society, there is nothing which it *could* be for political outcomes to be neutral. If this, *mutatis mutandis*, is what outcome neutrality requires in its application to specific contentious areas of public policy, its applicability seems severely limited.

In response to this problem, outcome neutrality is often distinguished from its procedural counterpart. Consider games as distributive mechanisms, differentially allocating goods to those who participate in them. It is implausible to regard the *outcome* of a chess game as neutral, when one player decisively defeats the other. Nonetheless, the rules of chess may be thought of as a neutral *mechanism* in accordance with which outcomes are determined, in this sense: the rules themselves do not favour one player over the other – except insofar as they may be said to advantage the gifted chess player over the rabbit (I shall consider the implications of this qualification in a moment). So the rules of the game provide a mechanism which is neutral, leaving aside differences in chess-playing ability, for generating outcomes. The neutrality of a tournament official is not compromised, for example, if the official conscientiously enforces a rule which, in the circumstances, works to the advantage of one player over the other. So, it may be said, the rules of games provide a paradigm case of procedural neutrality.

However, the neutrality of an outcome (again, viewed purely *qua* outcome) will not be guaranteed by its having been produced by a neutral procedure, whether or not it is right to say that neutral outcomes may sometimes be produced by *non*-neutral procedures. If so, in this respect neutrality differs from justice, as a property of procedures. For (at least in some distributive situations, such as lotteries) if an outcome has been produced by a just procedure, then the outcome itself is just.[7] This need not mean that there is no method which can be applied directly to the outcome (whether or not a set of holdings of goods, say, conforms to a certain pattern) to determine whether outcomes are just; though if this is so, there may be some feature of the method which ensures that it maps onto all and only those outcomes which are procedurally just, in the same way as there may be an on-inspection test for theoremhood in a formal system, which picks out all and only those strings validly produced from the axioms via the derivation rules. We can thus distinguish between *on-inspection* criteria of neutrality, and *derivative* criteria – in other words, respectively between criteria linked to what is produced by a certain method, argument or procedure, and criteria applied to the method, argument or procedure itself. I return to this distinction later.

The impossibility of non-neutral outcomes does not preclude neutrality. But the neutrality of outcomes cannot consist solely in their having been produced by a neutral procedure. For if it did, then, *per impossibile*, the neutrality of the procedure's outcome on a policy question such as that of abortion would follow immediately from the neutrality of the procedure. But even if there is one, appeal to neutrality alone will not be enough to resolve the decision about policy. In the face of diverse conceptions of the good life, neutrality must fail to enter into justifications of public policy. The policy of legalising abortion will be defended on grounds such as the following: that 'back-street' abortions will happen anyway, to promote freedom of choice, and so on, and similarly with the justifications for outlawing abortion. The justification for public policy, in such cases, will not be that the policy itself is neutral.

There is a fairly obvious problem with the move from outcome to procedural neutrality. The former apparently relies on an independent, intuitively based conception of what counts as a neutral outcome; and if so, we need to know more about the relation between the criteria on the basis of which procedures and outcomes are judged to be neutral. Where there are no neutral outcomes, the danger is that a given procedure's neutrality will be challenged on the grounds that it will foreseeably yield a certain non-neutral outcome. If so, the neutral procedure must be rendered immune to such challenge. The procedure must be justified on grounds which themselves do not themselves breach neutrality – indeed (and *a fortiori* given the unavoidability of non-neutral outcomes) it is hard to see how a procedure justified on grounds which did breach neutrality could itself *count* as neutral. This broaches the possibility of a side-constraint conception of neutrality, discussed below.

A further difficulty is suggested by the expository analogy drawn earlier, between procedural neutrality and the rules of a game such as chess. As I noted, there was a way in which even the procedures could be seen as *non*-neutral distributive mechanisms – namely the fact that these mechanisms select non-neutrally as regards differences in chess-playing ability. Unlike chess or other games, whether given differences can justifiably produce differential distributive shares may itself be what is politically at issue. It may be said, of course, that there are practices such as handicapping which, although to one side's advantage, are acceptable to each of the participants, who will abide by the outcome; but this only sharpens the question which the qualification raises. In relation to *what* ulterior conception of fairness, or other external standard, are the game's rules (whether or not they are modified to allow for devices such as handicapping) deemed to be procedurally neutral? This suggests that the chess analogy may be question-begging. For it explicates the intuitive content of procedural neutrality only if the procedures laid down by the rules of the game conform to a pre-conceived standard. The standard cannot simply be read off from the rules' *de facto* standing *as* rules. And it is only relative to the concern which gives a procedure its point – such as a handicapping device – that procedural neutrality can be judged. But, in any case, what gives point to a procedure may itself be politically contentious. That the rules can be seen as procedurally neutral – for example, in virtue of their applying equally to both sides – itself rests on a prior conception of neutrality, to which the rules must conform if they are to be procedurally neutral.

Side-constraint neutrality

So far I have considered neutrality as a property of what may broadly be called *political objects* – that is, as a property of outcomes or states of affairs, and as a property of political procedures. We can however regard neutrality differently – as (in Nozick's sense)[8] a *side-constraint* on justification. Neutrality here operates as a philosophical constraint on the forms of argument which can be relied upon to reach any conclusion about political design. The device of the veil of ignorance, imposed by Rawls on negotiators in the Original Position in *A Theory of Justice*, conforms to a side-constraint conception of neutrality (although Rawls holds the negotiations themselves to be procedurally neutral, the reason why this matters is because it expresses in reflective equilibrium the co-equal moral personhood of the negotiators).

Neutrality as a side-constraint is to be distinguished in general from interpreting it as an object of justification. We can see this again from *A Theory of Justice*, where it would be possible to claim that the actual political objects held to be justified by the Original Position (as distinct from the negotiation-procedures in the Position itself) were non-neutral. One possibility would be that non-neutral political objects were required by side-constraint neutrality, for example, as restitution for past injustices suffered by groups or individuals. Thus restitution via non-neutral political structures now might be held to be demanded by neutrality, construed as a side-constraint operating *sub specie aeternitatis*. Or it might be held that the practice of toleration, for example, was irreconcilable with neutrality as an object of justification, since it required that the groups or opinions tolerated were viewed by the state as legitimate targets of moral disapproval, and thus that the state was not neutral towards them; nevertheless this policy might be ultimately motivated by second-level considerations which were regarded as imposing a neutral side-constraint on justifications for policy.[9] Nonetheless, since disapproval is a condition of tolerating a practice, the object of justification remains non-neutral between those who approve and those who disapprove of it.

The non-partiality advantage secured by side-constraint neutrality demands an insufficient-reason argument.[10] Side-constraint neutrality has to show that there is insufficient reason[11] to favour one conception of the good over its rivals. If there were sufficient reason to favour one conception (for example, because it was true, or demonstrably superior to its rivals), non-partiality would be forfeited, even if favouring one conception is justified. If the side-constraint is to be satisfied, the justification will screen out arguments favouring one side or the other. This is not to say that there could be no good argument showing that there was sufficient reason to favour one side – that, after all, is what a good argument is. But in that case there would be no justification for neutrality. So the non-partiality advantage requires that there be insufficient reason to favour any one conception of the good over all others.

We can now see a relevant difference between the neutralist side-constraint and procedural neutrality. There we noted, when pursuing the game analogy, that the neutrality of a game's rules was not compromised merely because the game produced a determinate outcome: the rules of chess can be seen as a neutral procedure capable of producing non-neutral outcomes. However, it does follow from the fact that a given justification favours one conception over the others, that it fails the neutralist side-constraint. So, if there are justified non-neutral outcomes, the neutralist side-constraint cannot be a condition of justification itself. Note that these comments apply to justification at a given level: it bears on the arguments for neutrality at a certain level of generality, and does not preclude departures from neutrality at a lower level. This flexibility, however, allows the side-constraint to play a protean role in political justification, as we shall see.

Moreover, any justification which satisfies the side-constraint will still be non-neutral between neutralist and non-neutralist objects of justification. Its outcome is a determinate object, and the justification will not be neutral with respect to those who reject such an object. The distinction between on-inspection and derivative criteria for assessing neutrality, which as we saw could be made for procedural neutrality, lapses in this case. For if there is an on-inspection criterion which shows that the object of justification is non-neutral, this entails that the means by which it was determined violated the neutralist side-constraint. I return to this point later (p. 154).

Insufficient reason

Thus the neutralist side-constraint on acceptable forms of justification, which secures the non-partiality advantage, is an insufficient-reason requirement. I now examine versions of this requirement.

Value-pluralism

It may seem natural to think that neutrality is a response called for by value-pluralism. The following argument tries to draw on Charles Larmore's definition of value-pluralism to show that there is insufficient reason for the state to do other than remain, as far as possible, neutral between the relevant conceptions of the good life (CGLs). According to Larmore's definition of value-pluralism:

VP: There are many viable CGLs that neither represent different versions of some single, homogeneous good, nor fall into any discernible hierarchy.[12]

The definition is defective in that it remains agnostic between value-pluralism and other meta-ethical positions which entail its falsity, such as moral scepticism, or nihilism. For value-pluralism must be committed to a claim beyond the conjunction of the two negative propositions expressed by VP; in particular, it must adopt a realist view of the goods, or values, forming the object of the conceptions of the good life. From this we can construct an insufficient-reason argument in favour of neutrality, as follows. This argumentative frame, as we shall see later, can also be adapted to accommodate premisses other than VP.

(1) By VP, there are many CGLs which fall into no discernible hierarchy.

So,

(2) there is insufficient reason to prefer any one of the CGLs referred to in (1) to any other one mentioned there.

So, by (2)

(3) there is insufficient reason for any political structure to prefer any one of the CGLs referred to in (1).

But,

(4) if a given political structure is justified [in the sense in which 'justify' is an achievement verb], then there is sufficient reason for it.

So,

(5) it is not justified for any political structure to prefer any one of the CGLs referred to in (1).

For all x, y, not to prefer x to y is to remain neutral between them. So,

(6) no political structure which is not neutral between the CGLs referred to in (1) is justified.

The argument must show that there is insufficient reason to favour one conception over its rivals, thereby respecting the neutralist side-constraint. It assumes that political justification must be confined to the relative worth of the conceptions of the good life, whereas there may be external grounds (conferring 'sufficient reason') for preferring one such conception over another. The argument works only insofar as we attend purely to the relative standing of the conceptions themselves. But it remains to be shown that this is the sole or even prime consideration in justifying the political structures. The step from (1) to (2) can only be justified with a further assumption about the political *priority* which these conceptions (or the relations between them) enjoy. Without an assumption of this kind, there is nothing for the insufficient-reason version of the neutralist side-constraint to work upon.

More fundamentally, the initial description of the problem to which neutrality provides a solution makes assumptions about the status of political actors – that they arrive with disparate conceptions of the good which vie for public goods, and between which a political solution must arbitrate. The actors are conceived of as equal, and the relevant aspect of their equality consists in their status as conceivers of the good. But we can ask in virtue of what conception of the good this status enjoys the primacy it does. After all, it is not merely that equality is not given priority in some conceptions of the good; it is that even where it is, the equality is often not construed as equality between conceivers of the good. Then the question is whether the neutralist side-constraint will sanction that priority. The side-constraint has to ratify not just the derivation of political structures from the initial situation, but the favoured description of that situation itself. We can of course always meet a violation of the side-constraint, and hence neutrality at a given level, by citing a higher-order neutrality in which the side-constraint is respected, as in the move from outcome to procedural neutrality. But that will only work if either status-neutrality between conceptions of the good is respected, or departures from it can be justified in a way that respects the side-constraint.

Scepticism

By contrast with Larmore, Barry's *Justice As Impartiality* rejects pluralistic foundations for neutrality in favour of epistemic scepticism about conceptions of the good. Before considering Barry's argument, it is important to be clear about what this scepticism involves. Although Barry does not seek to ground his argument in an appeal to pluralism, the fact that there are diverse and conflicting conceptions of the good in society provides the starting-point of his argument: it is this fact which is held to call for the implementation of a conception of justice in the first place. An important facet of the conflicts to which diverse conceptions of the good may give rise is political conflict over resource allocation, entitlement to legal immunities, powers, and so on. So the political rationale for the theory is to provide means of mediation between actual conceptions of the good when they give rise to competing claims on public resources.

A version of argument (1)–(6) above can be constructed which eschews the specific claims about the metaphysical structure of value to which pluralism is committed. This revised version seemingly limits theoretical commitment, by requiring no resolution of philosophically intractable disputes about value. Faced with moral conflict, and no obvious means of rationally resolving it, we avoid deciding who, if anyone, is right. We then take the conflict at face value, and cast about for means of resolving it.

The version of the neutrality argument which will then emerge will be along the following lines. Instead of the original (1), we begin instead from the following premisses. We can reach the same conclusions as before, given either moral scepticism:

SK: in disputes such as that between proponents of different CGLs, there is no knowable truth of the matter, regarding whose conception is better or best;

or moral nihilism:

NH: in disputes such as that between proponents of different CGLs, there is nothing which it could be for one party to be right.

From each of SK and NH, it follows that there can be no discernible hierarchy of conceptions of the good life. For, given SK, there is no *discernible* hierarchy, even if such a hierarchy (unknowably) exists; and given NH, there is nothing which it could be for the conceptions to fall into such a hierarchy. So from these premisses, we can rewrite the original premiss (1) as follows:

(1)* by SK or by NH, there are many CGLs which fall into no discernible hierarchy.

Consequently,

(2)* there is insufficient reason to prefer any one of the CGLs referred to in (1)* to any other one.

From here we can proceed to the original steps (3), (4) and (5) and thence to the conclusion (6), that there is no justifiable policy non-neutral as between the relevant conceptions of the good. So we can, *mutatis mutandis*, provide arguments from moral scepticism and moral nihilism to the same conclusion as that derived from value-pluralism. The argument of Barry's *Justice As Impartiality*, for instance, apparently proceeds to a (6)-like conclusion from a version of SK. As Barry says,

> it has to be accepted that there is no reasonable prospect of closure in these arguments [regarding the relative merits of rival conceptions of the good] ... We must therefore anticipate that the normal state of affairs will be one in which there is no consensus on the nature of the good.[13]

The scepticism which Barry endorses is not of that ancient form which claims that belief is ill-founded.[14] Rather, Barry's scepticism holds that, in matters controversial between the conceptions of the good, any claim to 'certainty is ill-founded', so that

(B_1) there is no CGL such that nobody could reasonably reject it.[15]

This does the work of VP, SK, or NH in the first premiss of the argument schema. It pares down the commitments incurred by arguments from value-pluralism: since the relevant facts about value are held to be unknowable, it is unknowable whether the diverse conceptions of the good correspond to a real diversity of values. This is not of course to say that the scepticism espoused by Barry incurs no controversial commitments.

Barry's positive argument for neutrality relies on an additional premiss, that

(B_2) there is a desire [that is, shared by the partisans of each CGL] to reach agreement with others on terms that nobody could reasonably reject.[16]

Given this, the conclusion follows that there is no agreement which both satisfies the desire to reach agreement with others on terms that nobody could reasonably reject and is based on a particular conception of the good. If we wish to satisfy the desire mentioned in (B_2), there is insufficient reason to favour any political structure favouring one CGL over another. Thus, effectively, Barry's argument arrives at neutrality (justice as impartiality).

This does not show that there is any agreement capable of satisfying the desire mentioned above; but if there is, it must be one which is impartial to the extent that it is not based on any particular controversial conception of the good; or, more accurately, not based on any aspect of a conception of the good controversial with respect to other conceptions. The latter qualification opens up the more optimistic prospect that there may be a basis for agreement in the shared content of the various conceptions – a variant on Rawls's overlapping consensus. Difficulties however arise before we get this far.

One problem with (B_2) as a premiss is that there is no reason to think that such a desire exists. What Barry needs is something stronger than (B_2), such as the claim that it is not reasonable to lack such a desire. Otherwise there is no reason to deny that secessionists or anarchists may reasonably abstain from any purportedly 'impartial' agreement, whether or not it is based on controversial ideas about the good. Even those who have a desire to reach agreement as in (B_2) may have stronger opposing desires – for example, not to betray the faith to the infidel, risk eternal perdition, and so forth. These considerations jeopardise a maximinimal justification of (B_2), which would claim that the desire is reasonable because reaching reasonable agreement is a condition of securing the minimum that partisans of each conception would reasonably desire to secure. It is, accordingly, very doubtful that the desire exists or that it has the force required to do the work which Barry's argument demands of it.

Part of Barry's response to these problems is to augment the normative content of 'reasonable'. Barry says: '[c]learly, I have introduced substantive moral ideas in the course of talking about what could reasonably be rejected'.[17] The major substantive moral idea is that of equality. There are obviously conceptions of the good in which equality plays no very important role, and indeed many conceptions in which it does play a part have radically different views about equality's extension. This is if anything harder to understand in view of the fact that Barry makes explicit allowance for a range of conceptions of the good, distinguished, for example, by their contrasting views of human beings' status in relation to the biosphere.

Thus Barry's argument admits of two divergent interpretations. The first, relying on a thinner conception of reasonableness, is in effect an insufficient-reason argument along the lines already canvassed, with Barry's sceptical premiss (B_1) doing the work of SK. But, as we have seen, the thinned-out conception of reasonableness fails to exclude any conceptions from the initial contracting or bargaining situation, and in particular fails to exclude those conceptions for which the pursuit of reasonable agreement is not a priority.[18] There may be reasonable disagreement about which conceptions of the good are reasonable, and about how much importance they attach to reasonable agreement.

The second interpretation relies on an extended conception of reasonableness embodying substantive moral commitments. This bases neutrality on claims about the *status* of those between whom (it is held) we should be equal. The status of the participants determines what the procedures are neutral *between*, and explains why conceptions of the good held by some persons are privileged over those held by none.[19] The justification of procedural neutrality relies on a conception of a status-neutral starting-point, on which the procedures set to work.[20] We have already seen a similar assumption at work in Larmore's argument. Barry's neo-Scanlonian argument cites the desire to meet agreement on terms which nobody can reasonably reject: formally, status-neutrality is assumed with regard to this desire. It is not just that each contractor is assumed to have the desire, but also that it has the same weight, or the same status in justifying political arrangements, for each contractor. So status-neutrality figures twice in Barry's argument, in the specification of the political problem (competing conceptions of the good, none of which is such that it cannot be reasonably rejected) and in one of the key premisses towards its solution (B_1). Here again we lack a reason to think that the side-constraint ratifies the problem, and its solution, as status-neutral.

Ackerman: dialogue

Ackerman's *Social Justice and the Liberal State* provides a case for neutrality which explicitly endorses the side-constraint interpretation. Ackerman imposes two requirements on justificatory reasons.

> *Neutrality.* No reason is a good reason if it requires the power holder to assert: (a) that his conception of the good is better than that asserted

> by any of his citizens; *or* (b) that, regardless of his conception of the good, he is intrinsically superior to one or more of his fellow citizens.[21]

These are combined, at the start of the book, with requirements of rationality and consistency, which together demand that the use of power is justified by reasons consistent with other reasons invoked elsewhere in support of the use of power. What this licenses, in the rest of the book, is a dialogic conception of political neutrality. According to this, conceptions of the good must allow of conversational justification in which claims are subjected to the rational scrutiny of fellow-citizens, each of whom bears a personal and perhaps different conception of the good. The significance of the dialogic conception with regard to the forms of neutrality distinguished earlier is that it combines a version of object neutrality (in this case, neutrality of procedure) with side-constraint neutrality. For the dialogic model is commended as being procedurally neutral, while the model's serviceability in support of neutrality itself is dependent on the philosophical argument's being subject to the neutrality side-constraint (a) and the further condition (b).

Ackerman applies these conditions on dialogue not merely to common-or-garden political debates, but the argument for neutrality itself: this is how he ensures that the argument for neutrality is itself a neutral one, so that the side-constraint on justification is satisfied. This is made clear at Section 70 where Ackerman says:

> [t]here is a perfect parallelism, then, between the role of political conversation *within* a liberal state, and the role of philosophical conversation *in defense of* a liberal state ... The task of *philosophical* conversation is to make it possible for a person to reason his way to neutrality without declaring that the path he has chosen is intrinsically superior to any other route to liberalism.[22]

Various simplifications mark Ackerman's account, including the assumption that the objects of claims on public resources can be telescoped into a single good which Ackerman calls 'manna' (essentially a homogenised form of Rawlsian primary good), and that these claims are necessarily claims mounted by individuals on their own behalf. There is no compulsion to accept either of these assumptions – in the sense that Ackerman's own criteria allow for their being reasonably challenged. Indeed, these two assumptions skew Ackerman's conclusions unjustifiably towards neutrality. Once primary goods are homogenised, one source of political disagreement is immediately removed – namely the fact that political decisions may take, or at least appear to take, the form of choices between different kinds of good.

Equally, it is unclear why only claims mounted by individuals on their own behalf (rather than others, or the community as a whole) are admissible. Since a neutral political order forms part of only some conceptions of the good life, it is hard to see why they do not succumb to Ackerman's principle (a) above. This explains how neutrality fails to leave room for the political. For neutrality is only defensible in its own terms if it excludes the *political* component of conceptions of the good from the terms of the argument, although argument over the nature of politics itself is fundamental to political engagement (which helps to explain the failure of attempts to provide descriptive and decompositional analyses of the political). Ackerman also fails to allow for the underdetermination by reason of political decisions: it is not obvious that a uniquely reasonable solution will always emerge from the dialogic process. It is also hard to see how any form of political dialogue *could* conform to Ackerman's neutrality requirement. For this dialogue paradigmatically involves the commendation of certain conceptions of the good as better than their rivals.

So far I have considered only condition (a). Why does Ackerman also need (b)? Without it we lack a substantive basis for reaching political decisions. In view of the parallelism already noted, this will afflict not only substantive political decisions, but the *philosophical* argument for political design as well. Argumentative stasis is only avoidable if the condition, which ostensibly operates as a *side-constraint* on justification, is amplified so that it permits substantive conceptions of the good as valid inputs into political design. For the stasis which (a) threatens can only be averted if a particular conception of the good is mobilised in political design – that conception which holds that human beings have equal standing, a version of status neutrality. If the side-constraint is interpreted purely as an insufficient-reason argument against non-neutrality, it proves ineffective both at the political and philosophical level of justification. Only if the neutrality side-constraint permits an argument from equal standing will the conception of the good embodied in the latter survive (a).

The only way of making this move is to claim that this conception of the good is privileged with respect to the others. The only obvious way in which this can be done is by appealing to a certain conception of the person. This is in effect a conception of the person embodied in status neutrality. This can be seen by recalling the political circumstances which neutrality is designed to address. When we know that there are different conceptions of the good at large in society, we still need some reason why we should take notice of this fact. The fact that they may generate conflict may be sufficient grounds for taking political action, but it is insufficient to mandate a neutralist political solution. However, only if the *bearers* of the conceptions are regarded as being equal in standing will the problem even exist in the form which it must take for neutrality to be a possible solution to it. Only if the initial problem is cast as one in which different conceptions have equal standing is neutrality eligible as a solution to the problem of diversity (it might be held that the conceptions could have value in their own right, but the political problem only arises if the conceptions are attached to bearers). The problem is then framed by the fact that while specific conceptions of the good are held insufficient to justify non-neutral political design, there is a fundamental ethical commitment to equality.

Only with such a commitment can side-constraint neutrality be satisfied with a sceptical or pluralistic view of the values involved. In addition, only thus will it be possible to specify a controversial form of political design – controversial, for example, between liberal and non-liberal conceptions of the good. For the latter's veto on the former works, within condition (a), as powerfully as the former's on the latter. We need, then, a *moral* rather than a political reason to think that diversity requires the neutralist solution. To generate substantive conclusions, side-constraint neutrality requires status neutrality.

Politics

The upshot is that insufficient-reason arguments seem to be unable to justify neutrality in any context in which it is the subject of political dispute. There is however a further problem, which may be seen as the practical counterpart of this difficulty, and which makes particularly clear the political difficulties facing neutrality.

In political conflicts such as that in Northern Ireland,[23] there is no reason to think that a neutral outcome is possible or, if it is, that it is politically desirable from the standpoint of the protagonists. Earlier I considered the possibility that neutrality could be understood procedurally; the same may now be said of the example under discussion. In relation to the political conflict over sovereignty in Northern Ireland, however, it is far from clear how neutrality of procedure is to be understood. It is not immediately clear how this fact, if it is one, enters into the determination of the problem. A stance of neutrality between nationalism and unionism simply fails to deliver any clear verdict on the political issue.

One obvious problem, given the unavailability of a neutral outcome to the political conflict over sovereignty, lies in the argument considered earlier for moving from neutrality of outcome to that of procedure: since a neutral outcome is unavailable, the conflicting parties will be unlikely to regard as neutral any procedure liable to result in the outcome they oppose. It is plausible to think, for example, that concerns of this nature inform the long-standing nationalist rejection of a purely plebiscitary mechanism for determining sovereignty.[24] In addition, given the nature of the political conflict, it is very likely that the contending parties will have different views as to what *constitutes* a neutral procedure; in this case, the *grounds* for rejecting the procedure just are that it will precipitate this unfavoured outcome. The *Satanic Verses* controversy, for example, led to conflicts between secular liberals and British Muslims as to how a neutralisation of English blasphemy law should proceed – the former favouring abolition; the latter favouring extension of Anglicanism's legal indemnity to the Islamic faith.[25]

As regards these political conflicts, the dilemma facing neutrality seems to be this: viewed *merely* as a side-constraint, neutrality is too thin to determine a political outcome. This is particularly clear in circumstances where conflict is deep, and the contestedness of outcomes infects the procedures to generate them. But attempts to supplement it, for example with a form of status neutrality, are liable to miscarry in these circumstances, since the conflict itself is (at least in part) over the status which the protagonists should be granted politically. A graphic illustration of this in the Northern Ireland conflict has been the political conflict over 'political' status itself (for example, that of paramilitary prisoners).

In a number of respects, moreover, the side-constraint neutrality favoured by many conversational or 'dialogic' models, such as Ackerman's and Habermas's,[26] ignores the terms of political engagement. Barber argues that the essential contestability doctrine subverts neutrality,[27] but matters are in fact less clear-cut than this. The point is not whether a commitment to neutrality remains possible in the face of a given contestable concept but, to the extent that it does enter into political dialogue, whether it resolves political conflicts manifested in conflicting interpretations of the concept. The problem would be particularly acute, of course, if neutrality were itself essentially contestable. Even if the essential contestability thesis is false, however (or at least false of neutrality), there is little reason to think that neutrality provides a basis for arbitration where reasonable persons have different views of what a contested concept demands. Side-constraint neutrality provides no clue as to how to deal with a situation in which a given concept is subject to conflicting political interpretations, or in which there is a clash between different conceptions of the political good.

Barry's reliance on scepticism seems to point towards an insufficient-reason justification of neutrality. But this is vulnerable to the objection that there may be considerations, unrelated to the relative merits of the conceptions of the good in play, for favouring a certain kind of political order over others: a certain kind of non-neutral political order may be Pareto-optimal with respect to all neutral orders, for example, in which case representatives of each conception presumably could rationally agree to it. The argument assumes that scepticism about conceptions of the good is suspended when we turn to consider their purely political aspect. But the sceptical arguments which Barry applies to the conceptions in general surely apply with equal force here. And, as we have seen, Barry relies on specific normative assumptions about reasonableness in order to arrive at his conclusions.

His project of establishing political principles on neutral grounds therefore has to eliminate from conceptions of the good that aspect of them which concerns the *political* good. This is also true of other neutralist theories such as that of Rawls's *Political Liberalism*. It has to exclude them because the neutralist political order itself plainly *cannot* be neutral between neutralist and perfectionist (or other non-neutralist) conceptions of the political good. In the language of Barry's central argument, what is required is a political order which nobody could reasonably reject. The neutralist order is held to fulfil this requirement. But it is far from clear why its rejection by those who favour a non-neutralist political good is *necessarily* unreasonable, or in other words why neutrality is a political order which nobody can reasonably reject. According to Barry, this is necessarily the case. The effect of Barry's argument is to remove the possibility of there being a political good from the terms of political engagement.

It is tempting to conclude that neutralists like Larmore who base their argument on this plurality in fact have in view a claim about the status of the *bearers* of those conceptions. Most commonly, this is a version of status neutrality, such as that of equal respect for persons, embodied in formal procedures for determining political outcomes. Again, it is unclear how status neutrality bears on the design of negotiating procedures in this situation.

However, there is then a danger that the project of justification will simply beg the question. In spelling out the concrete form which ground rules for negotiation should take, given a commitment to procedural neutrality, appeal is made to equal respect for persons, or some other conception of status neutrality; but then the most obvious move (one made explicit by dialogic and some contractual accounts of neutrality) is to stipulate that the ground rules are the object of rational agreement by negotiators who are suitably constrained, by the principle of equality of respect, or whatever other principle is held to secure status neutrality. This, in effect, is the methodology of the Original Position in Rawls's *A Theory of Justice*. One problem for the advocate of status neutrality is whether the parties involved would opt for the constraining principle itself, and how it can be shown to be reasonable on grounds which do not implicitly identify reasonableness with the disposition to accept the constraining principle. More fundamentally, it remains to be explained how the parties can do the negotiating before they can do the negotiating.

The neutralist side-constraint takes the form of an insufficient reason argument. To generate substantive conclusions the side-constraint on justification requires a commitment to status neutrality, to determine what, *ab origine*, is eligible to enter the philosophical discussion of political design. It is only as it bears on persons' conceptions of the good that the side-constraint is held to apply. This is true of all forms of object neutrality, not merely of the outcome-based version. But once we consider the normative force of status, it is either uncontroversial – as in the insufficient-reason form of argument examined above – but also of little help in resolving questions of political design; or it needs a fuller account of normativity whose content can only be spelt out politically.

Conclusion

This pre-empts political processes.[28] It also requires that the distinctively political content of conceptions of the good be debarred from the argument, and in effect denies that deep normative commitments can be embodied in a controversial conception of the political itself. And, while apparently according normative primacy to conceptions of the good, it must exclude the idea, fundamental to many such conceptions, that politics itself can be a good.

The reason why political structures should remain neutral between conceptions of the good is not to be found in considerations intrinsic to the conceptions themselves; it is the very undecidability of the conflicts to which those conceptions give rise that motivates neutrality in the first place. But, it should be noted, the bare fact of undecidability is not by itself capable of justifying substantive political structures. The most it warrants is a *limit* to justification. In fact, however, as we saw, the insufficient-reason considerations fail even to justify limits on justification, since it is gratuitous to suppose that the conditions on political justification must be set solely by the relative standing of the conceptions of the good which prevail in society. It may be simply that an insufficient-reason argument applies insofar as we attend *exclusively* to the standing of those conceptions; but there is no reason to think that these are the sole or decisive considerations which determine the limits of political justification. As I suggested in Chapter 4, those who draw such conclusions are usually thinking elliptically – that is, they are assuming the equality of status of the *bearers* of the conceptions, rather than the conceptions themselves.

It is, after all, not politically pressing to consider what claims on public resources, and so on, are posed by conceptions of the good to which nobody subscribes: the political issue is determined by the existence of persons *qua* self-originating sources of claims on these resources. Thus arguments for neutrality, in their most defensible version, are traceable to an assumption about status, the assumption being that persons enjoy *equal* status with respect to one another. The setting up of the initial position embodies normative commitments, about the worth of persons and their ideas about value. These are liable either to depart from neutrality, or leave the practical problem unsolved. In trying to arbitrate political disputes, it is not clear how viable appeals to these commitments are. Insofar as neutrality attempts to provide a *political* resolution, it has, in facing the intractability of real political disputes, either to say that no justification exists, or to retreat from these disputes to an attempted philosophical resolution, based on what protagonists ought to do, if they were (say) rational, or moral agents. But politics itself makes it problematic whether these concepts are sufficient to resolve the practical disputes.

Part of the attraction of procedural versions of neutrality is that they seem to offer simulacra of actual political deliberation – that they seem to provide a *philosophical* model of real political processes. The problem with the object version of neutrality, however, is that the outcome version of object neutrality is often unattainable – that is, actual political outcomes will fail to embody neutrality. The response to this is to outline *ideal* procedures worked out pre-politically, intended as a response to the *political* problems in implementing object neutrality. What then informs the structuring of the procedural version is not the reasons on which the contending parties, are in fact motivated to act: this, after all, sets the terms of the problem, rather than of its solution. The procedural structuring will not, then, itself be determined politically, as this would require, as I have argued, that the business of politics was completed prior to politics. So the procedural conception of neutrality will not begin from the circumstances of actual political agents.

As regards non-compliance, neutrality differs from justification. A certain *justification* of political design might be valid even though certain political actors reject it. But if an object is not regarded as being neutral between actual political protagonists, there is a clear sense in which it no longer *is* neutral. To accept that it is justified by philosophical arguments whose validity some may be insufficiently enlightened to accept may not undermine the arguments themselves, but impugns the description of them as neutral. The problem goes deeper. It results directly from the normative commitment embodied in status neutrality, since this describes the political problem by reference to the conceptions of the good to which actual protagonists subscribe. This may include conflicting reasonable conceptions of the political – some thin, some with quite distinct thick conceptions. But there is no political order which could be neutral at this level, and neutrality's attempt to resolve such conflicts is therefore chimerical.

7
Rawls and Habermas: Liberalism versus Politics

Introduction

As was argued in Chapter 5, political theorists often move from explaining political phenomena to prescribing how politics should be organised. One reason for this is that they work with highly theorised conceptions of ideal reasons for action. These tend either to underplay pure explanation in theory, since what is in view is a set of reasons on which agents ideally *would* act, rather than those which are in fact motivationally effective. Moreover, as argued in Chapter 4, over-optimism about the capacity of alleged truths in meta-ethics, such as that of value-pluralism, to establish conclusions about political design ignores problems in reconciling actual agents to these conclusions: propositions about the nature of value may and often will not be deliberatively effective for holders of specific conceptions of the good. And, as I argued in Chapter 6, neutralist theorists often rely on rather specific motivational assumptions – in Barry's case, for example, a desire for reasonable agreement; or in that of Ackerman, a desire not to regard other conceptions of the good as inferior. Since there is no reason to think that these desires are universal, or that all of those who do have them give them the priority which their argumentative role requires them to have, the arguments fail unless they make idealising assumptions about motivation.

In this chapter I examine the work of theorists who have aimed to provide substantive conclusions about political design, and in particular Rawls and Habermas. My main conclusion will be that these theorists provide conceptions of political design which are post-political: the societies they describe are societies after politics. These conceptions, if implemented, would contain little political content. I shall argue for this conclusion by way of a semi-formalised model of the political, appeal to which is as I argue fundamental to the theories of both Habermas and Rawls. The *political conceptions* (as I shall refer to them) at work in their theories are intended to furnish an understanding of public justification. I shall however argue that this depends on conditions which will only be met if decisions, which in fact admit only of political determination, are made pre-politically.

My remarks will be confined to Rawls's and Habermas's more recent work, and will address their work only insofar as it bears on the main theme of this book. Both these theorists have a post-political conception of the aims of political philosophy. Once political philosophy moves away from description, or explanation, towards a normative account of reasons for action, it looks towards a 'well-ordered' or ideal state of society in which fundamental political issues have been either resolved or side-lined. The warrant for this is presumably thought to be that philosophical argument will have shown that the beliefs of those engaging in actual political argument were mistaken – mistaken in that they will then have proved to embody false conceptions of justice, or false conceptions of what *can* justifiably enter into political debate. So the implicit conception of the political – of what is eligible for political discussion, and the terms on which political actors engage – already embodies theoretical restrictions on the scope of political engagement.

But it does not regard the resultant prescriptions as inputs into political discussion, where they will be confronted by those offering rival prescriptions of their own – for example, about justice, or the contribution of rival conceptions of the good towards political design. The prescriptions are thought of as framing the terms on which to engage politically, rather than its being the case that the political terms of engagement frame the discussion of the prescriptions. The procedural models on which Rawls and Habermas draw are not to be thought of as simulacra of actual political procedures, but as pre-empting them – because the ground rules governing participation in the procedures are fixed pre-politically. As I shall argue with respect to both Rawls and Habermas, however, the procedures' resemblance to actual decision-making processes is misleading: they replace and do not merely model them.

The nature of the political conception

The term 'political conception' is due to Rawls. He relies on a purely 'political' conception of the argument's justification-conditions, which means (unlike the view of the Reflective Equilibrium apparatus of *Theory of Justice*)[1] that he now thinks it does not aim to achieve moral consensus, but as seeking to cope with the fact of irreducible differences in moral outlook or conceptions of the good in civil society. What it is for a conception to count as *political*, accordingly, is that it embodies a framework for agreement which can recommend itself to the interested parties by accommodating the moral outlook of each. It does this by being either void of moral commitments, or at least void of moral commitments controversial between the parties (Rawls's 'overlapping consensus');[2] variants of this idea recur frequently in contemporary liberalism, particularly in its neutralist versions. In Rawls's case 'political' is tacitly contrasted with 'moral': with the controversial ideas about the good embodied in particular 'comprehensive doctrines'.

As I shall understand it, 'political conception' refers to that conception which, given an account of relevant background conditions (for example, that society contains a number of distinct and incompatible conceptions of the good) is held to constrain or determine the content of a philosophical understanding of the nature of public justification within the society.

The notion of justification applies at two distinct levels: first, at a political level, and second, at a philosophical one. We can, accordingly, ask what can justifiably be said within political discussion itself, but we can also ask what justifies the philosophical conditions determining or constraining the nature of justification within this discussion. Thus, on the interpretation given here, a political conception concerns what *can* be justified ('constrain or determine'), according to philosophical analysis of the nature of public justification. It may be asked why the definition talks of constraining or determining 'the content of a *philosophical* understanding of the nature of public justification', rather than its simply constraining or determining 'the nature of public justification' directly. The content of political argument is to be distinguished from a philosophical analysis of the *conditions* to be satisfied if that argument is justifiable (that is, what counts as an eligible consideration within public deliberation).

In some accounts, these coincide. The intention behind the definition, however, is to leave room for the possibility that they do not; on some views (such as Plato's in *Republic*) there is no basis in general for thinking that what can be justified intrapolitically, must coincide with the justification of a philosophical claim about the conditions *within* which political justification should operate. An illustration of this is provided by the political theory of the *Republic* itself: the considerations in respect of which it is deemed justifiable for the philosopher-guardians to exercise authority are held distinct from those which are eligible for citation by the guardians to those whom they rule, which is as close as the *Republic* gets to a notion of intrapolitical justification. That is the rationale of the 'noble lie'. It should not however be inferred from this that the distinction must take the form of a partial-information or paternalistic public culture.

An immediate illustration of the distinction's relevance can be taken from Rawls's *Political Liberalism*: 'our exercise of political power is proper and hence justifiable only when it is exercised in accordance with a constitution the essentials of which all citizens may reasonably be expected to endorse in the light of principles and ideals acceptable to them as reasonable and rational'.[3] This explicitly sets out an account of what, philosophically, is held to determine or constrain the nature of public justification within the well-ordered society; in fact, Rawls allows[4] for a two-tier account of public reason, in which the comprehensive doctrines may be adduced at a substantive level, while questions of constitutional interpretation, and so on, require the philosophical account of justification itself. Thus in Rawls's case the political conception holds that public justification is to be understood as contingent upon the exercise of power through procedures which immediately are in accordance with the constitution, and mediately can be reasonably and rationally accepted by all citizens.

We can also apply the definition already given to the theory of public deliberation presented by Habermas in recent work. The crucial part of the theory for present purposes is encapsulated in Habermas's principle 'U', as follows:

> a norm is valid when the foreseeable consequences and side effects of its general observance for the interests and value-orientations of *each individual* could be freely accepted *jointly* by *all* concerned.[5]

Thus principle U sets a condition on what can be justified intrapolitically: only those norms are justifiable or valid which can be accepted on the terms stated (it is clear from remarks elsewhere that Habermas believes it 'free' acceptance to entail 'rational' acceptance).

The term 'political conception' demands further elucidation. First, it is a term of art, not to be confused with 'conception of the political' or 'conception of politics'. Not every political subject-matter directly concerns the nature of public justification. Voting behaviour, for instance, treated as a raw datum of democratic polities' life, does not, nor do the activities of pressure groups, nor does the electoral system actually used by a democratic polity. The notion rather concerns the relation between the nature of the justificatory procedures within polities and their image in philosophical conceptions of those procedures.

Second, a political conception is not, on this definition, straightforwardly to be identified with a philosophical justification of a particular set of political arrangements, policies, institutions, and so on. The definition's field of operation is located one stage further back. It concerns that *in virtue of which* a given account of philosophical justification (as applied to these arrangements, and so on) is itself argued for, or held to be justifiable.

Third, an ambiguity in the phrase 'public justification' needs to be clarified. On the face of it, this may refer either to those forms of justification which are used in the public realm (which may vary from one context to another, as for example Aristotle believed that forms of rhetoric varied as between forensic, epideictic and political contexts of public argument); or to what kinds of public arrangments (including, for example, the prevalence of these contextual variations) are justifiable. That these are different follows at once from the fact that no conception of justification held to be subject to these contextual variations could be used to justify the fact of variation itself, whereas this is a job for which justification, on the second interpretation, is pre-eminently suited. It will then be asked which interpretation is intended by the definition. However, for the time being I want to leave this ambiguity unresolved. It will be seen in due course that both Rawls and Habermas adhere to political conceptions which in effect regard the two interpretations as equivalent. The important point to note for the time being is that they need not be so regarded. Clearly the specificity of any given political conception is itself in need of justification. One way to go about this (not the only one) is to argue that the considerations supporting the political conception – that is, the philosophical justification for adopting a political conception with just that content – are none other than those which satisfy the conditions on public justification as articulated *within* the conception itself.

As has already been observed, Rawls's own theory in *Political Liberalism* provides a clear illustration of the notion of a political conception. In this theory, the philosophical understanding of justification in the operative political conception holds that only those political structures commanding the free acceptance of each representative group, when it is subjected to certain epistemic constraints, will pass the test of public acceptability. Many political conceptions embody filtration devices of this kind. Again, in the political conception of Barry's *Justice As Impartiality*, the relevant filter is that the negotiating parties abjure claims to certainty on behalf of any particular conception of the good.[6] As in these examples, and in Habermas's recent writings, filtration is often effected by means of certain favoured meta-ethical concepts, particularly those of the *right* or the *obligatory*. The political conception of Habermas's *Between Facts and Norms*, for example, treats conceptions of the good as 'epistemic inputs' into a public decision-making process, subject to a unanimity constraint.[7]

On some interpretations, neutrality requires that the political conception be morally evacuated, rather than merely requiring that the political conception embody at most values or moral principles commanding general assent among the parties. This stronger conception seems to lie behind the identification of a theory like that of Raz's *The Morality of Freedom* as non-neutral; Raz's theory in fact recommends autonomy as a value which can command general assent in the face of value-pluralism, and so satisfies the thinner conception of neutrality.[8] What characterises the political conception is its embodying a framework of principles capable of commanding general agreement – though in practice this is invariably taken to mean general *rational* agreement, or in other words what the relevant parties would agree to if they were fully rational.

This relies on meta-ethical positions which have already been questioned in Chapter 5. A common route to this version of the political conception is to provide a philosophical argument (such as a normative one) for a certain view of political society and then commend it as the only one which the parties *could* be justified in accepting if they were fully rational: so, *a fortiori*, it is the one which they *would* accept, if fully rational. Many contractarian theories are of this form.[9] I shall refer to this political conception as the *onefold route*.

These interpretations of the political conception, however, ignore another possibility. Perhaps there is *no* political conception satisfying the demands of the onefold route. The grounds on which this might be asserted could include claims about the nature of value, such as pluralism, or nihilism, or scepticism, or the essential contestability thesis. For example, someone might hold that the onefold route failed because there was a plurality of values, with a concomitant plurality of justifiable political conceptions; or, at the other end of the scale, because there were no values at all (or no knowable truths about value), and so no justifiable political conception. We can note in passing that the claim that there are no knowable truths about value is sometimes taken as the starting-point for justifications of political neutrality. Or it might be held that since nothing about value was knowable, there could be no public justification. In each case, the upshot is that the onefold route fails, because rational justification fails to determine a unique political conception.

For now I shall note simply that we can *define* alternative political conceptions, and that one mark of difference lies in the implied relation between the justification of the conception itself, and the account of public justification embodied within it. On one showing, these justifications coincide, or at least are non-contingently related; we could call this the *compact* version of a political conception. But on another, there is no necessary tie-up between the justification of the political conception itself, and the philosophical account of the nature of public justification (including, for example, filtration devices, and so on). This is the *two-stage* version. Plato's *Republic* is a clear example of a two-stage theory. The distinction depends on whether or not the content of the *philosophical* justification of the political conception is held to coincide with the content of public justification itself. The compact version of the political conception holds that it is; the two-stage version holds that it need not do so.

Note that this distinction is quite different from the justifiability or otherwise of the onefold route. The horizontal distinction between the onefold and (as it may be called) the manifold routes concerns the possible plurality of *philosophical* justifications of political design, while the vertical distinction between the compact and two-stage justifications concerns its (or their) nature. Even if the onefold route is justifiable, it may be that its only justifiable form is a two-stage version of the political conception. On the other hand, if there were an argument to show that *only* the compact version was justifiable (for example, given the commitment to democracy mentioned at the start of this chapter), it might show why the onefold route was unavailable: for, if that was a condition of justifying a political conception, the background conditions might provide, in effect, a *reductio* of it – showing that no philosophical account could frame the terms of public justification, given certain of the background conditions.

An illustration of this point is the 'agonistic' liberalism attributed by Gray to Isaiah Berlin, and latterly espoused by Gray himself.[10] The fundamental idea behind this is that it is a consequence of value-pluralism that the onefold route fails. However, since value-pluralism is *par excellence* a philosophical theory – one purportedly disclosing truths about the metaphysics of value – a two-stage political conception might consistently deny that this by itself determined the content of public justification; but then, *if* it could be shown that only the compact version were itself justifiable (for example, within a commitment to democratic theory), we would have an explanation of why the onefold route fails. I return to this possibility in the next chapter.

Habermas

Habermas's recent work, such as his paper 'On the Cognitive Content of Morality', brings these points more clearly into focus. His starting-point, like that of Barry, Rawls, Ackerman and others, is the proliferation of diverse conceptions of the good in society, from which results a search for principles, acceptable to the partisans of each conception, capable of mediating politically between the interest-groups they represent. On Habermas's neo-constructivist view, moral principles are those generated by suitable dialogic procedures – the criterion of suitability of any candidate procedure being its acceptability to negotiating parties representing the actual conceptions of the good present in society, when subject to certain epistemic constraints. Thus Habermas's conception of the initial negotiating situation follows the Rawlsian veil of ignorance quite closely. The aim of these procedures is to determine principles of *right* which alone, in Habermas's view, are capable of winning unanimous acceptance given the diverse conceptions of the good in society. The neo-constructivist element consists in the fact that acceptable principles, generated by means of procedures conforming to the above specifications, are held to be constructed from the negotiating process according to the decision-principle U already mentioned.

This is a procedurally neutral principle. Neutrality is guaranteed by the epistemic constraints designed to check special pleading by interest-groups, and so on, on their own behalf. This not only precludes non-neutral *outcomes,* but also embodies restrictions on knowledge which are indifferent as between the interest-groups concerned. Furthermore, the method by which outcomes are determined relies on a procedurally neutral mechanism – though the verbal formula given above is beset by ambiguities, familiar from Rousseau, concerning the nature and extent of individuals' vetoes.

Habermas's theory marks a thoroughgoing shift to neutralist liberalism from the Frankfurt school Marxism of his earlier writings. Though he is not always clear as to whether the negotiating process should be understood, Habermas apparently regards it as an actual, rather than merely hypothetical process. Nonetheless, the different conceptions of the good are explicitly treated as *epistemic* inputs into the discussion:

> Pragmatic and ethical reasons, which retain their internal connection to the interests and self-understanding of individual persons ... no longer *count* as the motives and value-orientations of individual persons but as epistemic contributions to a discourse in which the norms are examined with the aim of reaching a communicative agreement.[11]

There is no reason in principle why the conceptions of the good *qua* inputs into the discussion should be made by those who adhere to them. Then, given that the construction is a purely epistemic one, it is unclear why the negotiating procedure must be actual rather than hypothetical. For if it is possible to adduce the value-orientations as propositional inputs to discussion, it is irrelevant whether those making them actually subscribe to them. Political decision-making then becomes a process by which an inquirer might seek to reduce a set of beliefs to consistency.

The political problem arises, as was noted in Chapter 4, not because there are several conceptions of the good in society, but because they sometimes conflict. This will, for example, yield rival options for public policy, and not infrequently the clash between these opinions will not be contingent (as it may be, for instance, where the conflict arises from limited public resources), but necessary – some conceptions of the good are essentially conceptions of the *badness* of other conceptions of the good. Then there will necessarily be more than one way of resolving the policy dispute: given that there are at least two beliefs in conflict, it must be possible to dispose of the conflict by rejecting the one belief, or the other, and similarly with beliefs about public policy.

However, the problems facing Habermas begin one stage further back, with the justification of the constructivist procedure itself. This gives rise to at least two problems. First, his resolution understates the refractoriness of political conflicts, and of the differences in ethical outlook which may characterise them. The conception of normativity informing the structure of the negotiating procedures is itself questionable. If what licenses the procedures is that they conform to certain substantive ethical principles, those may themselves be the subject of dispute. The moral commitments which are to structure discussion are better seen as outputs *from* the discussion, rather than inputs *to* it. Similarly, the belief that the political problem consists in constructing policy according to consensual principles of *right* reflects a questionable set of meta-ethical priorities. Of course, once the problem has been identified as a conflict between conceptions of the good, then conceptions of the good (or at least, *those* conceptions) will not be able to resolve them. This is a pattern of reasoning which, as we shall see, is also present in Rawls's work. But there may equally be conflict between conceptions of the right as well. The attempt at procedural structuring is liable to pre-empt decisions which can only be arrived at through political action. Seen in this light, the attempt to provide a pre-political framework for political negotiation itself seems open to challenge.

Secondly, Habermas presupposes a quite specific model of normativity and practical deliberation. We have encountered a version of this model before, when discussing arguments for political obligation which attempt to satisfy requirement TD in Chapter 3: the requirement that reasons for political obligations be transparent and apply to each citizen subject to them. In understanding the assumptions underlying the model it is important to distinguish two levels at which ethical inquiry can proceed. In Chapter 3, I explored different views of practical deliberation and its relation to political obligations. It is an assumption, in need of justification, that the theoretical modelling of moral concepts (such as that of *obligation*) provided by philosophy must coincide with the reflex of these concepts in actual examples of agents' practical deliberations.

Habermas's constructivist model, like some other forms of discursively-based neutrality, attempts to close a perceived gap between theoretical justification and actual deliberation. The requirement that the conceptions of the good be treated as epistemic inputs prejudices both the deliberative framework's ability to model political negotiations and the willingness of rational individuals to make themselves a party to it. Some such conceptions, after all, are held more vigorously than others, and rational individuals may not much favour a procedural framework which fails to take this into account (they may also balk at endorsing a procedure in the knowledge that it may yield results uncongenial to their own conception of the good).

Given diverse conceptions of the good, a neutralist political resolution appears attractive, and it may be supported by reasons such as those considered in the last chapter. I contended earlier that the most obvious form which the argument might take – the insufficient-reason argument considered in Chapter 6 – is unconvincing. But even if it were shown that neutrality was the only justifiable political answer to civil-society diversity, it would not prove that there was any political structure which was in fact justified. On one view, politics just *is* the public decision-making mechanism deployed when justification gives out.[12]

The attraction of *discursive* forms of procedural neutrality is that they appear to offer a link between theoretical justification and agent-deliberation. Ackerman's dialogic neutrality seems designed partly with this in mind, as do Larmore's arguments for neutrality. Discursive neutrality thus offers a form of justification which both is compact and follows the onefold route. It is compact, in the sense given above, because it purports to model justification on the deliberation of real agents – agents engaged in political decision-making. There is thus no gap between the justifications which philosophically can be given for a form of political design, and justifications which operate infra-politically. The discursive approach apparently follows the onefold route, because it holds that justification is *constructed* from the discursive procedures, duly mediated by the discursive conditions (such as principle U).

However, this constructive approach faces grave problems, most of which are exemplified by principle U. Habermas's proposal that validity depends on what *could* be accepted on individuals' behalf blurs important issues, as do the conditions under which individuals can be described as 'freely' accepting the deliverances of the deliberative structures. This 'could' looks like the hypothetical conditional, and if so, we need some specification of the relevant conditions to be fulfilled. It may be taken to mean simply that each individual could freely accept the deliberative outcome if they accepted Habermas's constructivism, or accepted some other general model of normative rationality. But, of course, this only redirects attention to the question why individuals should accept *that*. As already noted, Habermas's aim is to provide regulative principles capable of dealing with diversity in 'thick' normative beliefs, and he apparently favours a practical rather than hypothetical interpretation of the principles' operation. But he gives no indication of how the adherents of the ethical beliefs are to describe a deliberative path leading them from the 'thick' normativity of their acculturated belief-systems into endorsement of principle U. As with the justification-condition set by Barry's neutralist theory, there is no reason to assume that there is *any* set of political arrangements which conform to the condition, and sustain the first-order commitments which gave rise to the conflict in the first place.

In what conditions can power be legitimately exercised? Any attempt to model politics on discourse has to accept that real political actors often disagree and conflict with each other.[13] The model then has to decide how much disagreement and conflict is left in, with the following dilemma. Either the discursive model no longer attempts to represent this fundamental aspect of political engagement; or it does, with the likelihood that agreement is unattainable. On any plausible view (not merely value-pluralism), disagreement will occur.[14] The procedures envisaged have to provide some means of generating a decision. Then it will be a matter of *enforcing* an agreement, or at least a decision, on parties who are otherwise not disposed to reach one. That, of course, is an entrenched feature of political decision-making. But it no longer answers the requirement that the discursive processes yield judgements which command the rational and unforced agreement of those who participate in them, as demanded by principle U. It seems that the only way this can be avoided is by so limiting the initial 'inputs' that the scope for conflict and disagreement no longer exists; but that simply evades the problem, and pre-empts the outcome of the discussion. The upshot is that free agreement can be reached only if the procedures which yield it are no longer modelled on politics.

The conception of rational agreement underlying Habermas's view of politics assumes in effect that the motivations of political actors are indefinitely susceptible of cognitive manipulation. Given that Habermas's is a constructivist model, it presumably holds that the fact of its having been delivered by the procedure is itself what underwrites the truth of a given judgement. For the initial epistemic predicament is one in which there is no independent agreed method of determining the truth or falsity of judgements. The discursive procedure is the *proxy* for such a method, since it generates an output from the initial epistemic inputs, to which those taking part are held to be committed by dint of the fact that they freely participate in it. If this *were* the case, and there were some independent grounds for believing that rational agents should participate in the procedure, it would be the case that rational agents were committed to accepting the judgements delivered by it. But no such grounds have been given.

What the free agreement model ignores is the role of power and force in reaching political decisions. For where there are *only* free and uncoerced agreements, difficult questions about power need not arise.

On the other hand, when the political process is characterised by disagreement and conflict, the use of political power is required in order to bring matters to a decision, and support for this will then necessarily *not* be freely given by those at odds with it. As noted in Chapter 6, the parties may eschew any ostensibly 'neutral' procedure for conflict-resolution precisely because they fear it will lead to an outcome which they reject. The use of power, too, will presuppose a framework within which political decisions can be reached in the face of disagreement. But it is fantastical to believe that these can be decided pre-politically, since deciding such matters is itself a political matter. Allocating powers and responsibilities is not a regrettably necessary prelude to the real business of politics: it *is* the regrettably necessary business of politics.

The model requires that political questions be resolved prior to politics itself.[15] When we consider how the deliberative framework would operate in practice, a wide range of highly contentious political issues come into view. Among these are, for example, awkward questions concerning ownership and opportunity. As regards the distribution of power, Habermas seems to envisage a cantilevered set of structures, rising from low-level deliberative forums in which each person has the opportunity to participate, to larger bodies with presumably more extensive decision-making authority. The balance of power between these bodies, and their decision-making competence, are matters themselves requiring a political decision. Either this competence will be wide enough to address the fundamental issues themselves, or it will not be. If not, it is evident that the structures envisaged are only in an attenuated sense political ones. But if their competence is sufficiently wide, fundamental issues about the distribution of power will already have been resolved: the conditions for undistorted communication require that. So the discursive structures will be in place only when these pervasive and highly divisive political issues have been resolved. The discursive structures arrive too late; they only arrive after politics.

Rawls

In his recent work Rawls explicitly contrasts the 'political' with what he refers to as 'comprehensive' doctrines – contentious moral and metaphysical belief-systems which (usually) carry with them commitment to a particular, and controversial, conception of the good life. It is, moreover, held to be a truth about the relation between these comprehensive doctrines that 'reasonable pluralism' prevails: in other words, 'a basic feature of democracy is ... the fact that a plurality of conflicting reasonable comprehensive doctrines, religious, philosophical, and moral, is the normal result of its culture of free institutions'.[16] For Rawls, the political task is to determine public principles, commanding the reasonable assent of those subscribing to the comprehensive doctrines, capable of governing the society as a fair system of cooperation for mutual benefit, and mediating between them when they conflict.

This position is widely accepted within modern liberal philosophy.[17] But it invites a fairly obvious objection. If the different comprehensive doctrines are 'conflicting', but each is reasonable in at least the sense that it cannot be shown to be less reasonable than its rivals, then belief in any particular such doctrine must be unreasonable. For if the comprehensive doctrines conflict, but none can be shown to be less reasonable than the others, then reason must conclude that belief in *none* of them is reasonable. Since they conflict, to accept a particular doctrine is *ipso facto* to reject the others, but that is to reject what reasonable pluralism tells us are no less reasonable doctrines. It is notable that what Rawls elsewhere seems to regard as a purely descriptive claim[18] about modern societies has become a normative epistemic claim. What begins as a datum delivered mainly by political experience – namely the fact of disagreement – is conflated with a normative doctrine about reasonableness which, although incoherent, is then itself invoked to circumscribe politics. For it is the 'reasonable pluralism' doctrine which determines what is eligible for political discussion.

In what follows I shall consider the suggestion in *Political Liberalism* – a clear departure from Rawls's earlier view in *A Theory of Justice* – that the well-ordered society is no longer characterised by agreement over substantive moral principles, but seeks to formulate, in the face of pervasive and unresolvable moral disagreement, an 'overlapping consensus' on principles of political justice. My aims in discussing Rawls are confined to the following. First, I examine the moral presuppositions of the argument of *A Theory of Justice*, and the transformation of this part of the theory in *Political Liberalism*. Then, in the light of this, I evaluate further Rawls's contention that the later work marks a shift to a 'political' conception of justice. Finally, I shall relate the discussion to the critique articulated in the foregoing chapters.

A Theory of Justice subscribed to a theory, albeit 'thin', of the good. This survives in transmuted form in *Political Liberalism*.[19] In the latter work, Rawls insists that overlapping consensus is not merely a *modus vivendi* reached when no single comprehensive doctrine holds sway: 'a political conception supported by an overlapping consensus is a moral conception affirmed on moral grounds';[20] Rawls adds elsewhere that 'the political conception of justice, is itself a moral conception ... affirmed on moral grounds'.[21] These grounds are that 'it [that is, the political conception of justice] includes conceptions of society and of citizens as persons, as well as principles of justice, and an account of the political virtues through which those principles are embodied'.[22] In reply to Habermas's objection[23] that political liberalism cannot avoid questions of truth and contentious issues raised by the philosophical conception of the person, Rawls says: 'I do not see why not. Political liberalism avoids reliance on both of these ideas and substitutes others – the reasonable, in one case, and the conception of persons as citizens viewed as free and equal, in the other.'[24]

Citizens have 'two moral powers. The first is a capacity for a sense of justice' enabling them to formulate and implement principles of justice, and the second 'is a capacity for a conception of the good'.[25] Later in this passage Rawls comments on the methodological status of the 'constructivist'[26] procedure which he now favours:

> not everything ... is constructed; we must have some material, as it were, from which to begin ... In a more literal sense, only the substantive principles specifying content of political right and justice are constructed. The procedure itself is simply laid out using as starting points the basic conceptions of society and person, the principles of practical reason, and the public role of a political conception of justice.[27]

So, despite the 'political' character which Rawls now imputes to his argument for the principles of justice, this does not preclude – indeed it presupposes – a role for specifically moral ideals in the process of construction: as Rawls says, 'a political conception of justice is a normative and moral conception, and so is the domain of the political, as well as all the other political conceptions',[28] and 'political rights and duties are moral rights and duties, for they are part of a political conception that is a normative (moral) conception with its own intrinsic ideal, though not itself a comprehensive doctrine'.[29]

The two lines of inquiry which I shall pursue concern first Rawls's constructivist methodology, and second the 'political' conception of justice which Rawls derives from it. The major development since the publication of *A Theory of Justice* in Rawls's interpretation of the problem which political philosophy sets out to solve is that he now believes that there is a plurality of incompatible but reasonable comprehensive doctrines, and that philosophical argument will not reduce these different doctrines to reasonable agreement. This poses a puzzle, since Rawls repeatedly affirms that a political conception of justice is a moral conception, on which the partisans of different comprehensive doctrines can concur. Accordingly Rawls's idea must be that the political conception coexists with a plurality of comprehensive doctrines. Rawls is at pains to emphasise that the principles constitutive of the overlapping consensus can be given different justifications, depending on the perspective afforded by particular comprehensive doctrines.[30]

I shall not examine how far Rawls's claim that overlapping consensus commands reasonable assent can be sustained. There is however room for considerable doubt as to whether the principles of justice and the modelling procedure which generate them are subject to the consensus to which their theoretical role requires that they conform. It should be noted that this difficulty exists regardless of whether or not the 'political conception' demands convergence on fundamental values (that is, those values which Rawls assigns to the 'comprehensive doctrines'): it remains to be shown that there will be scope for reasonable agreement on a political conception when variations in the comprehensive doctrines have been taken into account. Even if there is agreement on the values constitutive of the political conception, there may be reasonable disagreement about the role which these values should play in determining its content. Moving further out, there may simply not be reasonable agreement on the values themselves. None of this requires any metaphysical commitment, such as value-pluralism; all it requires is the failure of reasonable people to reach agreement. Political issues remain even if people who espouse conflicting comprehensive doctrines are not reasonable.

The question is how to understand the procedure from which the overlapping consensus is held to result, and particularly with the claim that there are consensual *political* principles capable of regimenting the plurality of comprehensive doctrines which prevail in civil society: 'the comprehensive philosophical and moral views we are wont to use in debating fundamental political issues should give way in public life. Public reason ... is now best guided by a political conception the principles and values of which all citizens can endorse.'[31]

There is a terminological oddity in Rawls's use of the term 'political'. In his understanding, what is 'political' is the content of justice, that is, the object of an overlapping consensus between comprehensive doctrines.[32] But in fact the content of justice is determined purely philosophically: it is delivered prior to politics, which it at least partially pre-empts. The theory demarcates the space within which politics is to operate. This presupposes no very controversial understanding of the political: at the limit, it requires no more than that it involves interpersonal transactions. The crucial question is begged by saying that what is under discussion is what *ought* to be political; as far as that goes, the Rawlsian account of justice is merely one voice in the multitude. The attempt to cordon off as 'political' the domain of overlapping consensus forestalls what are properly political questions.

In the version of the Original Position given in *Political Liberalism*, Rawls's assumption is that it is a 'device of representation' which aims 'to model both freedom and equality'.[33] Similarly, the Original Position as it appeared in *A Theory of Justice* was designed to model systematically a certain moral conception. So the nature of the 'political' as it appears in the 'political conception' is not such that it precludes normative commitments. What is intended to exact rational agreement to the principles of justice which result from the Original Position? In *Political Liberalism*, as in *A Theory of Justice*, it is that the principles would reasonably and rationally be chosen by parties in a negotiating situation which models the relevant normative commitments.

The fact that there is a plurality of reasonable comprehensive doctrines does not play a direct role in the derivation of the principles. As was noted in Chapter 4, where liberals use pluralistic premisses to establish substantive conclusions about political design, it often indicates that they are appealing to a value, such as that of equality of respect or moral personhood, which explains why the diverse actually existing conceptions of the good (or 'comprehensive doctrines') demand a certain kind of political accommodation.[34] Similarly, what matters for Rawls's argument is not that there is a plurality of comprehensive doctrines, but that there is a common normative core which is substantial enough to play its heuristic role. Without this, there is no reason to think that there will be a theoretical basis ratifiable by this procedure for the overlapping consensus.

This raises an important question regarding the reasonableness of the device itself, in relation to the plurality of reasonable comprehensive doctrines. On one reading, the basis for deciding whether the doctrines are reasonable is whether or not those subscribing to them *assent* to the reasonableness of the device, as embodying a model conception from whose perspective theirs is reasonable. On the other hand, it may be that there is an independent way to decide the model's reasonableness, and we then proceed to adjudicate, on a case-by-case basis, whether the adherents of individual comprehensive doctrines (which may or may not be themselves reasonable) are able to recognise this fact.

We might refer to these possibilities, respectively, as the narrow and the wide understandings of reasonableness. On the narrow reading, since conformability to the normative content of the pre-commitments issuing in the political conception is the criterion of reasonableness, this fact (that is, that the doctrines are so conformable) cannot be invoked to justify the normative content itself. But if we move to the wide reading, then it is clearly possible that there may be some doctrines, themselves reasonable, which fail to ratify the content of the normative pre-commitments. If that is true, Rawls's aim – to set out an overlapping consensus which partisans of reasonable comprehensive doctrines can agree as reasonable – will not be met.

Rawls perhaps never makes explicit his preference between the wide and the narrow readings. But his remarks about 'the political conception of the person', and in particular the normative commitments involved in identifying moral persons as citizens, equipped with the two moral powers (the capacity to have a conception of the good and to have a sense of justice) are held already to embody the specific values of liberty and equality. Since there are comprehensive doctrines which reject this conception of the person, those who subscribe to them will presumably reject or at least have no reason to accept the principles of justice resulting from the Original Position developed from this conception. If so, then it seems that those conceptions which fail to recognise this are not reasonable. Then it seems that adherence to the specific values is a condition of reasonableness. There is also, as Joseph Raz has pointed out, the ambiguous status of the conception of justice which results from the argument of *Political Liberalism*, in relation to the comprehensive doctrines. As we have already seen, what it means for the conception to count as 'political' is that it is held apart from these doctrines, which are regarded as being inherently disputable.[35]

Nonetheless, it is held to be one of the advantages of the 'overlapping consensus' conception of justice that it can be integrated into very different and mutually incompatible comprehensive doctrines. But then, clearly, the conception is not free-standing as Rawls intends, but a proper part of the comprehensive doctrines. If justice as fairness were merely a *modus vivendi*, negotiated by the representatives of the comprehensive doctrines to guarantee civil peace, it would not need to be integrated into the doctrines, being merely a device for mutual benefit. But Rawls explicitly rules this out: 'it is not sufficient that [the holders of] these doctrines accept a democratic regime merely as a *modus vivendi*. Rather, they must accept it as members of a reasonable overlapping consensus.'[36]

This suggests that the political design envisaged in *Political Liberalism* is a 'weak' form of neutrality, as that was defined in Chapter 6. In other words, neutrality will result not from a blanket abstention from normative commitments, but from the fact that these commitments are uncontroversial between the comprehensive doctrines. But, as already noted, since there are doctrines which reject the commitments, it seems that acceptance of them is a condition of reasonableness. Then we can by what conception of reasonableness this is held to be justified – and justified on the grounds of *neutrality*. It is not enough to say that the right is prior to the good, as Rawls and other neo-Kantians argue. There are at least apparently reasonable comprehensive doctrines which deny this priority, and so we need to know why the political conception is fashioned to fit it. Even if some such explanation is forthcoming, there may well be a plurality of conceptions of the right, as well as of conceptions of the good. The assumption that there is not may be based on the thought that there can only ever be one thing which it is *right* to do, whereas there may be any number of things which it would be *good* to do. But there can be disagreement about what that right thing is, and so pointing to the 'priority' of the right will not produce a onefold route to political design.[37]

As we saw in Chapter 6 with other versions of neutrality, we can also ask why the 'political' is excluded entirely from the remit of the 'comprehensive doctrines' (on the free-standing interpretation mentioned above), or else excludes those doctrines whose political content is at odds with Rawls's political liberalism itself (if political liberalism, as the object of the overlapping consensus, is held to be part of the comprehensive doctrines). There is a more obvious consequence of this, on which previous commentators have remarked.[38] It is far from clear that politics, in Rawls's understanding of it, has any *deliberative* content. This is perhaps more apparent in the Original Position in *A Theory of Justice*, where the deliberators – or what amounts to the same thing, the solitary deliberator – fix the basic shape of society. Within the framework of the two principles, the scope for decision-making seems to be confined to administration. For if politics is the main public arena within which deliberative conflicts are enacted, then it follows that any theory which attempts to produce a framework for basic public agreement, as Rawls does in both *A Theory of Justice* and *Political Liberalism*, will not operate with a conception of politics: it will have moved from the government of people to the administration of things.

Theory, motivation and reason

In Chapter 5 I offered a theoretical explanation for the anti-political methodology of political philosophy, and for the post-political ambitions of much work in the discipline. That explanation drew attention to the lack of psychological realism in contemporary ethical theory, and in particular its relative neglect of agents' actual motivations. In *Political Liberalism* Rawls asks: 'How is one to fix limits on what people might be moved by in thought and deliberation and hence may act from?',[39] and answers as follows:

> once conception-dependent desires are admitted as elements of what Williams calls 'a person's motivational set' ... then the line between his allegedly Humean view of motivation and Kant's view, or ones related to it, begins to dissolve. To see this we have only to suppose that Kant's idea of the categorical imperative is coherent and say that a person with a good will is someone effectively moved by the conception-dependent desire to act as that imperative requires ... if it is asked how principle- and conception-dependent desires become elements in people's motivational sets in the first place, then the superficial answer ... is that they are learned from the public political culture. This is part of the ideal of publicity.[40]

Rawls's aim here is to show that the 'internal' conception of reasons must allow for executive or in other words 'conception-dependent' motivations, a consequence of which is that an agent with them may have reason to act in ways in which he is unmotivated to act, so that having a reason to act cannot be identified with having the relevant motivation. The first-level reasons-statements which Rawls envisages are nonetheless dependent on a motivation, namely the executive desire itself. It fails to establish that an agent lacking an executive desire to act morally still has a reason to do so. Even so, the standing of moral propositions as reasons need not be impugned by the absence of appropriate motivations.

Rawls attempts in the passage just quoted to link internalism with his own favoured view of political design. It would not follow from the fact that someone lacked certain executive desires that he had reasons to act in ways in which he was unmotivated to act. It may empirically be true that exposure to a political culture in which certain executive desires are valued will inculcate them in citizens who would otherwise lack them. But of course this assumes that the business of political design has already been accomplished and certain kinds of desires accordingly are valued within the culture. More significantly, perhaps, the motivations must enjoy appropriate priority with respect to other ones – for example, those associated with particular comprehensive doctrines to which citizens may subscribe.

Since the working out of public disputes arising from these competing motivations is of the essence of politics, a form of political design which excludes it is in effect post-political: it envisions a state of the world in which a prime cause of political conflict has been removed, or short-circuited. This is because the fundamental principles of justice, embodied in a Rawlsian overlapping consensus, are decided pre-politically. Rawls relies on a political conception in which the ground-rules for public justification are determined prior to politics.

Though it is a form of object neutrality, since what he envisages is a set of 'basic institutions' and instruments of 'public policy' which are 'not to be designed to favor any particular comprehensive doctrine',[41] Rawls's version of neutrality is designed also to meet the side-constraint on justification discussed in Chapter 6. That, after all, is what the idea of an overlapping consensus involves. It is quite possible that there is in fact no basis for the consensus at all, just as Barry's requirement that political design be based on principles which no one could reasonably reject leaves it open that there is then no justified form of political design.[42] The response to someone who finds that their conception of the good or comprehensive doctrine excludes the area of agreement defined by the overlapping consensus, seems to be that they will in fact become motivated to act within the consensus once it is enshrined in the public political culture, since they will then acquire 'conception-dependent' desires. More concretely, the principles of justice may fail to entrench themselves precisely because they are embodied in large-scale institutions whose operations are regarded as impersonal and in certain respects arbitrary. We can then ask whether their entrenchment is better secured by hoping that motivation will follow the institutionally embodied principles, rather than by working from the inside out.[43]

The outside-in approach, on the other hand, tends to remove by fiat the motivational facts which give rise to political conflict in the first place. A similar move is evident in Habermas's recent work. As we saw, his constructivist version of cognitivism treats the circumstances of politics purely as 'epistemic inputs' to the decision-making process: the relevant normative truths are constructed out of these raw materials, by quasi-discursive means.[44] Its emergence from the process is what confers truth on a given discursively-produced norm, just as in formal systems the very fact of derivability from the axioms via the rules of inference confers truth on a given sentence of the system. As Gaus points out, however, 'common sense' reasoning is not immune from fallacious inferences.[45] So if it is to construct truths, actual dialogue has to be filtered. This is not to claim that real-world participants should adhere to conclusions yielded by faulty inferences, though they may reasonably decide its yielding a certain conclusion by *valid* inference is a good reason for rejecting a certain premiss. But there is no reason to think that the process of reducing 'epistemic inputs' to consistency will yield a unique outcome; more commonly it will not. What will then happen is an attempt to circumscribe the 'inputs' themselves, so as produce a result. This will put strain not only on the procedure's claim to 'construct' truths, but also on its capacity, once the truths are constructed, to elicit the support of those subject to it.

Roberto Alejandro has made a systematic attempt to set out the respects in which Rawls's (and by extension, others') theory of justice might or might not be judged to be political. In defending the view that Rawls's theory may after all be properly regarded as political, Alejandro states that:

> Rawls's doctrine is deeply political in (1) his attempt to articulate a conception of justice on the basis of values that are part of the history and culture of constitutional democracies; (2) his effort to provide a wide space for the accommodation of conflicting understandings of the human good; (3) his goal of promoting the political values of cooperation, stability, and order through the regulation or avoidance of conflicts.[46]

These remarks embody a confusion of categories. It is not obviously wrong to say that aims (1)–(3) set out in the quotation above may be political aims. That is, aims to set out a conception of justice, accommodate conflict, and promote stability, cooperation, and so on, may be essayed by practical politicians. But these are aims *within* politics itself. Rawls's theory, on the other hand, sets out these goals before practical politics exists, so as to circumscribe the space within which it operates. Thus the fact that the aims (1)–(3) may be ones which political actors have in their sights fails to prove that Rawls's is, after all, a political conception of justice: on the contrary, it defines a *limit* to politics.[47]

Alejandro argues that, contrary to the standard interpretation, justice as fairness is itself a perfectionist doctrine.[48] There are indeed passages in Rawls's later writings which support this view.[49] That justice as fairness is a form of perfectionism does not, however, prove that Rawls's understanding of it is political. Since there are rival conceptions of the good, some of which include rival conceptions of the political, we need an explanation as to why the issue between Rawlsian perfectionism (if such it be) and other conceptions of the good is ineligible for political debate. Indeed, Alejandro subsequently admits that:

> Honig's claim[50] that Rawlsian justice displaces politics in favor of administrative procedures is *partially* true ... Rawlsian liberalism is predicated upon a juridical vision of politics ... the possibility of exploring an agreement on a political conception of the human good is excluded ... politics as the public deliberation about power has no place within the confines of Rawlsian political liberalism. In the Rawlsian paradigm, there is no discussion of power.[51]

Attempts to derive substantive conclusions about political design from claims about the nature of value fail, because they rely on a conception of public justification (one usually thought of as licensing a liberal conception of political design) which either leaves all possibilities in play – that is, it is politically vacuous – or else relies on premisses consistent with, if not actually entailing, monism. Again we are left with a gap between what is supposedly justifiable on the strength of particular philosophical claims – here those about the metaphysics of value – and what public justification will support. One response to failures of justification such as this is to espouse neutrality. But since the nature and scope of the political is itself a matter for political dispute, the neutralist order circumscribes politics itself. Some neutralist theorists, like Rawls and Habermas, adopt an explicitly political conception of the circumstances of justification. They rely, however, like other neutralists on an implicitly moralised interpretation of the circumstances of justification.

Now it may be said that these remarks are irrelevant to neutralist theories such as those of Rawls, Barry and Habermas, because in each case the starting-position and rationale for neutrality is precisely that substantive normative ideas, or conceptions of the good, are an inadequate basis on which to found political design. There is just a plurality of 'comprehensive doctrines' or conceptions of the good, the truth of any of which it is reasonable to deny; so a basis for reasonable agreement must lie elsewhere than in these conceptions. Moreover, as I argued in Chapter 6, neutrality itself requires a neutral foundation if it is not to fail in its own terms. So it may be said, the arguments of

Chapter 5 regarding the application of normative theory to political philosophy are irrelevant to neutrality.

It should, however, be clear from the argument earlier in this chapter that this criticism fails. For as we saw, the only argument for neutrality which satisfies its own side-constraint is or entails an insufficient-reason claim: this applied irrespective of whether neutrality was interpreted as being normatively 'thin' (that is, devoid of normativity *tout court*) or 'thick' (that is, not so devoid, but embodying only consensually acceptable normative conceptions). For on the thin interpretation, *any* form of political design which embodies normative commitments is *ipso facto* neutrality-violating, since the thin interpretation demands that political design be devoid of normative commitment. Since on this view there is insufficient reason to write into political design any normative commitments, there must, *a fortiori*, be insufficient reason to favour a particular commitment, *qua* conception of the good, over others. On the other hand, while the thick interpretation allows for normative commitments, the latter must be uncontroversial between different comprehensive doctrines. The normative content of political design must therefore be limited to commitments which are neutral between the competing doctrines.

So, either way, there is insufficient reason to favour any one controversial doctrine over the others. We can see this from the discussion of the theorists already mentioned. As I argued in Chapter 6, the insufficient-reason argument fails to justify substantive conclusions about political design. Barry's main argument for neutrality is ostensibly an insufficient-reason argument, since it holds that no particular conception of the good will satisfy the desire for reasonable agreement: that is because it is reasonable to deny, of any such conception, that it is reasonable. However, given the weakness of the insufficient-reason argument, Barry as we saw relies on a thickened conception of 'reasonableness', which expands its normative content. The danger then is that thickening will only restore substantive content by incurring controversial normative commitments.

Of course, one possibility is to move to the thick conception of neutrality. Rawls's overlapping consensus provides an example of this, subject to the qualification that the adherents of different comprehensive doctrines may each interpret the principles differently from their own normative standpoint. This does not however mean that the thick Rawlsian conception of neutrality avoids normative commitments. As such, there is reason to doubt, as I have argued, whether there will be any non-vacuous principles commanding consensual agreement. It should be recalled that these principles need not only to be the object of universal assent, but need to be *prioritised* in order to play the role required of them by Rawls's argument: that is, they must be principles which the parties not only accept in some hypothetical way, but regard as sufficiently important to serve as (in Rawls's sense) 'political' principles for the society.

Appendix: Gaus and public justification

In his recent book *Justificatory Liberalism* Gaus argues that liberal theorists such as Rawls have imposed it as a condition on candidate principles of justice that they be capable of eliciting the actual assent of the contracting parties.[52] Since, however, people are prone to make inferential errors (for reasons which in Gaus's view may be either good or bad ones), it cannot in his view be a condition on the justifiability of the principles that they command the assent even of reasonable people: reasonable people often ignore excellent reasons.

Gaus's major argument is that reasonable persons may fail to be swayed by justifications which are themselves reasonable. In his sights are those theories, such as Rawls's, which are concerned only to arrive at a basis for agreement between reasonable people. Everyday reasoning often relies on 'quick and dirty' rule-of-thumb modes of inference, which often yield unreasonable results. Gaus draws on studies which, for instance, track the success-rate of ordinary reasoners in working with rules of inference such as *modus ponens*, noting that this is lower than one hundred per cent. Equally, it may be the consequence of globally justifiable belief systems that individuals arrive at some beliefs which are unjustified. Hence, in Gaus's view, we should reject Rawls's view that political philosophy should aim to secure agreement, postponing contentious epistemological issues such as those concerned with justification. Gaus adds:

> I believe this [that is, the postponement of controversial epistemic issues] to be a fundamental error. If public justification is the core of liberalism – and because there is no such thing as an uncontentious theory of justification – an adequately articulated liberalism must clarify and defend its conception of justified belief – its epistemology ... it does not follow from this that settling on a particular conception of public justification is to settle questions that are *properly political*. If we have provided a sound case for employing a particular conception of public justification, we are in a position to insist that substantive

> political views that cannot be justified within this conception are properly ruled out. That, for instance, the proper theory of public justification makes it easier to justify liberal than statist views does not show that we are preempting 'properly' political questions; it shows, rather, that the proper domain of the political is circumscribed by the ideal of public justification.[53]

Gaus adopts a form of 'weak foundationalism' which is inconsistent with merely coherentist accounts of justified belief, and hence rejects the claim that there are no non-inferentially justified beliefs. At the same time, however, Gaus argues against the stronger version of foundationalism, which holds that there is some set of beliefs on which rational believers as such should converge. In this passage Gaus, drawing on some remarks by F.B. d'Agostino,[54] introduces a field of agency somewhat akin to politics, but different from it, namely the domain of the 'properly' political. How far the philosophical enterprise of delimiting politics in advance so that its remit is confined, by a theory of public justification, to the domain of the 'properly' political depends on how far a theory of public justification can avoid being political. If it cannot, then as far as this question goes, the bounds of the properly political will not be something which can be settled prior to politics. But according to the minimalist account given in Chapter 2, it cannot avoid this, since what is deemed to be political itself falls within the extension of the term 'political'. Accordingly, the scope of the political is itself (whether 'properly' or not is in the nature of the case indeterminate) a political matter.

One question which Gaus's approach raises is how much *could* be demonstrated by a more epistemically orientated account of public justification than those he criticises, given that 'there is no such thing as an uncontentious theory of justification' – and even though later in the same passage Gaus slides into talking of 'the proper theory of public justification'- which 'makes it easier to justify liberal than statist views'. In Rawls's defence, it might be said that the 'political' (in his sense) account of liberalism was devised precisely in order to handle problems of this nature, which arise from justificatory indeterminacy. If reasonable persons may disagree about theories of justification themselves, there is little prospect that they will succeed, even insofar as they are reasonable, in arriving at an account of public justification which circumscribes the proper domain of the political.

This is so even if we remain within a commitment to the core values of liberalism. *Autonomy* is often (though not always) upheld as one of its core values. That requires that the circumstances are created in which individuals are (in a sense to be supplied by the given theory) self-directing. It is however plausible to think that it is a necessary, if not sufficient, condition of autonomy that individuals think and act on reasons which are good reasons *for them*. The fact that reasonable persons may ignore good (or best) reasons on occasion does not show that the value of autonomy is adequately served by circumscribing the content of the political so that sub-optimal reasons are excluded from political design. The fact that some aberrant views command acceptance is plausibly regarded as the consequence of their exercising autonomy. Even if political views such as the statist ones were demonstrably wrong, it would not follow that implementing the views which *were* countenanced by an account of public justification such as Gaus's would be consistent with their autonomy. They may even be unable to *grasp* the content of the justifiable principles, or of the arguments which justify them. It then remains to be shown how the foreclosing of certain political options can be justified in a way that is consistent with respecting autonomy.

It may be said that autonomy cannot be inconsistent with the imposition of certain political values on Gaus's account, since the forms of political design which are justified are those which can alone be autonomously willed. This claim however has to be argued for, on pain of begging the question. It also, of course, runs the risk of reducing to nullity the sense in which agents' actions and beliefs are genuinely self-directed, as is clear when we consider those who are unable to follow a purported justification limiting political design. This point becomes particularly sharp when we ask what level of coercion would be justified in order to bring such individuals round to agreement with this limitation. When to use force is a matter for political discussion. Gaus, like Rawls and Habermas, makes no attempt to decide what negotiation with the justificatory principles has to be made when we confront questions of implementation and the use of power. D'Agostino writes:

> [t]o settle on a particular conception of public justification, it is ... necessary to settle questions, at least to our own satisfaction, which are themselves properly political questions. The project of public justification therefore cannot be beyond or prior to politics itself. It is not a

meta-political project, as some have wishfully thought; it is, rather, itself a part of properly political argumentation.[55]

While Gaus is right to say that what is justified cannot be beholden to the inferential or other errors to which even reasonable people are sometimes prone, it does not follow from this that what is justified can be determined prior to politics. The next chapter considers the demand for political justification in more detail.

8
Political Philosophy Without Foundations?

Introduction

Richard Rorty and John Gray represent deviant tendencies within modern liberalism. For the purposes of this book's argument they are important not merely because they are both significant political theorists, but because their work is more sceptical about the project of philosophical design than the other liberal theorists such as Rawls, Habermas, Larmore, Gray, Raz and Barry, who have been criticised earlier in this book. In Rorty's case this is fairly clearly derived from more general philosophical positions which he espoused in his earlier, non-political philosophy, but Gray's more recent writings (specifically in *Enlightenment's Wake*) mark a departure from his earlier work.[1]

Rorty has identified the writings of theorists such as those just mentioned as 'foundationalist', and commended an alternative 'anti-foundationalist' or 'post-metaphysical' mode of political philosophising in which non-alethic (and in particular aesthetic) considerations are accorded more importance than they currently enjoy in political philosophy. In addition, he has argued for the 'priority' of politics to philosophy, so that the very project of political design proves to be quixotic. This prompts the question what role, if any, is left for political philosophy. While Rorty is certainly aware of this issue, I shall argue that his response to it renders unstable his polemical distinction between philosophical and non-philosophical discourse.

Gray's recent work has also taken the form of a thorough-going critique of contemporary liberal philosophy and its methodological aspirations. Like Rorty, Gray believes that the prospects for foundationalism in liberalism are bleak. In Gray's case, however, this is held to follow from the self-defeatingness of the foundationalist project, given the premisses from which it proceeds; thus the argument takes the form of a *reductio*. This is clearly a distinct position from Rorty's, since Gray holds that a certain claim is true, namely value-pluralism, and this is a philosophical claim *par excellence*. It may be, however, as I shall suggest, that Gray is not fully aware of these commitments. Gray argues that the truth of pluralism spells doom for the 'foundationalist' philosophical enterprise undertaken by Rawls, Nozick, Dworkin, Ackerman, Raz, Larmore, Barry, Habermas and others. In the following I will consider the work of Rorty and Gray in more detail. What marks off their work from that of other philosophical liberals is their scepticism about the power of philosophy to deliver substantial conclusions about political design; as far as this goes, of course, their views accord with the sceptical position adopted in the present book. In what follows I shall argue that, despite this scepticism, their work still has difficulty in accommodating the political.

Rorty and post-philosophical politics

In some respects, accordingly, the writings of Richard Rorty, and in particular *Contingency, Irony, and Solidarity*, constitute an exception or counter-example to the post-political tendency in modern political philosophy. In *Contingency, Irony, and Solidarity*[2] and in his papers 'The Priority of Democracy to Philosophy' and 'Postmodernist Bourgeois Liberalism', collected in *Objectivity, Relativism, and Truth*, Rorty applies the anti-foundationalist arguments developed in earlier works such as *Philosophy and the Mirror of Nature* and *The Consequences of Pragmatism* to political philosophy. In Rorty's understanding, a philosophical position is 'anti-foundationalist' if it holds that:

> the notion of a 'philosophical foundation' goes when the vocabulary of Enlightenment rationalism goes. These accounts [that is, those which Rorty attributes to Donald Davidson and to Wittgenstein] do not *ground* democracy, but they do permit its practices and its goals to be *redescribed*.[3]

This passage sets out a guiding idea of Rorty's political philosophy: that the merits of given samples of discourse are not to be determined by how accurately they correspond to an independently given (for example, normative) reality, such as the nature of the physical world, realistically construed, but according to criteria which are fundamentally aesthetic. In the terminology of Mary Hesse borrowed by Rorty, the serviceability of new scientific theories is that they offer us 'metaphoric redescriptions' of nature rather than affording us insights into its intrinsic constitution.[4] On this view, the innovative natural scientist's contribution will be more akin to that of a creative artist, rather than disclosing some hitherto undiscovered aspect of an independently existing reality.

Towards the end of *Contingency, Irony, and Solidarity* Rorty provides an example of political philosophy conducted in the mode which he favours. This draws on Wilfrid Sellars's 'analysis of moral obligation in terms of "we-intentions"', which 'takes the basic explanatory notion in this area to be "one of us"', a claim which is 'typically contrastive in the sense that it contrasts with a "they"', presumably excluded from the moral community.[5] Rorty goes on to contrast Sellars's view of moral obligations with the universalistic aspirations of Enlightenment, and specifically Kantian, understandings of their scope. For Rorty, the more inclusive criteria of eligibility for the moral community which have developed in the last two centuries are therefore warranted not by the discovery of 'a core self, the human essence' in those hitherto excluded (such as slaves).[6] This shift is rather to be understood as a form of redescription – in this case, redescription of 'they' (those hitherto thought of as inferior, slaves, and so on) as 'we'. The mistake of traditional philosophising consists in thinking of this new propensity as dependent on criteria which are themselves world-driven. Language to this extent does not represent an independent reality. A fundamental mistake is therefore committed by those moral and political philosophers who set out to identify independent foundations for morality, or political design.

Insofar as the argument attends to a specific moral concept, that of obligation, it relies on a form of *analysis* – namely Sellars's proposal concerning 'we-intentions'. In other words, Rorty is offering a philosophical claim. Despite his scepticism about the methods of analytical philosophy, this is in fact an orthodox methodological move, one which offers its own foundationalist trope, in the form of a 'basic explanatory notion', which is then pressed into the service of conceptual clarification. Taken as such, however, the proposal must be wrong. No doubt there are uses, some of them familiar, of phrases such as 'we' and 'one of us' which identify a locus of moral obligation; but the purpose of conceptual analysis is to secure something stronger – a claim about the concept *obligation* which entails that counter-usages are incoherent.[7] But there is at most a rough match between a speaker's identification of in- and out-groups, and the ascription to their members of moral obligations. There is no incoherence in saying, 'We don't have any obligations to one another', or in saying, 'We (as a group) have obligations to them' – indeed, people frequently say such things. If the proposed analysis were correct, such utterances would be incoherent or at least – the Rortyan counterpart to conceptual incoherence – not the sort of utterance we come out with, around here; but they are not. To this extent, it emerges not, modestly, as a philosophical gloss on actual discourse, but something more theoretically ambitious – a philosophical *theory*, which if it is to retain plausibility will have to be firmly corrective of that discourse.

This raises wider questions about the methodological assumptions behind Rorty's argument, as I explain below. Sellars's and Rorty's proposal is nothing if not an ordinary-language analysis, and it fails by the test of ordinary language itself. Politicians' discourse is indeed replete with positional pronouns in the first and third person, but by itself this is far too thin a basis for the very thick category of reasons for action which (as I argued at greater length in Chapter 3) is identified by the concept *obligation*. Rorty's problems are inherent in the project of post-philosophical philosophising: that is, in disavowing philosophy as such, and then for local argumentative purposes purveying specimens of philosophical theory.

The sole response to abandoning hope for philosophy which avoids pragmatic contradiction, is (as Wittgenstein did after writing the *Tractatus*) to go and do something else. If as Rorty says in the Introduction to *The Consequences of Pragmatism*,[8] the most that 'post-philosophical' philosophy can hope to do is to study 'the comparative advantages and disadvantages of the various ways of talking which our race has invented', that applies equally to ways of talking about talking. Since philosophy is conducted in language, that either leaves the whole of philosophy intact; or it leaves no room for Rorty's version of it, having shut the door on itself.

The Rortyanised Rawls of Rorty's essay 'The Priority of Democracy to Philosophy' – to which, at least, the Rawls of *Political Liberalism* approximates less remotely than the Rawls of *A Theory of Justice* – holds that '[t]ruth', in the form of 'what Rawls calls "an order antecedent and given to us" is simply not relevant to democratic politics. So philosophy, as the explanation of the relation between such an order and human nature, is not relevant either. When the two come into conflict, democracy takes precedence over philosophy.'[9] On this view, the truth-seeking activity constitutive of philosophy is firmly subordinated to the project of seeking a democratic consensus. In fact, it is unclear that in Rorty's view there is much to be sought, once the community itself has been identified, since the analysis of truth offered in *Philosophy and the Mirror of Nature* and subsequent writings makes the effective community (as it exists, *inter alia*, for the purposes of reaching collective decisions democratically) co-extensive with the site of intersubjective agreement on norms. We have already seen the effects of this identification when applied to the concept *obligation*.

I will not consider whether Rorty's interpretation of Rawls is accurate. The more important question is whether Rorty's position, which he sees mirrored in Rawls, is independently sustainable. It is certainly true, not only of certain aspects of the later Rawls, but also of several other theorists examined in this book, that normative truth is regarded as problematic, and that a prime motivation behind theory is to provide the means to cope with this. The work of Barry, Habermas, Larmore and others is, to an important extent, designed with this in mind. Insofar as all these theorists, like Rorty, aim to establish a basis on which democratic consensus can be reached, they believe in 'the priority of democracy to philosophy', if that description is applicable to Rawls. I shall now argue, however, that the description raises more specific problems facing Rorty's methodological emphasis on redescription.

Commentators such as Stephen Macedo[10] have plausibly argued that Rorty exaggerates the extent of normative consensus in existing political societies. This threatens to undermine the basis on which Rorty's belief in democracy's 'priority' to politics is founded, since it shifts the locus of normative consensus away from the political community itself. The starting-point for much political, as well as philosophical, debate is the existence in political societies of distinct and conflicting norms, and a Wittgensteinian appeal to 'forms of life' in order to underwrite normative claims is – at least as far as this issue goes – unhelpful. This is a criticism often levelled, with justice, at 'communitarian' accounts of the basis of normativity – it is, for example, a notorious difficulty for MacIntyre's tradition-relativised account of rationality in *Whose Justice? Which Rationality?*,[11] which has somehow to explain the fact that here and now (if the diagnosis of modernity's ills presented there and in MacIntyre's other writings is right),[12] the product of the traditions' current state of historical development is one of normative incoherence.

Equally, Rorty's theory provides few resources with which to address, or even articulate, this incoherence. This underlines the point already made in discussing his account of obligation, that the politically effective community is more extensive than the locus of normative agreement in modern democratic societies: as we have seen repeatedly in this book, this is indeed the fundamental problem addressed by liberal political philosophy. To ignore this is not to solve the problem by moving to a more knowing conception of the philosophical enterprise, but merely to ignore it.

Since it is mistaken in Rorty's view to think that there is a 'given' – something in the nature of things which, for example, determines the extension of terms used in political argument – there is always the scope for rationally interminable disagreement, in political cultures committed to the principle enshrined in the First Amendment. If so, the analysis offered must be inadequate, since the discourse in these circumstances lacks the basis which Rorty claims for it. The problem here is that Rorty offers a *rival* philosophical theory, rather than simply refraining from philosophical theorising *tout court*. That theory sees itself as freed from foundationalist illusions because it sees no basis for truth-claims apart from the fact of consensus about the claims. Nonetheless, Rorty still offers a foundation for them in the brute fact of operative consensus, which leaves him open to objections of a kind familiar in attempts at foundationalist analysis of discourse elsewhere in philosophy – that the explanation offered fails, because the discourse may subsist even where the claimed foundations for it are absent.[13] Rorty's argument follows a pattern noticeable in other anti-foundationalist, relativist and communitarian writings, where the rejection of universalism accompanies – indeed, in some cases, is held to follow from – local consensus, heuristically exaggerated: 'agreement in judgements' looks a more eligible proxy for traditional foundations than *dis*agreement in judgements.

More saliently for the present purpose, Rorty's appropriation of Rawls leads to awkward problems when we examine the implied relation between philosophising and politics. Since a normative commitment to the value of democracy may intelligibly be countered by espousing other forms of political decision-making (aristocratic, timocratic, absolutist, and so on), Rorty's view is presumably that there is a consensus-validated basis within this (American, or more generally, western bourgeois) society for democracy. This, to be sure, is a pre-philosophical commitment in the sense that it is held by many people who are unversed in philosophy. But it is not free of philosophical commitment when put to the use which Rorty requires of it.

Rorty says that one of the ways in which the 'liberal ironist' is distinguished from the 'liberal metaphysician' is not their differing propensities to indulge in redescription, but how redescription is understood:

> the metaphysician typically backs up his redescription with argument – or, as the ironist redescribes the process, disguises his redescription under the cover of argument ... [T]o offer an argument in support of one's redescription amounts to telling the audience that they are being educated, rather than simply reprogrammed – that the Truth was already in them and merely needed to be drawn out into the light ... The metaphysician in short, thinks that there is a connection between redescription and power, and that the right redescription can make us free. The ironist offers no similar reassurance.[14]

This passage raises a number of questions – for example, whether that form of redescription which transmutes 'argument' into 'redescription' should be preferred to a form which redescribes some forms of 'redescription' (but not others) as 'arguments'. If the answer to that question is 'Yes', we need to know the basis on which some redescriptions are regarded as being preferable to others, given that Rorty's dismissal of foundationalism in philosophy consists in rejecting the very idea of justifying philosophical claims by appealing to a 'basis on which'. But without some such basis, there are no grounds for preferring one form of redescription over another; Rorty's underlying conception of the basis for choice between available descriptions seems to be an aesthetic one, which if it is not to collapse into radical subjectivism will have to rely (as Rorty does) on neo-Wittgensteinian 'agreement in judgements'.

This suggests that there is a deeper reason for Rorty's exaggeration of consensus in liberal democratic societies: without it the redescriptive meta-philosophy he favours itself lacks warrant. It assumes that the explanation provided by 'agreement in judgements' stands in for explanatory foundations, but in the absence of such agreement Rorty has no way of justifying redescription itself – in particular, no way of justifying it against rival prevalent descriptions of the philosophical enterprise itself. If not, Rorty's view of philosophising is vulnerable to those who favour descriptions of philosophy which portray it using the familiar maieutic metaphors, or of the truth's lying latent within the philosophical initiate, waiting only to be 'drawn out into the light'. It is, accordingly, unclear how Rorty's meta-philosophical position justifies itself. As it stands, it appears prone to refutation by the mere fact that there is someone who disagrees with it.

More importantly, Rorty's assumption is that the only form which philosophising about politics could assume is a normative one. Then, given Rorty's view, drawn from Sellars and the later Wittgenstein, that the roots of normativity lie in intersubjective consensus, rather than in cognisable external truths, the task of political philosophy must be impossible – that of generating substantive normative conclusions 'monologically' via philosophical argument, when in fact the only means by which these conclusions could be reached is consensually, and *ex post facto* at that. This however merely ignores the possibility of a non-normative form of theorising – perhaps surprisingly, in view of Rorty's emphasis on redescription as his preferred alternative to more traditional conceptions of philosophical argument. This is surprising to the extent that Rorty goes to some lengths elsewhere in his work to make room, in other areas of philosophy, for a redescriptive account of conceptual development free of any normative commitment. However, in the case of political philosophy, it seems that the preferred methodology sanctions only the replacement of one form of normative vocabulary by another. In criticising philosophical orthodoxy, Rorty unwittingly relies on one of its core assumptions.

Some of the more obvious counter-examples to Rorty's descriptive account of normative judgements involve attempted redescriptions which are politically sensitive. For example, following the Soviet invasion of Czechoslovakia in the wake of the 'Prague Spring' in 1968, *Pravda* described the invasion as 'a spontaneous, ardently welcomed defence of popular freedom'. This was a redescription which many at the time and since have found unpersuasive. It is more than usually clear, in relation to this example, that relying on attitudes towards this redescription, in order to define the community with respect to whose agreement a consensual basis can be found for normative judgements (such as this one), is viciously circular.

There is however a more intractable problem than mere circularity. The problem is not that Rorty lacks an explanation of the truth-predicate's place in everyday discourse; I shall say more about this at the end of this section. It is that attitudes towards the provenance of normative judgements could not be as they are if those making the judgements took a Rortyan view of them. If the verification of a normative judgement or redescription, such as that above, consisted purely in the existence of a community defined by its propensity to assert that judgement, they would not be in disagreement with those who deny it. But they do regard themselves as being in disagreement, so the philosophical claim cannot take a wholly *post factum* attitude towards this form of discourse – it must also, in part at least, be corrective of it. It will be noticed that similar problems beset the essential contestability thesis, when the phenomenon of political disagreement is placed alongside what, according to the thesis, provides its explanation.

This casts doubt on Rorty's view of the relation between political and philosophical activity. As we have seen, he emphasises the 'priority' of democratic politics over philosophy. This is articulated through a view of philosophising drawn from Wittgenstein which holds that the sole legitimate aim of philosophising is self-supersession – that is, to arrive at a point where the desire to philosophise has been banished – the fly liberated from the bottle, in Wittgenstein's well-known analogy – by a form of conceptual therapy. Rorty's version of this is to redescribe philosophical theorising as Lyotardian 'metanarratives', to which the appropriate response is 'distrust'.[15]

It is however far from clear that the line between philosophical and non-philosophical discourse can be held, at least for Rorty's purposes. As has already been noted, his objection to foundationalist philosophy is that it relies on ontic commitments – to a conception of human 'essence', for example – which it ultimately cannot honour. What remains, once we recognise this failure, is a criterionless play of metaphoric vocabularies. The problem, however, is that Rortyan meta-meta-narrative is not simply to be identified with unvarnished narrative; the vantage-point of the Rortyan liberal ironist is one which aspires to be not lower, but loftier than that of the philosophers who have yet to rid themselves of their foundationalist delusions. To achieve this vantage-point is not, then, to recover a world of pre-ironic innocence. 'Distrust towards metanarratives', 'we-intentions', and so on, are as much terms of art as philosophical vocabulary like 'clear and distinct ideas' or 'the transcendental unity of apperception'. They are a philosopher's piece of talk, not the lingua franca of the Clapham Omnibus. When we know what we need to know in order to be Rortyan liberal ironists, we have not returned to pre-philosophical innocence, but transcended the higher innocence of foundationalist philosophy.

This is not a merely *ad hominem* point. Ordinary discourse is not, *pace* Rorty and (on some views) the later Wittgenstein, the talk of noble savages unsullied by philosophy and its obfuscation. It carries metaphysical commitments, which are most plausibly understood – perhaps even more obviously in normative discourse than elsewhere – as commitments to naive realism. Few who unreflectively employ the 'thick' vocabulary of moral commendation and disapprobation regard themselves as merely indulging in a local patois of redescription. To take only the most obvious and significant example, the truth-predicate is not a term of art, but part of ordinary discourse, and its playing the role it does depends on a non-Rortyan understanding of it. Once again we encounter an esoteric doctrine.

This imports further explanatory problems when accounting for normative disagreement. Rorty's position might seem obviously wrong: innovation in the history of philosophy has characteristically involved redescription, and therefore there is nothing to this history of innovation but redescription. Since, however, redescription by itself does not entail contradiction – if the sentences used by A and B to express some proposition differ only in B's use of a different, but co-designating, expression used (but not mentioned) by A, then there is no disagreement between them – we require an explanation of the phenomenology of disagreement, both in philosophy and in non-philosophical areas of discourse where disagreement is rife.

This, it will be recalled, was the major explanatory problem encountered by the essential contestability thesis. As I argued in Chapter 2, the thesis founders because its objective, of explaining why there are apparently interminable disputes involving fundamental justificatory concepts, is in conflict with the explanatory mechanism on which it relies – alleged truths about conceptual structure: for these should be truths on which the disputants could agree. The thesis can then only sustain itself as an esoteric doctrine, one which draws a sharp line between the philosophical explanation of political disagreement, and the self-understanding of political actors. Similarly, in Rorty's case, the condition of the possibility of explanation – agreement in judgements – must also be an esoteric doctrine, since if the disputants believed that this condition obtained, they would to that extent no longer see themselves as being in disagreement. Thus it is not merely that Rorty's belief in the 'priority' of democracy to philosophy underestimates the anti-Rortyan metaphysical commitments of non-philosophical discourse; it is also that, as applied to political discourse, his account cannot intelligibly recover its content. The consequence is that, so far from prioritising democracy over philosophy, Rorty's anti-theory ends up by rehearsing the inverse priority, favoured by traditional 'foundationalism'. His is another philosophical corrective to the philosophically untutored discourse of the layman.

In the discussion so far I have set out the basic shape of Rorty's redescriptive account of 'postmodernist bourgeois liberalism', and argued that it relies, as do many 'communitarian' theorists, on an excessively consensual view of actual normative beliefs.[16] This generates an implausible account of particular concepts, such as that of obligation. More fundamentally, it exposes a paradox at the heart of the Rortyan programme itself: it suggests that Rorty's proposed substitution of redescriptions for the extra-discursive foundations sought after by traditional modes of philosophising cannot be justified in its own terms. Rorty needs some basis for the widespread perception – as pervasive in normative discourse as elsewhere – that some redescriptions are better (more apposite, and indeed truer) than others. The anti-foundationalist way of doing this is to regard agreement in judgements as explaining this differential grading of redescriptions. But the appeal to agreement in judgements to do duty for the extra-discursive foundations will fail, when applied to the redescriptive project itself. More awkwardly for the project of prioritising democracy over philosophy, the efficacy of what Rorty (following Williams)[17] calls 'the morality system' depends on people's propensity to make anti-Rortyan assumptions about the nature of normativity.

Finally in discussing Rortyan political philosophy, I want to relate the criticisms above more closely to the main argument of this book, and in particular to Chapter 5. Rorty asserts[18] in *Objectivity, Relativism and Truth* that to make a truth-claim is merely to bestow a mark of commendation. As with the example of obligation earlier, this offers a form of analysis, which in effect transfers the old-style emotivist treatment of moral discourse to truth: just as '*X* is good' under Stevensonian emotivism came out as 'I approve of *X*; do so as well',[19] so '*p* is true', for Rorty, is analysable as 'I commend *p* to you as worthy of belief', or something along these lines. Again, my concern is not with the plausibility of Rorty's analysis; one question worth pressing, however, is whether this analysis delivers what Rorty wants from it – which, I take it, is to keep his hands clean of the ontification sullying 'foundationalist' conceptions of the philosophical enterprise. The analysis will commit itself to objects like beliefs, commendations, propositions, and so forth, which entails that there are at least these things, of which claims (for example, about the semantics of truth-claims themselves) can be true. But my aim is to show how it aligns him, appearances to the contrary notwithstanding, with other theorists considered in the book so far.

It is important to keep in mind that what is on offer here is, again, a philosophical theory, not (as Rorty is often inclined to suggest) an alternative to it. Rorty's analysis of moral obligation is, as we have seen, one which identifies its extension – those to whom speakers using the concept regard obligations as being owed – with a locus of affect. This leaves us with a fairly straightforward version of emotivism, coupled with a general rubric to the effect that Rorty is only offering a redescription, rather than some more cognitively aspiring form of theory. Since, however, unschooled moral intuition fails, as we have seen, to deliver agreement in judgements, Rorty's substantive political theory has left to it only a bare prescriptiveness which cannot be justified in his own terms: the intuitions which the moral community with which he identifies himself ought to accept, such as revulsion at cruelty, solidaristic humanism, and so forth. The non-cognitivist rhetoric is thus slightly misleading: despite the fact that their objects are held to be redescriptions, moral beliefs remain, which would be lacking without the relevant affect. Whether these beliefs are, in standard cognitivist parlance, treated as beliefs about matters of fact is, in the nature of the case, a moot point; the issue falls under the general imponderability which arises when we ask whether a piece of first-order talk in good standing, with metaphysical commitments, is something which Rorty can find it within himself to repeat. Most obviously this arises with truth itself. If as a pragmatist, Rorty thinks that what is counted as true is what we have found it convenient to say, the question is why Rorty does not say it as well.

I have suggested that there are intractable difficulties confronting Rorty's belief in the 'priority' of democracy to philosophy, when combined with his wider methodological stance. Nonetheless, Rorty's views may appear sufficiently similar to those expressed in this book to make it advisable to contrast our positions. Like Rorty, I have doubted whether the project of providing normative foundations for political philosophy, as attempted by liberals in the past few decades, succeeds. In addition, I have echoed Rorty's view that the prospects for this form of philosophising are dim, and that philosophers should be more aware of the political context within which theory is produced. To this extent Rorty's work constitutes an exception to the material covered so far in this book. It may also seem to provide a counter-example to my main argument, since Rorty explicitly stresses the 'priority' of politics to philosophy. I shall now argue, however, that this appearance is misleading.

Since Rorty disavows truth as a means of assessing the relative merits of different redescriptions, his account is not well placed to pronounce on the merits of rival (that is, illiberal or anti-liberal) descriptions. Nor does it leave any space for immanent critique – for example, of the role which sheer power may play in gerrymandering consensus. Laclau argues,[20] with reference to the essential contestability thesis, that given the practical indeterminacy of key concepts within the normative political vocabulary, there must be a deficit of rationality when politicians seek to justify a particular interpretation of one of them – a deficit which is characteristically made good through the exercise of power. Then we are in the condition described by Humpty Dumpty in *Through the Looking-Glass*, who says: 'When I use a word, it means exactly what I choose it to mean, neither more nor less', and when challenged by Alice, goes on to say that the question is, 'who is to be master – that's all'.[21] I certainly do not mean to deny that political power may be used to make good this deficit where it exists. Indeed, as rationalistic constructs, political theories necessarily fail to make sense of power as a means of making good the rational deficit. One problem with Rorty's account, as far as this issue goes, is that it seems to make a critique such as Chomsky's of 'manufactured consensus' conceptually impossible;[22] but (whatever else may be said of this critique) it is surely not incoherent. One way in which the priority of politics to philosophy might be stressed is by considering the part played by power in effecting conceptual change, or in pushing through a particular interpretation of a politically controversial concept. But Rorty's account leaves us no resources with which to make sense of this. As a result, his assessment of how politics is prior to philosophy ignores what any political sociologist would regard as essential to understanding political action, namely the use of power and indeed on occasion brute force. That the exercise of power is often thought to be necessary often testifies to the absence of an effective normative consensus within political society; but, as we have seen, this is something which Rorty is ill-placed to acknowledge.

Again, this aligns Rorty's view of the political with 'foundationalist' theorists like Rawls, Habermas, Barry, Larmore, Ackerman, Scanlon and Dworkin: the political is the realm of consensus, where normative disagreement is put to one side – whether this is effected contractually (in the case of Scanlon and Rawls), or by a neutralist order which reasonable persons can unite in accepting (Dworkin, Larmore, Habermas, Ackerman and Barry). What defines the content of such conceptions as political is that they purport to provide public principles, usually combined with associated institutions and procedures, which command rational or reasonable consensus. Whether it is in fact possible to identify such a locus of principled agreement for the purposes of articulating a conception of the political is a different question from whether it is desirable. Next, I consider a theorist who certainly answers the first question in the negative, and who would probably see this as a reason for answering the second one in the same way.

Gray and post-liberalism

John Gray holds a view of philosophy's relation to politics which is in some ways similar to that of Rorty. Despite some clear methodological differences between Gray's and Rorty's approach to philosophising itself, however, there is a clear convergence in their view of this relation. Unlike Rorty, Gray does not regard himself as eschewing philosophical commitments as such: indeed, as I have already noted in earlier chapters, his recent work commits itself to quite specific philosophical claims. From this rather different starting-point, however, Gray arrives at conclusions which may appear, like Rorty, to constitute an exception to the general thesis of this book. This is not only because Gray, like Rorty, identifies himself as writing in the liberal tradition – indeed, latterly, Gray has described himself a 'post-liberal'.[23] The more significant point of convergence is that both Gray and Rorty are sceptical about the foundational enterprise itself, and thus about the prospects for a philosophically justified liberalism satisfying the universalistic aspirations of Enlightenment and post-Enlightenment thinkers. I shall however argue that, like Rorty, Gray finds himself endorsing some of the wider assumptions about the relation between philosophy and politics criticised earlier in this book. I shall begin by examining the implicit understanding of the political in Gray's work, as a preliminary to assessing its significance (as he sees it) for philosophical theorising about it.

As we saw in Chapter 7, there are different ways of conceptualising politics philosophically. A rather specific way of doing so was captured by Rawls's version of a 'political conception' – that understanding of politics which, in conjunction with certain relevant background conditions, is held to determine the content of a philosophical account of public justification. Much depended, as we saw, on the criteria of relevance by means of which the background conditions were decided, and on the independent justification of the conditions themselves. As I argued, this compromised Rawls's claim that his work since 'Kantian Constructivism in Moral Theory' embodies a 'political' rather than a moral argument for the two principles of justice, since it is normative claims which, appearances to the contrary notwithstanding, are doing the real argumentative work. As I argued in Chapter 4, it is false to assume that an argument based on the purely descriptive claim that there is a plurality of conceptions of the good or comprehensive doctrines in society will have any independent justificatory force, unless it is conjoined with a normative thesis about the value of those conceptions. This does not mean that the definition of a 'political conception' must take this normative form, only that the shape of the argument depends on the background conditions themselves.

According to one conception of politics, the reason why political theories such as those considered in this book fail is because of its ineluctably conflict-ridden or (as it is sometimes termed) its *agonistic* character. As we have seen, one ground on which this view could be asserted is the essential contestability thesis. Barber takes this view,[24] as does Gray himself. But essential contestability need not be the grounds for asserting that politics is agonistic; many other possibilities suggest themselves. For example, it may be said that this follows from the fact that there are inevitably different classes, or interests, represented in the polity. Or it may be said that the rationale for the public political forum is to dramatise the conflict between different courses of action, in which their relative merits may be gauged; in Rousseau's terms, *agon* is an essential precondition of the General Will's determining a content for itself. It may be said that there are different and incompatible outlooks, or ideologies, and we cannot know which is true. So the public forum inevitably witnesses clashes between them, which are rationally interminable. One version of this is MacIntyre's analysis of the 'emotivist' character of political disagreement in *After Virtue*.[25] Or it may be held to be a fundamental fact about making decisions that there are alternative courses of action, and this already contains the possibility of conflict.

Gray seems disposed to accept some of these justifications for his agonistic conception of the political. The more important reason for Gray's agonistic view of politics, however, is his belief in value-pluralism. Gray remarks that '[t]he implications of [Isaiah] Berlin's value-pluralism for political philosophy have gone curiously unnoticed by most, partly, no doubt, because they undermine so much in recent liberal thought'.[26] Elsewhere Gray draws the consequences of Berlin's 'radical' value-pluralism for liberal political philosophy. In 'What is Living and What is Dead in Liberalism?', Gray says that modern liberals such as Dworkin and Rawls cannot 'withstand the force of strong indeterminacy and radical incommensurability among values. Considered as a position in political philosophy, accordingly, liberalism is a failed project'.[27]

In his study *Isaiah Berlin* Gray endorses Joseph Raz's claim that '[i]ncommensurability among values discloses itself ... as a breakdown or failure in transitivity. "Two valuable options are incommensurable if 1) neither is better than the other, and 2) there is (or could be) another option which is better than one but is not better than the other".'[28] I have already addressed Raz's account of value-incommensurability in

Chapter 4, the details of which I shall not rehearse again here. The important point is what, in Gray's view, follows from the 'fact' that there are incommensurable, and therefore plural, values. A preliminary point, which follows directly from the argument of Chapter 4, is that Razian incommensurability cannot be taken to support Larmore's definition of value-pluralism as the view that values do not form a hierarchy, because of the possibility of lexical ordering: goods embodying the relevant values are incommensurable because a loss, however small, of the one good outweighs a gain, however large, of the other. Value-pluralism might be true because there was one value which enjoyed this paramount status with respect to all the others; in this case, the consequence for political design would be that political structures should be arranged so as to maximally embody or promote that value.

Presumably, however, this is not what Gray and Raz have in mind when assessing the consequences of value-pluralism for political design. The truth of the value-pluralism at the heart of Berlin's liberalism, which Gray acclaims as 'by far the most formidable and plausible [version of liberalism] so far advanced',[29] has an 'agonistic character' resulting from 'its acknowledgement of an irreducible diversity of rivalrous goods'.[30] Thus the form of value-pluralism ascribed by Gray to Berlin, and to which Gray himself subscribes, is taken to entail that 'the state can never have sufficient rational justification for imposing any particular ranking or values on people',[31] and refutes also theories, such as Rawls's, which wrongly assume 'that principles of liberty or justice can be insulated from the force of value-incommensurability';[32] it is likewise thought to doom Lockean and Kantian versions of liberalism. The question is whether any conception of liberalism survives an acceptance of value-pluralism, and if so, what form it takes.

Gray considers a number of arguments which seek to base liberalism on value-pluralism, and argues that each fails, 'because the range of worthwhile forms of life is ... wider than any that can be contained within liberal society' and 'liberal institutions can have no universal authority'; this is held to be entailed directly by the thesis of the incommensurability of values.[33] As Gray acknowledges, there is little reason to think that, for example, the 'negative liberty' conception of liberalism proves any hardier in the environment of value-pluralism than other forms of liberal or non-liberal ideology – most obviously because the sources of value are not all plausibly thought of as liberal ones.

If value-pluralism is true all the way down, then it follows that the identity of practitioners of a liberal form of life is a contingent matter, not a privileged expression of universal human nature. If there is value-conflict all the way down, then there is contingency all the way down, too.[34] The pervasiveness of value-based conflict is regarded as having direct consequences for the viability of liberalism itself, one of whose constitutive features, as Gray sees it, is its aspiration to universality.[35] If this is so, then as Gray acknowledges,[36] attempts by recent theorists like Raz, Rorty and the later Rawls to provide a contingent and historically local justification for liberalism must be self-defeating. This characterisation of liberalism (apart from any independent objections that might be urged against it), does not however explain Gray's main objection to the localised versions of justification.

His objection to this lowering of aspirations, from the universalism aimed at by the 'Enlightenment Project' to a more localised conception of justification, is not that the latter is insufficiently universalistic, but that it will fail even in its less aspiring form, because it underestimates the pervasiveness of value-based conflict. Gray concludes that the universalistic aspirations of liberalism's Enlightenment progenitors will have to be discarded and its ambitions scaled down to 'finding a *modus vivendi* for diverse cultural forms, liberal and non-liberal'.[37] In its place will be a 'postliberal political thought' aiming at this coexistence without 'any claim to universal authority', aiming to 'live in harmony, with other, non-liberal cultures and polities'.[38] Additionally, in his most recent work, Gray espouses substantive values which seemingly have cross-cultural validity.[39]

These concerns are amplified in the chapter entitled 'Agonistic Liberalism' in *Enlightenment's Wake*. There Gray argues again that values are 'incommensurable', apparently in the sense attached to that term by Raz[40] which was discussed in Chapter 4. A conspicuous merit of Gray's discussion is its clear-headedness about the philosophical commitments entailed by value-pluralism itself.

> [I]f value-pluralism is correct, then these are truths, correct moral beliefs about the world. The thesis of the incommensurability of values is then not a version of relativism, of subjectivism or of moral scepticism ... it is a species of moral realism.[41]

I shall not rehearse the problems with value-pluralism, and with the particular form which it takes in Raz's *Morality of Freedom* (on which Gray's arguments explicitly rely). My immediate concern is with the use to which Gray puts value-pluralism in establishing his 'post-liberal' position, which is based on the claim that 'value-pluralism defeats traditional liberalism'.[42] There is no reason to suppose that Gray thinks that this consequence follows from value-pluralism as such. The idea instead is that the particular values which liberalism is committed to – pre-eminently that of liberty – cannot be insulated from value-pluralism. There is according to Gray no way out of the problem via neutrality, since 'the ideal of neutrality with respect to rival conceptions of the good is itself incoherent'.[43]

I assume that Gray's argument is intended to take roughly the following form. It is entailed by the fact that at least some values are incommensurable that those values are plural. One of the consequences of the plurality of values is that practical decisions involving options embodying different values may be underdetermined by reference to the values alone, since there is no way to decide which among these options is best. As a result, there is no reason to think that in practical choices between actions involving these values there must be a uniquely best action. But the core values of liberalism are themselves incommensurable with other, non-liberal values. Thus from Gray's point of view it follows from the truth of value-pluralism that liberalism cannot be shown to be the best option in taking decisions about political design.

This is a speculative reconstruction, and indeed some things that Gray says stand in some tension with it. The argument cannot be that the values to which liberals subscribe are incommensurable with each other, since that would give no reason to deny that the set of values which characterise liberalism are superior to other values. It would also, as we have seen, give no reason to deny that a value may, while being incommensurable with another, nonetheless be lexically superior to it; so incommensurability does not entail that practical choices between options embodying incommensurable values must be underdetermined by reference to the values. Gray does say, however, paraphrasing remarks of Berlin, that 'liberties – in this case, negative liberties – are not only rivalrous but also sometimes incommensurable values'.[44] Presumably this means not (as it might be interpreted) that the value of liberty may conflict with itself – which, as we saw in Chapter 4, is consistent with value-monism – but that traditional liberal ways of entrenching certain moral concerns (for example, through apportioning rights) are undermined by value-pluralism. There is no optimal set of rights, or other forms of institutional entrenchment, which best embodies the incommensurable values. This is a denial of the onefold route to political justification.

This is however consistent with the view that there may be a set of mutually incompatible schedules of rights, each of which schedules embodies the values in question, and which, taken together, are such that none better embodies the values than any of the other ones; but nevertheless (it may be added), each schedule is a liberal one, and is judged superior to others lying outside this set. Thus, for example, the values of freedom of expression and privacy may be thought of as incommensurable with each other, and on these grounds it may be said that the values generate mutually incompatible schedules of rights. But, it may also be said, each of these schedules is liberal (because each embodies liberal first-level values) and is superior to any other schedule outside the set, which does not embody these values. Looked at like this, Gray's argument demonstrates not that value-pluralism undermines liberalism, but that it underdetermines the decision as to which version of liberalism is, on the strength of the values alone, to be preferred. A number of theorists have thought that it is precisely its ability to cater for value-pluralism which makes liberalism superior to its rivals.

There is, as a result, reason to question the following stages of Gray's argument: to doubt that incommensurability entails value-pluralism, that (even if values are plurally incommensurable) practical choice between options embodying incommensurable values is underdetermined, and that where such underdetermination exists, it entails that the superiority of liberalism to non-liberalism is unprovable. Its superiority may of course be unprovable – it may even not be the case that liberalism is superior – but if so, that does not follow from the fact (if it is one) that liberal values are mutually incommensurable.

Some, though not all, of these problems can be dealt with by a closer specification of value-pluralism itself: for example, the lexical form of incommensurability can be explicitly ruled out, and then the argument can be rephrased to say that non-lexically incommensurable values yield practical indeterminacy. It should be noted, however, that this cannot be coherently identified with the claim that the values concerned (or, more accurately, the options embodying them) are equal, since equality entails commensurability. There is simply nothing to be said about the relative merits of the options concerned, since they embody incommensurable values. As a result, practical choice is indeed underdetermined by reference to the values concerned, but this does not show that liberalism is merely one contingent ideology among others. It may, again, be that in order to avoid the blunder of Buridan's ass, any one of the options which are incommensurably related in the way just described is preferable to any other option. Or there may be other (for example, pragmatic) reasons for preferring one form of political design to others.

Gray's diagnosis of liberalism's prospects derives from at least two sources. First, as we have seen, it rests on the belief that there is an irreducible plurality of real values. Secondly, however, Gray adduces in its support the fact that there is an indefinite number of different cultures, many of which are non-liberal, and with which liberal regimes such as those of the 'west' must coexist. This second claim is however a pragmatic one; nothing follows about the purely theoretical viability of liberalism from the fact that there are non-liberal regimes in the world. What poses theoretical problems for liberalism is the distinct claim that non-liberal value-systems, existing, for example, as discrete subcultures within liberal societies, may themselves be bearers of value. This claim itself does not follow from value-pluralism in itself, since the plural values may all be values which liberals as such embrace; the plural values may simply fail to include non-liberal cultures. Accordingly, if this sort of value-pluralism were true, it would not follow that liberalism was not superior to its rivals; there might merely be a plurality of different possible liberal regimes compatible with the values concerned.

Thus Gray conflates a philosophical thesis about the nature of value with some descriptive claims about the circumstances of modern politics: that liberal cultures exist alongside, and that they include, value-systems alien and sometimes hostile to liberalism. We have already seen this conflation at work in Chapter 4. Gray's conclusion is, however, that value-pluralism subverts liberal foundationalism, rather than supporting it; his grounds for this conclusion are that if value-pluralism is true, then it follows that there is an indefinite number of forms of political design, none of which can be shown to be superior to its rivals. In this sense, value-pluralism means that reason underdetermines political design. In the terminology of Chapter 7, this means that there is no onefold route to political justification. It should be stressed, however, that the argument becomes much stronger when the basis for underdetermination is scepticism rather than value-pluralism. That scepticism can rest content with claiming that there is no definitive rational basis on which reasonable persons can be forced to consent about the structure of political design, and so no philosophical resolution of this structure.

It can be noted in passing that this conclusion withstands the main argument advanced in Gaus's *Justificatory Liberalism*,[45] that liberal theorists can rest content with providing arguments which *in fact* justify liberal political design, rather than being obliged also to show that these arguments would command the assent of reasonable persons (as, for example, Barry's *Justice As Impartiality* requires). Gaus's fundamental point is that even reasonable persons are sometimes impervious to rational argument, so that liberals need only furnish justifications which would command their assent *insofar as* they were rational. However, it is Gray's contention that even maximally reasonable persons may arrive at radically different conclusions about the form which political design should take, and included within the set of equal-best or equally-reasonable alternatives are non-liberal procedures and structures; hence the argument does not acknowledge a gap between what reasonable people may in fact accept and the conditions satisfied by a justification which counterfactually they would accept if perfectly rational. It rather relies on *justificatory pluralism* – in effect, the rejection of the onefold route to justification. Thus the onefold route may fail even if it is accepted that the conclusions which reasonable people in fact accept may differ from those which follow from a rational account of justification. Gray's point is precisely that rationality may be value-led, in the sense that what *counts* as rationality in this context is geared to truths about values; and since the latter are plural, there is no onefold route.

Gaus's point that reasonable persons fail on occasion to accept rational justifications does not apply to Gray, therefore, because Gray takes it to be a consequence of value-pluralism that there is, or there need be, no single best (that is, most rational) form of philosophical argument for political design. That is not because there is no gap of the kind which Gaus's point relies on, between the justifications which reasonable persons in fact accept, and those which it would be rational for them to accept: there may well be forms of justification which *no one* who was rational would accept, even if there are plural values. The important point is, however, that for Gray these conclusions about political design follow from alleged facts about the nature of value – that is, from a theoretical claim about ethical objects.

Gray seems to underestimate the degree of conflict present in the agonistic model of politics. One reason for this is (perhaps surprisingly) that the account of value-pluralism which supports it understates the scope for value-based conflict.[46] Sometimes conflicts take the form of a *denial* that the value espoused by the other side has any weight, or that the object concerned really is valuable: in this case it is hard to sustain a *realistically*-construed value-pluralism as an explanation of the conflict. Again, though often Gray seems to understand the practical face of pluralism as the partitioning of the world into discrete and various cultures, each espousing local value(s), he often regards the cultures viewed *locally* as homogeneous, which we also saw in Rorty's case. The capacity of value to generate conflict arises less *within* liberal cultures, than *between* liberal and non-liberal ones. And as already noted, his recent work seems to signal a move towards a needs-based or otherwise naturalised political ideology committed to a homogeneity of interest not merely among the human species, but the biosphere.[47] If, however, value-pluralism is as pervasive as Gray maintains, it is as likely to surface in different conceptions of humans' due relationship with the natural world as anywhere else. Even the search for a *modus vivendi* as the paradigmatic goal of post-liberal, or post-Enlightenment politics, requires a shared commitment to the Hobbesian goal of seeking peace, and underlying Gray's move away from his earlier Hayekian commitment to *laissez-faire* economics is antipathy to the social degeneration which he attributes to capitalism, and its destruction of an earlier (if mythic) stability.[48]

Conclusion

As should be clear from the analysis above, both Rorty and Gray depart in significant respects from the justificatory project engaged in by most contemporary liberal political philosophers. The point of contact between them lies in their shared scepticism about the viability of philosophical attempts to justify liberalism, of the sort engaged in by Rawls, Nozick, Dworkin, Ackerman, Raz, Larmore, Habermas, Barry and others. Rorty's work can be plausibly regarded as less an exercise in justification, than a critique of the very idea that conclusions about political design can be justified in the way conceived of by liberal philosophy. While this does not, as Rorty sees it, undermine his adherence to the locally prevalent ideology (East Coast liberalism), in Gray's case the scepticism derives, not from questioning the very possibility of justification, but from endorsing value-pluralism. As we have seen, this in Gray's view severely limits the aspirations of liberal theory itself.

By now it should be clear, however, that despite the overt and undeniable points of difference between the more mainstream liberal theorists and the views of Rorty and Gray, there are also relevant similarities. In Gray's case, as we have seen, the 'fact' of pluralism supports a rejection of the onefold route to political justification. But pluralism's being true is quite consistent with its being a belief which *nobody* holds – society may simply be partitioned into distinct groups, each of which espouses a single (and in their view unique) value; it may be true that each is indeed a value (though, obviously, not the unique one). We can then ask why pluralism should guide anyone's conception of political design. In Rorty's liberalism, the disavowal of foundations is held not to question or undermine that which would have rested on the foundations – that is, ambient normative belief – but to reinforce it.[49] The question which prompted the foundationalist enterprise was whether beliefs of this sort were justified. But it is hard to see how the realisation that there was nothing which could end the search for foundations would *answer* that question. What replaces foundations is an exaggeratedly consensual account of normative belief, anchored in the motivations which are supposed to be effective in the relevant communities. The exaggeration of consensus operates as a device to create the relevant motivations where they are lacking.[50]

Neither Gray nor Rorty concludes that political philosophers might usefully engage in other forms of normative theorising than those practised by exponents of the traditional justificatory project, or in non-normative theorising. There is, particularly in Rorty's case, an acknowledgement that the activity of theorising itself may have its limitations, but this is taken to show that philosophising about politics is liable to be futile – rather than merely that form of philosophising which attempts to dispense theory. As these remarks are intended to suggest, these possibilities are worth exploring, and future contributions to political philosophy should try to do so.

In conclusion, what is needed in political philosophy is more engagement with politics, and in particular with the fact of power and the fact of conflict. These are not contingent or eliminable features of the political scene. They are its essence. To appreciate this – and to see in it not cause for regret, but rather regret's transcendental condition[51] – is the first step to regarding politics not just as a method for ordering goods, or avoiding bads, but as a good in its own right. That has been too little acknowledged in recent political philosophy, especially in liberalism.[52] One irony of recent liberal theory has been its neglect of the insight – to be detected in the work of early liberals like Walwyn, Milton and Locke – that life is constitutively imperfect, and that fact constrains any political project. In recent political philosophy politics has usually been thought as the means for *containing* imperfection. What is less common in the liberal tradition is the recognition that politics may *express* that imperfection, but also be a good. Once that is acknowledged, the good of politics can be accepted without going as far as perfectionism. There is then room for a new view of the political subject, which is ampler than the conceivers of the good envisaged in contemporary liberalism. The ampler view is not of the fantasised omnipotent and private selves of the liberal imagination – such as the fearful subjects of Hobbes's state – but self-interpreters and self-transformers. That requires a more imaginative view of the subject, of politics, and of imagination itself. What it reveals can as well be greeted with optimism as equanimity: bad as it may be, life with politics is as good as it gets.

Notes

Introduction

1. I. Berlin, 'Does Political Theory Still Exist?', in P. Laslett and W.G. Runciman (eds) *Philosophy, Politics, and Society*, 2nd series (Oxford: Oxford University Press 1962). Other theorists writing during this period assumed more or less openly that the remit of the discipline was confined to those 'problems' thought to admit of solution by the methods of conceptual analysis: for example, Anthony Quinton's *Political Philosophy* (Oxford: Oxford University Press 1967) and T.D. Weldon's *Vocabulary of Politics* (Middlesex: Penguin 1953). As applied to *specific* 'problems' in the discipline, the results of this methodological bias were often unhelpful, as in Margaret Macdonald's and Hannah Pitkin's belief that the 'problem of political obligation' admitted of a purely lexicographical solution (see Chapter 3).
2. P. Laslett, editor's introduction to *Philosophy, Politics and Society*, 1st series (Oxford: Oxford University Press 1956), p. vii.
3. T. Ball, *Reappraising Political Theory* (Oxford: Oxford University Press 1995), p. 45.
4. J. Rawls, *A Theory of Justice* (Oxford: Oxford University Press 1971).
5. Cf. Ball, *Reappraising Political Theory*, p. 45. Ball apparently shares some of the criticisms of the discipline presented below. For example, see p. 53: '[a] troubling sign is to be found in political theory's increasing isolation from its own subject-matter, which it supposedly shares with political science – namely, politics'.
6. Though, as I shall argue below (Chapter 5), another form of reductivism about motivation is important in explaining the *theoretical* neglect of politics by political philosophers.
7. As the subtitle of this book suggests, my main focus is on liberal political philosophy. Hence when I speak of 'political philosophy' without qualification, it can be taken as referring to *liberal* political philosophy unless otherwise stated explicitly. My justification for this is that liberalism in its various guises is the dominant political philosophy espoused in the academy. This qualification does not mean, of course, that none of the arguments I make in the following pages applies to any of the philosophies conceived of as antithetical to liberalism.
8. Examples of this conflation may be detected even in areas where (it might be thought) normative claims are held in check. For example, those forms of revealed preference theory which try to construct preference schedules purely from agents' observed choices need to provide some non-question-begging way to choose between these two possibilities: the schedules are consistent, given some projection of the intrapersonal utilities; and the schedules are, as a matter of brute fact, inconsistent (irreducible to any single utility metric).
9. For a feminist statement, see for example C. Mouffe, *The Return of the Political* (London: Verso 1993), and E. Frazer, *The Problems of Communitarian Politics*

(Oxford: Oxford University Press 1999). B. Honig, *Political Theory and the Displacement of Politics* (Ithaca, NY: Cornell University Press 1993) offers a neo-Arendtian perspective. For Marxism, see for example E. Laclau, *New Reflections on the Revolution of Our Time* (London: Verso 1990), and B. Barber, *The Conquest of Politics* (Princeton, NJ: Princeton University Press 1988). The *locus classicus* for one form of conservative position is M. Oakeshott, 'Rationalism in Politics', reprinted in Oakeshott, *Rationalism in Politics and Other Essays* (London: Methuen 1962). A rather different form of conservatism is C. Schmitt, *The Concept of the Political*, trans. G. Schwab (New Brunswick, NJ: Rutgers University Press 1976). Also relevant is J. Kekes, *Against Liberalism* (Ithaca, NY: Cornell University Press 1997).

10. One explanation is that a fundamental feature of citizens' relation to their state is that the latter imposes legal obligations on them. But this masks a confusion about the justificatory role which the concept of *obligation* has been used to fill in discussions of the problem: between its playing a *direct* justificatory role, as an inherently reason-giving category of reasons for action, and an *indirect* role, where it is assumed that further reasons, which justify the obligations themselves, are sought. The problem with the direct approach is that it always demands further (that is, indirect) justification, while the indirect approach cannot but couple a *sui generis* class of reasons for action which apply unconditionally, with a categorially distinct and contingent class of supporting reasons – regardless of whether the latter are couched in terms of prudence, gratitude, and so on. There is no more reason to think that individuals' relations with the state are characterisable exclusively in terms of obligations than their relations with one another.
11. This version of the argument for the state is due most notably to Hannah Pitkin. See her 'Obligation and Consent', *American Political Science Review* 55 IV (1965) and 'Obligation and Consent II', *American Political Science Review* 56 I (1966). Also Pitkin, 'Obligation and Consent', in P. Laslett, W.G. Runciman and Q. Skinner (eds), *Philosophy, Politics and Society*, 4th series (Oxford: Blackwell 1972). For helpful discussion of Pitkin, see J. Horton, *Political Obligation* (London: Macmillan 1992), pp. 40–1 and pp. 84–6.
12. There is now a voluminous literature on the subject, with considerable divergences over how 'pluralism' should be interpreted. The writings of Isaiah Berlin are the modern *locus classicus*, which in turn claims its inspiration from the work of J.S. Mill and Herder. See Berlin, 'John Stuart Mill and the Ends of Life' and 'Two Concepts of Liberty', in Berlin, *Four Essays on Liberty* (Oxford: Oxford University Press 1969), and 'From Hope and Fear Set Free' in Berlin, *Concepts and Categories* (Oxford: Oxford University Press 1978). See also J. Raz, *The Morality of Freedom* (Oxford: Oxford University Press 1986); S. Hampshire, 'Morality and Conflict' in Hampshire, *Morality and Conflict* (Cambridge: Cambridge University Press 1983); J. Kekes, *the Morality of Pluralism* (Princeton, NJ: Princeton University Press 1993); B. Williams, 'Conflicts of Values' and 'The Truth in Relativism', both reprinted in Williams, *Moral Luck* (Cambridge: Cambridge University Press 1981); Rawls, *A Theory of Justice*; C. Larmore, *Patterns of Moral Complexity* (Cambridge: Cambridge University Press 1987); T. Nagel, 'The Fragmentation of Value' in Nagel, *Mortal Questions* (Cambridge: Cambridge University Press 1979); M. Walzer, *Spheres of Justice* (New York: Basic Books 1983); M. Stocker, *Plural and*

Conflicting Values (Oxford: Oxford University Press 1990); R. Dworkin, 'Liberalism' in S. Hampshire (ed.), *Public and Private Morality* (Cambridge: Cambridge University Press 1978); S. Lukes, 'Making Sense of Moral Conflict' in N. Rosenblum (ed.), *Liberalism and the Moral Life* (Cambridge, MA: Harvard University Press 1989); D. Miller, *Principles of Social Justice* (Cambridge, MA: Harvard University Press 1999). For some helpful remarks, see J. Griffin, *Well Being* (Oxford: Oxford University Press 1986), Chapter 5; J. Gray, *Liberalisms: Essays in Political Philosophy* (London: Routledge 1989), and G. Crowder, 'Pluralism and Liberalism', *Political Studies* 43 (1994), pp. 293–305. See also I. Berlin and B. Williams, 'Pluralism and Liberalism: A Reply' in *ibid.*, pp. 306–9.

13. See Crowder, 'Pluralism and Liberalism', *passim*. Crowder plausibly argues that the mere commitment to meta-ethical pluralism is insufficient by itself to justify, or even favour, a liberal set of political arrangements. To regard a given value as being but one among others is not enough to justify liberalism; indeed, if we take seriously the claim made by many pluralists that pluralism is entailed by conflicts between values, it seems hard to see how political (or any other set of) arrangements could avoid favouring some values over others, as Crowder makes clear (pp. 296–7). Equally, since some values (for example, individualism) are *substantively* liberal ones, but others are not, the mere 'fact' of pluralism – that is, there is more than one value – does not show that each set of values must include liberal ones.
14. It is striking that many of those who, in asserting that there is a 'fact' of pluralism, take themselves to be making a metaphysical or meta-ethical rather than a merely anthropological claim, are nonetheless critical elsewhere of precisely those meta-ethical theories – for example, cognitivism – which hold that moral propositions are the kinds of objects assessable by their correspondence to an objective or realistic set of moral 'facts'.
15. A representative example of the argumentative gaps I have highlighted is P. Herzog and L. Foster (eds), *Defending Diversity: Contemporary Philosophical Perspectives on Multiculturalism* (Amherst, MA: University of Massachusetts Press 1994). There is a recurrent elision in the contributions to the book between *citing* the fact of diversity and demanding political, educational, and so on arrangements to cater for particular sectional interest groups. As such the book is clearly marked by the special-interest lobbying characteristic of American politics. For further criticism of the arguments in this volume see also G. Newey, 'Philosophical Aromatherapy', *Res Publica* II (1996), pp. 215–21.
16. Discourse ethics obviously takes much of its inspiration from the work of Jürgen Habermas. See in particular his *The Theory of Communicative Action*, vols I and II, trans. T. McCarthy (Cambridge MA: MIT Press 1984–7); *The Philosophical Discourse of Modernity*, trans. F. Lawrence (Cambridge: Polity Press 1987). Versions of the idea recur in B. Ackerman, *Social Justice and the Liberal State* (New Haven, CT: Yale University Press 1980), and Larmore, *Patterns of Moral Complexity*, as well as more recent theorists of 'discursive democracy'. On Habermas's discursively-based ethical theory see also S. Benhabib and F. Dallmayr, (eds) *The Communicative Ethics Controversy* (Cambridge, MA: MIT Press 1990), and W. Outhwaite, *Habermas* (Cambridge:

Polity Press 1994); also S. Chambers, *Reasonable Democracy: Jürgen Habermas and the Politics of Discourse* (Ithaca, NY: Cornell University Press 1996).

17. I discuss this further in Chapter 2.
18. Examples of neutrality in recent political philosophy include Ackerman, *Social Justice and the Liberal State*; Larmore, *Patterns of Moral Complexity*; R. Nozick, *Anarchy, State, and Utopia* (Oxford: Blackwell 1974). Rawls's theory is hybrid as regards neutrality to the extent that it aims to arrive by a procedurally neutral route at a 'thin' conception of the good consistent with a moderate form of perfectionism.
19. See Rawls, *Theory of Justice*, Section 69.
20. For the term 'partial compliance' and its significance see *ibid.*, p. 351.
21. J. Rawls, 'The Idea of an Overlapping Consensus', in Rawls, *Collected Papers*, ed. S. Freeman (Cambridge, MA: Harvard University Press 1999); see also Rawls, *Political Liberalism* (New York: Columbia University Press 1993), Chapter 4.
22. Political *theory* or political *philosophy*? Many who style themselves as political *theorists* belong to Philosophy faculties, publish in philosophical journals, and use the methods of analytical philosophy. There are, moreover, ways of theorising about politics which are not philosophical. In fact, this terminological confusion may encourage, by a predictable process of dialectical boundary-reinforcement, the marginalisation of political philosophy and philosophers within philosophy itself: political *theorists* by definition are not *philosophers*, unless they engage in *philosophical* theorising – but then since it may be claimed (plausibly enough) that the role for *this* sort of theorising about politics is unpromisingly limited, anyone who really wants to philosophise will have to decamp to a cognate area of the discipline (such as ethics). The *Oxford Dictionary of Philosophy* edited by Simon Blackburn (Oxford: Oxford University Press 1994) – while finding house-room for entries on *aesthetics, ethics, philosophy of mind, logic, philosophy of history, philosophy of science*, even *social philosophy* – lacks *any* entry on *politics*, or *political philosophy*, or indeed *political theory*. Similarly A.C. Grayling's recent general introduction to philosophy, which closely follows the University of London Philosophy curriculum and includes contributions from eminent London philosophers, has been expanded in its most recent edition to include entries on aesthetics and ethics, but not political philosophy; meanwhile many political philosophers live out a shadowy existence in the *demi-monde* of departments of Politics, Social and Political Sciences, History, and so on.

Chapter 1

1. This is not to claim that, judged by plausible professional and other institutional indices, there are no currently in-harness political philosophers at work producing such reflections. However, it seems to me that the following notable works of political philosophy offer little or no reflection of this kind. See J. Rawls, *A Theory of Justice* (Oxford: Oxford University Press 1971); also his articles, 'Kantian Constructivism in Moral Theory', 'The Priority of Right and Ideas of the Good', 'Justice As Fairness: Political, Not Metaphysical', and

others in Rawls, *Collected Papers*, ed. S. Freeman (Cambridge, MA: Harvard University Press 1999); *Political Liberalism* (New York: Columbia University Press 1993); R. Nozick, *Anarchy, State, and Utopia* (Oxford: Blackwell 1974) and *The Nature of Rationality* (Oxford: Oxford University Press 1989); R. Dworkin, *Taking Rights Seriously* (London: Duckworth 1977), *Law's Empire* (London: Fontana 1987), 'What is Equality? Part I', *Philosophy and Public Affairs* 10(iii) (1981), pp. 185–246 and 'What is Equality? Part 2: Equality of Resources', *Philosophy and Public Affairs* 10(iv) (1981), pp. 283–345; J. Raz, *The Morality of Freedom* (Oxford: Clarendon Press 1986); C. Larmore, *Patterns of Moral Complexity* (Cambridge: Cambridge University Press 1987); M. Walzer, *Spheres of Justice* (New York: Basic Books 1983); M. Sandel, *Liberalism and the Limits of Justice* (Cambridge: Cambridge University Press 1982); D. Parfit, *Reasons and Persons* (Oxford: Oxford University Press 1984); R. Rorty, *Contingency, Irony, and Solidarity* (Cambridge: Cambridge University Press 1989); B. Barry, *Theories of Justice* (Berkeley, CA: University of California Press 1989) and *Justice As Impartiality* (Oxford: Clarendon Press 1995); W. Kymlicka, *Contemporary Political Philosophy* (Oxford: Oxford University Press 1990), and *Multicultural Citizenship* (Oxford: Oxford University Press 1995); B. Ackerman, *Social Justice and the Liberal State* (New Haven, CT: Yale University Press 1980); D. Gauthier, *Morals By Agreement* (Oxford: Clarendon Press 1986); A. Gutmann, *Liberal Equality* (Cambridge: Cambridge University Press 1980); J. Habermas, *Between Facts and Norms* trans. W. Rehg (Cambridge: Polity Press 1996); W. Galston, *Justice and the Human Good* (Chicago, IL: University of Chicago Press 1980). Of course, listed above are many works of outstanding philosophical merit. As I stress in the text, I do not claim that philosophising about politics as it is must be the *sole*, or even the prime, focus of philosophers' concerns. What is striking is its almost complete neglect by them.

2. Rawls, *Theory of Justice*, p. 5: 'what is just and unjust is usually in dispute. Men disagree about which principles should define the basic terms of their association.'
3. See Rawls, *Theory of Justice*, p. 245ff.
4. K. Marx, *Theses on Feuerbach* XI, reprinted in D. McLellan (ed.), *Karl Marx: Selected Writings* (Oxford: Oxford University Press 1977), p. 158.
5. A good example of this is Donald Davidson's 'Weakness of Will', reprinted in Davidson, *Essays on Actions and Events* (Oxford: Oxford University Press 1980), which concludes that the *akrates*' behaviour is fundamentally 'surd'. This interestingly stands in some tension with Davidson's views on interpretation – in particular, his commitment to interpretative charity, and the view that observer-rational standards of intelligibility are the *only* basis on which interpretation can proceed.
6. This is particularly true for ethical *internalists*. The position is subject to local variations of definition, but is roughly characterised by the following claim: for any moral proposition p linking an agent A to a projected course of action ϕ, if A believes that p, A is motivated to ϕ. A trivial further condition on the entailment must be that A believes that he is the agent named in p; more substantive issues concern the force and status of the motive mentioned in the consequent. Externalists reject the entailment. As such they avoid the

obligation incurred by internalists to explain how agents fail to act on their moral beliefs.

7. A point made in B. Williams, *Ethics and the Limits of Philosophy* (London: Fontana 1985), Chapter 10. See also Williams, *Making Sense of Humanity* (Cambridge: Cambridge University Press 1995).
8. It need not be assumed that this means we should go on with a blithe disregard for the environmental costs of economic activity. Indeed, whatever else is to be said about the development of 'sustainable' environmental policies, they are precisely *not* an abdication of human control over nature.
9. See for example 'Agonistic Liberalism' in J. Gray, *Enlightenment's Wake* (London: Routledge 1995).
10. The doyen of the Cambridge school is Quentin Skinner. Among Skinner's methodological writings are the following: 'Meaning and Understanding in the History of Ideas', *History and Theory* 8 (1969), pp. 3–53; 'Conventions and the Understanding of Speech Acts', *Philosophical Quarterly* 20 (1970), pp. 118–38; 'On Performing and Explaining Linguistic Actions', *Philosophical Quarterly* 21 (1971), pp. 1–21; '"Social Meaning" and the Explanation of Social Action', in P. Laslett, W. Runciman and Q. Skinner (eds), *Philosophy, Politics and Society*, 4th series (Oxford: Blackwell 1972); also *The Foundations of Modern Political Thought*, 2 vols (Cambridge: Cambridge University Press 1978). For some criticism of Skinner, see J. Tully, *Meaning and Context: Quentin Skinner and his Critics* (Cambridge: Polity Press 1988).
11. Indeed this, *in nuce*, is the dispute between the 'Taylor-Warrender' interpretation of *Leviathan* (for example) and those like Gauthier and Hampton who take a less morally aspiring view of Hobbes's argument for the state.
12. Rawls, 'Kantian Constructivism in Moral Theory'.
13. See D. Gauthier, *The Logic of Leviathan* (Oxford: Oxford University Press 1969); J. Gray, *Mill on Liberty: A Defence* (London: Routledge 1983); Nozick, *Anarchy, State, and Utopia*, p. 175ff; Galston, *Justice and the Human Good*; G.A. Cohen, *Marx's Theory of History: A Defence* (Oxford: Oxford University Press 1978) and *Self-Ownership, Freedom and Equality* (Cambridge: Cambridge University Press 1996); C. Taylor, *Hegel* (Cambridge: Cambridge University Press 1975) and *Hegel and Modern Society* (Cambridge: Cambridge University Press 1978).
14. B. Williams, 'Moral Luck', in Williams, *Moral Luck: Philosophical Papers 1973–1980* (Cambridge: Cambridge University Press 1981).
15. T. Ball, *Reappraising Political Theory* (Oxford: Clarendon Press 1995), p. 45.
16. Compare, for example, the title of P.F. Strawson's *Individuals: An Essay in Descriptive Metaphysics* (London: Methuen 1959).
17. See D. Davidson, 'The Very Idea of a Conceptual Scheme', in Davidson, *Essays on Actions and Events*.
18. For this verdict, see P. Laslett, 'Introduction' to Laslett (ed.), *Philosophy, Politics and Society*, 1st series (Oxford: Blackwell 1956), p. vii; also Ball, *Reappraising Political Theory*, p. 41f. For a more sceptical contemporary view, see I. Berlin, 'Does Political Theory Still Exist?' in P. Laslett and W.G. Runciman (eds), *Philosophy, Politics and Society*, 2nd series (Oxford: Blackwell 1962).
19. For an example of this tendency, see the 'Introduction' by R. Goodin and P. Pettit (eds), *A Companion to Contemporary Political Philosophy* (Oxford:

Blackwell 1993). The editors, defending their selection criteria for the book, note (p. 3) that 'republicanism does not get in, because ... it has not had a substantial impact on public life', while on the other hand '[n]ationalism – still less racism, sexism or ageism – does not figure, on the grounds that it hardly counts as a principled way of thinking about things'. Whether or not a given person holds a 'principled' stance seems to depend here on whether the principles in question are ones the editors endorse (I owe this reference to John Horton).

20. A.C. MacIntyre, *After Virtue* (London: Duckworth 1981).
21. See I. Berlin, 'Two Concepts of Liberty' in Berlin, *Four Essays On Liberty* (Oxford: Oxford University Press 1969).
22. This is reflected in the well-entrenched misnomer for political philosophy or theory as 'political thought'. That *all* political study is the study of political thought parallels the truth in the Collingwoodian view that all history is the history of thought. See R. Collingwood, *The Idea of History* (Oxford: Clarendon Press 1941).
23. C.M. Korsgaard, 'Skepticism About Practical Reason', *Journal of Philosophy* 83 (1986), pp. 5–25.
24. For a contrary view, see B. Williams, 'Internal and External Reasons', in Williams, *Moral Luck*.
25. There is little discussion of power in contemporary political philosophy. For a few examples of such discussion, see T. Ball, 'Power' in Goodin and Pettit, *A Companion to Contemporary Political Philosophy*. Also P. Morriss, *Power: A Philosophical Analysis* (New York: St Martin's Press 1987), and S. Lukes, *Power: A Radical View* (London: Macmillan 1974).
26. For accounts of the attack on politics in contemporary political theory, see B. Barber, *The Conquest of Politics* (Princeton, NJ: Princeton University Press 1988); B. Honig, *Political Theory and the Displacement of Politics* (Ithaca, NY: Cornell University Press 1993).
27. This need not endorse the view that the very possibility of redescription makes it doubtful whether the gains which accrue from it can ever be 'cognitive' ones, as Richard Rorty seems to believe. See his *Contingency, Irony, and Solidarity* (Cambridge: Cambridge University Press 1989), which is also discussed in Chapter 8.
28. N. Machiavelli, *The Prince*, trans. G. Bull (Harmondsworth: Penguin 1961), p. 91. For a classic modern interpretation, see Skinner, *The Foundations of Modern Political Thought* I, p. 131ff. Interestingly, however, in criticising the Crocean interpretation which sees Machiavelli's originality as lying in his stress on the autonomy of the political, Skinner argues (p. 132f) that Machiavelli *agreed* with orthodox contemporaries on the ends of politics ('maintaining one's state', and so on), but disagreed only about the appropriate means. But surely this is the very distinction which Machiavelli's writings call into question. It is not that maintaining one's state, or achieving glory, or displaying *virtù* are goods which politics happens to promote, when it goes well. Rather these goods are intrinsically political ones, so that seeking them is simply what it is to engage in politics.
29. Aristotle, *Nicomachean Ethics*, 1106b6ff; on Aristotle's notion of a way of acting, see G.F. Newey, *Virtue, Reason and Toleration* (Edinburgh: University of Edinburgh Press 1999), Chapter 3.

30. See for example Parfit, *Reasons and Persons*; R.M. Hare, *Moral Thinking* (Oxford: Oxford University Press 1982).
31. Honig, *Political Theory and the Displacement of Politics*; J. Shklar, *Ordinary Vices* (Cambridge, MA: Harvard University Press 1984) and *Political Thought and Political Thinkers* (London: University of Chicago Press 1998).
32. M. Slote, *From Morality to Virtue* (Oxford: Oxford University Press 1995); J. McDowell, 'Virtue and Reason', reprinted in R. Crisp and M. Slote (eds), *Virtue Ethics* (Oxford: Oxford University Press 1997).
33. Sandel, *Liberalism and the Limits of Justice*, p. 192.
34. Traces of this view can be found, for instance, in the work of John Gray. See his *Liberalisms: Essays in Political Philosophy* (London: Routledge 1993) and *Enlightenment's Wake*. For a recent conservative statement of this view, see J. Kekes, *Against Liberalism* (Ithaca, NY: Cornell University Press 1997). See also Chapter 8 below.

Chapter 2

1. See W.B. Gallie, 'Essentially Contested Concepts', *Proceedings of the Aristotelian Society* 56 (1955–6), pp. 167–98; for others see below, note 7.
2. In the well-known phrase of John Rawls. See his *A Theory of Justice* (Oxford: Oxford University Press 1971), p. 3.
3. I examine this form of justification for neutrality in more detail in Chapter 6 below.
4. See J. Rawls, *Political Liberalism* (New York: Columbia University Press 1993); C. Larmore, *Patterns of Moral Complexity* (Cambridge: Cambridge University Press 1987); B. Barry, *Justice As Impartiality* (Oxford: Clarendon Press 1995); T. Scanlon, *What We Owe To Each Other* (Cambridge, MA: Harvard University Press 1999); J. Habermas, *Between Facts and Norms*, trans. W. Rehg (Cambridge: Polity Press 1996).
5. A. Leftwich, *Redefining Politics: People, Resources and Power* (London: Methuen 1983).
6. The term is applied to the debate over essential contestability by Christine Swanton. See Swanton, 'On the "Essential Contestedness" of Political Concepts', *Ethics* 95 (1985), pp. 811–27.
7. See D. Miller, 'Constraints on Freedom', *Ethics* 94 (1983), pp. 66–86, and 'Linguistic Philosophy and Political Theory' in D. Miller and L. Siedentop (eds), *The Nature of Political Theory* (Oxford: Basil Blackwell 1983); A.C. MacIntyre, 'The Essential Contestability of Some Social Concepts', *Ethics* 84 (1973–4), pp. 1–9; J. Gray, 'On the Essential Contestability of Some Social and Political Concepts', *Political Theory* V (1977), pp. 331–48, 'On Liberty, Liberalism and Essential Contestability', *British Journal of Political Science* 8 (1978), pp. 385–402, and 'Political Power, Social Theory and Essential Contestability', in Miller and Siedentop, *The Nature of Political Theory*; W. Connolly, *The Terms of Political Discourse*, 3rd edn. (Oxford: Blackwell 1993); Swanton, 'On the "Essential Contestedness" of Political Concepts'; A. Mason, 'On Explaining Political Disagreement: The Notion of an Essentially Contested Concept', *Inquiry* 33 (1990), pp. 81–98, and *Explaining Political Disagreement* (Cambridge: Cambridge University Press 1993). See also for

example S. Lukes, *Power: A Radical View* (London: Macmillan 1975); E. Laclau, 'Discourse' in R. Goodin and P. Pettit (eds), *A Companion to Contemporary Political Philosophy* (Oxford: Basil Blackwell 1993), pp. 431–7.

8. Connolly, *The Terms of Political Discourse* , p. 11.
9. Swanton, 'On the "Essential Contestedness"', pp. 813–14.
10. See note 1 above.
11. Connolly, *The Terms of Political Discourse*, p. 11.
12. Mason, *Explaining Political Disagreement*, p. 48.
13. *Ibid.*, p. 50.
14. *Ibid.*, p. 49; original emphasis. His specific point is that interpretations of the concepts will help to structure political design.
15. It should be noted that in earlier work, at least, Mason casts doubt on the capacity of the essential contestability thesis to explain the phenomena of political disagreement. See 'On Explaining Political Disagreement', for example p. 81, pp. 92–6. Mason's argument however proceeds directly from the possibility of independent explanations for political disagreement rather than from objections to the coherence of the thesis itself.
16. It may be suggested that the modal claim should simply be dispensed with. This would not, of course, block the earlier criticisms in this section regarding concept-possession and explanatory redundancy. But it would also not provide any means of refuting someone who denied that dispute was an *unavoidable* consequence of the concept's structure. Similar problems face Swanton's proposal that different interpretations be understood analogously with distinct Fregean senses of a common referent.
17. B. Barber, *The Conquest of Politics* (Princeton, NJ: Princeton University Press 1988), especially Chapter 5.
18. Swanton, 'On the "Essential Contestedness" of Political Concepts', p. 816.
19. *Ibid.*, p. 819.
20. *Ibid.*, p. 818.
21. *Ibid.*, p. 819.
22. Similar problems beset the attempts of Roy Bhaskar to preserve a realist, paradigm-transcendent ontology for theoretical developments in natural science by construing what is at issue between different theories or paradigms as concerning different senses of a unitary referent. But if theory-competition is construed like this, then the dispute between the theories precisely *cannot* be treated as one over truth-conditions. For if *all* that distinguishes them is the senses assigned to a unitary referent, then the corresponding propositions of their theory-languages can simply be conjoined; or, if this generates a contradiction, there is nothing to distinguish the picture from a quite standard ('naive') realist view of scientific development. The only way in which Bhaskar's picture could then be defended is by saying that the truth-conditions are generated intensionally. But then the existence of a putative extension for the respective theoretical vocabularies is no longer relevant to the determination of their truth-conditions.
23. M. Freeden, *Ideologies and Political Theory* (Oxford: Clarendon Press 1996), makes this point, p. 55f.
24. L. Wittgenstein, *Philosophical Investigations*, trans. and ed. G.E.M. Anscombe (Oxford: Blackwell 1953), § 241.

25. See, for example Wittgenstein's *Zettel*, ed. G.E.M. Anscombe and G.H. von Wright (Oxford: Blackwell 1967), § 567: 'What determines our judgements, our concepts and reactions, is not what *one* man is doing *now*, an individual action, but the whole hurly-burly of human actions' (original emphasis).
26. Wittgenstein, *Philosophical Investigations*, § 242.
27. *Ibid.*, § 217.
28. R. Alejandro, 'What is Political about Rawls's Political Liberalism?', *Journal of Politics* 58 (1996), pp. 1–24, p. 2.
29. G. Kavka, 'Why Even Morally Perfect People Would Need Government' in E. Paul, F. Miller and J. Paul (eds), *Contemporary Political and Social Philosophy* (Cambridge: Cambridge University Press 1995). The main reasons Kavka gives are that such beings would display cognitive limitations and reasonable differences in moral beliefs, and would face coordination problems.
30. Habermas's recent work is one example of this. See his *Between Facts and Norms*, for example, p. 107.
31. I discuss this example in more detail in my *Virtue, Reason and Toleration: The Place of Toleration in Ethical and Political Philosophy* (Edinburgh: Edinburgh University Press 1999), Chapter 5.
32. Only partial, because there are other concepts (for example, plausibly, *morality*) of which it is also true that disputes about their extension themselves fall within that extension (that is, in this example, the disputes are themselves moral disputes). But it does mark off *politics* from some other concepts, so is not empty. Disputes about the extension of *red* are not themselves red.
33. Perhaps the clearest illustration of this are the disputes which have occurred over whether sport should or should not be 'politicised', as in sporting boycotts of South Africa under apartheid, or of the 1980 Moscow Olympic Games following the Soviet invasion of Afghanistan. Whatever may be said about the claims made in those disputes, it is hard to deny that the disputes themselves were political ones.
34. As far as this goes, Locke is a foundational figure in the history of liberalism, in a respect rather different from that generally assumed. His private and ideational conception of meaning (*Essay Concerning Human Understanding*, Book III) nevertheless assumes interpersonal transparency and semantic convergence.
35. Barber, *The Conquest of Politics*, especially Chapter 5.
36. N. Machiavelli, *The Prince*, trans. G. Bull (Harmondsworth: Penguin 1961), p. 91.

Chapter 3

1. See B. Williams, 'Internal and External Reasons', in Williams, *Moral Luck* (Cambridge: Cambridge University Press 1981); see also J. McDowell, 'Might There Be External Reasons?' and Williams's 'Replies' in J. Altham and R. Harrison (eds), *World, Mind, and Ethics: Essays on the Ethical Philosophy of Bernard Williams* (Cambridge: Cambridge University Press 1995).

2. The phrase 'one thought too many' is taken from B. Williams, 'Persons, Character, and Morality' in R. Harrison (ed.), *Rational Action* (Cambridge: Cambridge University Press 1980), reprinted in *Moral Luck*, p. 18.
3. W.D. Ross introduced the apparatus of '*prima facie*' duties to try to preserve deontic coherence in a world where value is not exhaustively reducible to deontic concepts, and where obligations often clash. See Ross, *The Right and the Good* (Oxford: Clarendon Press 1930). For an application of this to political obligation, see W.A. Edmundson, *Three Anarchical Fallacies* (Cambridge: Cambridge University Press 1998), Chapter 1. Edmundson, too, says little to dispel the impression that *prima facie* obligations are merely defeasible reasons for action.
4. Cf. J. Rawls, *A Theory of Justice* (Oxford: Oxford University Press 1971); also Rawls, 'Kantian Constructivism in Moral Theory', *Journal of Philosophy* 77 (1980), pp. 515–72.
5. C. Larmore, *Patterns of Moral Complexity* (Cambridge: Cambridge University Press 1987).
6. For this claim, see B. Williams, *Ethics and the Limits of Philosophy* (London: Fontana 1985), for example p. 148.
7. Why not 'the *best* reasons ...'? This may be thought too demanding. The gap between best and justifying reasons is meant to allow for the possibility that there may be sets of reasons which justify obligation and can play the requisite role in generating action (that is, by citizens on their obligations), even though there are better reasons (more abstruse, or perhaps less motivationally efficacious) which also justify obligation. I have more to say on this below (pp. 71–2).
8. It should be clear that transparency and distributivity are distinct requirements. There could be transparent reasons which applied only at supra-individual level, without being reducible to true individual reasons; equally, reasons could be distributed without being transparent – for example, a Platonic style of theory might provide reasons why non-guardian citizens should act in certain ways, which *apply* to each such citizen without being transparent to them.
9. It may be said that (TD) is easily satisfied if law as such creates a reason for those subject to it to obey it. But this is surely less than liberal theory wants: by itself it fails to distinguish liberal from other regimes, because it is concerned purely with the formal attributes of positive law; and fails to allow for the possibility of procedurally impeccable but otherwise unacceptable legal obligations.
10. See Williams, 'Internal and External Reasons'; also J. Dancy, *Moral Reasons* (Oxford: Blackwell 1993), pp. 253–7; McDowell, 'Might There Be External Reasons?'; and C. Korsgaard, 'Skepticism About Practical Reason', in Korsgaard, *Creating the Kingdom of Ends* (Cambridge: Cambridge University Press 1996).
11. H. Pitkin, 'Obligation and Consent' in P. Laslett, W. Runciman and Q. Skinner (eds), *Philosophy, Politics and Society*, 4th series (Oxford: Blackwell 1972), argues that since it is in the nature of obligations that they apply whether or not those under them will them to, it must be futile to ask what *volitional* basis there is for an (for example, political) obligation. The argument also promises to meet the demand for transparency. For it says, in

effect, that any citizen capable of understanding what it is to be under an obligation will satisfy the demand. But just because it is senseless to ask why I should carry out an obligation of mine, it doesn't follow that it is senseless to ask why I am under the obligation. The latter question is no more senseless than asking 'Why go on holiday?' given the availability of the reply, 'Because it's in the nature of holidays that one goes on them.' This fails to show that it is senseless to ask why one should go on holiday, let alone to ask about the relative merits of different destinations. The 'conceptual' argument could have seemed apposite, given a certain view of the theoretical enterprise – that previous theorists tried to answer question (1) by appealing to the notion of an obligation, but then blundered by saddling themselves with the hopeless (2), for which the sole remedy was to point the hapless questioner at a dictionary. However, whatever the defects of formulations (3)–(7) inclusive, they at least make clear the unavailability of a purely lexicographic solution.

12. T. Hobbes, *Leviathan*, ed. R. Tuck (Cambridge: Cambridge University Press 1991), p. 91.
13. A clear statement of their distinctness is to be found in Williams, *Ethics and the Limits of Philosophy*, Chapter 10; also Williams, *Shame and Necessity* (Berkeley, CA: University of California Press 1996), Chapters 3–5.
14. C. Pateman, *The Problem of Political Obligation* (Cambridge: Polity Press 1985).
15. The definitions operate (by design) at a high level of generality. There are a number of issues raised by the definitions which cannot be addressed here: familiar ambiguities collect, for example, around token/type homonymy for the locutions 'same action' and perhaps also 'same reason'. One of the most important concerns the identity-conditions for reasons for action – a question which is particularly sharp for those theories assuming distribution. These difficulties are simply dodged in the definitions given above, which adopt a deliberately generous conception of reason-identity for argumentative purposes (the tighter the conditions are drawn, the harder it is for a would-be obligation-theorist to specify a set related by reasons meeting the given conditions on justification).
16. Usually; but there is no contradiction in the thought that someone might play to lose, for example, in order to indulge their friend.
17. For these types of agents and the problems they pose for internalism, see Dancy, *Moral Reasons*, p. 4ff.
18. This is not to deny that there may be cases in which I am justified in authorising actions whose rationale fails to meet these justificatory conditions; some professional/client relations are like this, though it is notable that the actions then are *mine* only in a prosthetic sense. It might be thought that we could derive an analogous account for *political* authorisation, with the sovereign mandated to act on reasons which are external to the authorising citizens. However, the analogy applies at the wrong point: professional/client relations, with accompanying prosthetic conceptions of agency, are made between competent agents to both of whom the reasons for *authorisation* are not external (they are not, for instance, in *Leviathan*, the most notable attempt to base a justification of the state on a prosthetic conception of agency) . There is indeed nothing wrong *per se* with contracting to authorise the state to act on reasons external to the citizens in some

situations (for example, official secrecy). But the point is that contractual or other professional authorisations are not in this way prosthetic.

19. Korsgaard, 'Skepticism About Practical Reason', especially p. 322.
20. Those tempted to argue that an external account of reasons will suffice to meet (TD) should reflect also that this may be hard to square with other conditions, not merely on *liberal* democracy, but on democracy *sans phrase*. If the external view is taken seriously with regard to this question, it imposes severe limits, for example, on democratic accountability. For those citizens to whom the justifying reasons for the state are in this sense external will be unable either to grasp the *content* of the reasons themselves, or the relevance of a citation of them in justifying political action. This is uncomfortably close to Plato's non-transparent hierarchic paternalism.
21. A point made clearly by Simmons; see A.J. Simmons, *Moral Principles and Political Obligations* (Princeton, NJ: Princeton University Press 1979), Chapter 1.
22. J. Horton, *Political Obligation* (London: Macmillan 1992), Chapter 6, pp. 145–71.
23. Edmundson (*Three Anarchical Fallacies*, Chapter 1) bases his argument on this very distinction between the grounds on which state authority is justified, and the justification of individual citizens' political obligations.
24. W. Hohfeld, *Fundamental Legal Conceptions as Applied in Judicial Reasoning* (New Haven, CT: Yale University Press 1919).
25. See H.A. Prichard, 'Does Modern Moral Philosophy Rest on a Mistake?', in J.O. Urmson (ed.) *Moral Obligation* (Oxford: Oxford University Press 1968). For an argument to a similar conclusion, see A.C. MacIntyre, *After Virtue* (London: Duckworth 1981), Chapter 5.

Chapter 4

1. See J. Rawls, 'The Priority of Right and Ideas of the Good', in Rawls, *Collected Papers*, ed. S. Freeman (Cambridge, MA: Harvard University Press 1999).
2. For sample statements of the claim, see for example the following: I. Berlin, 'Does Political Theory Still Exist?', in Berlin, *Concepts and Categories* (Oxford: Oxford University Press 1978), pp. 143–72; B. Williams, 'Conflicts of Values', in Williams, *Moral Luck* (Cambridge: Cambridge University Press 1981); C. Larmore, *Patterns of Moral Complexity* (Cambridge: Cambridge University Press 1987); J. Gray, *Enlightenment's Wake* (London: Routledge 1995); J. Kekes, *The Morality of Pluralism* (Princeton, NJ: Princeton University Press 1993); J. Raz, *The Morality of Freedom* (Oxford: Oxford University Press 1986), Chapters 13 and 14; M. Walzer, *Spheres of Justice* (New York: Basic Books 1983); J. Rawls, *Political Liberalism* (New York: Columbia University Press 1993), p. 153; S. Hampshire, *Morality and Pessimism* (Cambridge: Cambridge University Press 1972).
3. J. Gray, 'Agonistic Liberalism' in Gray, *Enlightenment's Wake*, pp. 68–9. It should be observed that Gray also says in this article that 'nothing follows inexorably, as a matter of strict implication or logical necessity, for the design of liberal institutions, from the truth of value-pluralism' (p. 74). But he adds that 'value-pluralism also undermines the implicit model of a liberal state

intimated in recent liberal political philosophy, as exemplified in the work of Rawls, Dworkin, Ackerman and their followers'. Roughly, Gray's view is that these liberals underestimate the force of value-pluralism, and its capacity to vitiate their own liberalism; whereas my view is that this may well be so if value-pluralism is true, but that the considerations standardly adduced in support of value-pluralism are quite consistent with monism. For more on this, see below, Chapter 8.

4. In what follows, whenever I use 'pluralism' without qualification, it should be understood as shorthand for 'value-pluralism', except where otherwise stated.
5. See above, note 2.
6. J. Gray, 'Toleration: A Post-Liberal Perspective' in Gray, *Enlightenment's Wake*, p. 28.
7. Larmore, *Patterns of Moral Complexity*, p. 23.
8. Sometimes this claim is distinguished from the claim that values are incomparable. I do not discuss this as a separate argument for pluralism, but briefly assess the consequences of incomparability-pluralism for political design (pp. 91–2, p. 103).
9. Raz, *The Morality of Freedom*, pp. 325–6. Raz offers a different set of formulations in his 'Autonomy, Toleration, and the Harm Principle' in S. Mendus (ed.), *Justifying Toleration* (Cambridge: Cambridge University Press 1988), pp. 155–75. There he defines what he calls 'weak' moral pluralism as the claim that 'there are various forms and styles of life which exemplify different virtues and which are incompatible'; forms of life are incompatible 'if, given reasonable assumptions about human nature, they cannot normally be exemplified in the same life' (p. 159). A similar formulation also appears in *Morality of Freedom*, pp. 396–7. But it is hard to see why the incompatibility between the forms of life should be thought to matter unless the virtues themselves are incompatible (as the mention of assumptions about human nature perhaps acknowledges). Compare the incompatibility between a life of courage as a soldier, and as a racing driver: these may be incompatible despite demanding similar moral qualities. It looks as though Raz's definition gestures towards a (psycho-)logical tightening capable of removing the contingent look of the incompatibility – a move similar to that discussed in relation to 'tragic conflicts' below.
10. It is sometimes said that the claim that quantities are incommensurable entails the claim that they are incomparable. This is in general false, at least if (as I take it) 'incomparability' is understood to mean that the quantities cannot be ranked. This can be seen from the example given earlier, of real numbers which are incommensurable with rational ones. No rational number is commensurable with $\sqrt{2}$, but any real number can be ranked (placed on the number line) with respect to it. However, if incommensurability is taken to be Razian (that is, there are a set of options, preferences between which cannot be ordered transitively), then that does entail incomparability. If *A*, *B*, *C* are such that *A* is preferred to *B*, but neither is it the case that *B* is preferred to *C*, nor *C* to *B*, nor *A* to *C* nor *C* to *A*, then there is *no* preference-ranking of *A* and *C*, and that is tantamount to saying that *A* and *C* cannot be compared – not compared, at any rate, in respect of that quality or those qualities relevant to determining their preference-ranking.

11. I here adapt an argument first presented in my paper 'Metaphysics Postponed: Liberalism, Pluralism and Neutrality', *Political Studies* 45 (1997), pp. 296–311.
12. For example, Bernard Williams; see his 'Ethical Consistency', in Williams, *Problems of the Self* (Cambridge: Cambridge University Press 1973), for example p. 173.
13. M. Stocker, *Plural and Conflicting Values* (Oxford: Oxford University Press 1990), for example pp. 268–9.
14. *Ibid.*, p. 268.
15. Sometimes it is said that *akrasia* gives grounds for belief in pluralism; but this is confused. The thought is that the *akrates*' predicament arises from the competing pull of distinct values. But what marks the *akrates* is failure to do what there is good reason to do. But that is obviously compatible with monism, though compatible also with lexical pluralism (see below). What it is *not* compatible with, is precisely that form of pluralism whose symptom is held to be reason's inability to decide between options embodying distinct values.
16. The guiding metaphor is that of sorting words into lexicographical order, so that (given an initial alphabetisation) each word can be assigned a unique place in the ordering, according to the following algorithm: (1) any word W with first letter x precedes any word W' with first letter y for all $x < y$ under the alphabetisation; (2) where the first letters are identically situated in the ordering, we proceed to the second letter, and in general where for each letter-place $\{l_1, l_2 \ldots l_n\}$ each letter x_i of W = each letter y_i of W', we order W over W' when, and only when, $x_{n+1} > y_{n+1}$. To be sure, this is a conventionalised ordering system. The conventional ordering ranks 'adzes', over 'zebec', for example, as would be shown by the fact that a mapping down the page would locate the start of 'adzes' north of that of 'zebec'. But this is sufficiently explained by the alphabetisation, since the reverse ranking is consistent with it. If we apply the following transform to the letter rankings, transposing l_i to $l_{i'}$, in line with the following arbitrary rule: $f(i)$: $i' = rem(i/5)+1$, we get a reversed order. Note that this occurs *within* the set lexical alphabetisation. This suggests that, even where we have lexical incommensurability, it still requires interpretation. Indeed, one ordering of objects may be reversed on a different interpretation. Talk of lexical ordering is metaphorical, and to that extent ambiguous.
17. J. Rawls, *A Theory of Justice* (Oxford: Oxford University Press 1971), p. 42f., p. 151f.
18. J. Griffin, 'Are There Incommensurable Values?', *Philosophy and Public Affairs* 6 (1977), p. 44f.; see also Griffin's *Well Being* (Oxford: Oxford University Press 1986), Chapter 5.
19. For the metaphor of meta-ethical 'shape', see J. Dancy, *Moral Reasons* (Oxford: Blackwell 1993), p. 112f.
20. J. Gray, 'From Post-Liberalism to Pluralism', in Gray, *Enlightenment's Wake*, p. 133.
21. Most obviously, that the argument seems to commit us to abandoning, on pain of incoherence, the possibility that there are conceptions of the good devoid of value, or with negative value.

22. Here, 'meta-political' conditions are those which (it is held) must be met by any legitimate form of political design.
23. See Newey, 'Metaphysics Postponed'; also Larmore, *Patterns of Moral Complexity*.
24. See Barry, *Justice As Impartiality*, p. 168.
25. Most notably in Rawls, *Political Liberalism*; see also Rawls, 'The Idea of an Overlapping Consensus', in Rawls, *Collected Papers*, ed. S. Freeman (Cambridge, MA: Harvard University Press 1999).
26. G. Gaus, *Justificatory Liberalism* (Oxford: Oxford University Press 1996), pp. 4–5.
27. For an example of this form of argument, see Larmore, *Patterns of Moral Complexity*, p. 51. Larmore contends that one way 'in which pluralism and disagreement with regard to the good life can be made to justify political neutrality' is that 'when ideals clash ... there is no reason to prefer any one of them, and so no government should seek to institutionalize them'.
28. The *Satanic Verses* controversy provided a clear illustration of this. See my '*Fatwa* and Fiction: Censorship and Toleration' in J. Horton (ed.) *Liberalism, Multiculturalism, and Toleration* (London: Macmillan 1993), pp. 178–92.
29. It is, moreover, unavailing to suggest that the truth of pluralism may generate higher-order mechanisms, such as that of procedural neutrality for resolving value-based conflict. See on this point Chapter 6.

Chapter 5

1. J. Rawls, *A Theory of Justice* (Oxford: Oxford University Press 1971). Rawls makes the often-quoted remark that 'justice is the first virtue of social institutions, as truth is of systems of thought' (p. 3). It is of course true that Rawls has latterly (in *Political Liberalism* (New York: Columbia University Press 1993), and in 'The Idea of Public Reason Revisited', in Rawls, *Collected Papers*, ed. S. Freeman (Cambridge, MA: Harvard University Press 1999)) reinterpreted his theory as 'political'. What, however, this means is that '[i]t leaves untouched all kinds of doctrines – religious, metaphysical, and moral ...' (*Political Liberalism*, p. 375). It is however doubtful whether Rawls can avoid the following dilemma: either the political conception is a part of the comprehensive moral doctrines, or else its autonomy from them is bought at the cost of not being grounded within them in the way that the 'overlapping consensus' idea requires.
2. B. Barry, *Justice As Impartiality* (Oxford: Clarendon Press 1995).
3. J. Raz, *The Morality of Freedom* (Oxford: Clarendon Press 1986). Raz calls his book 'an essay on the political morality of liberalism ... the essay will concentrate on the moral principles of political action, on the political morality of liberalism' (pp. 1–2).
4. R. Nozick, *Anarchy, State, and Utopia* (Oxford: Blackwell 1974). The first sentence of Nozick's book is 'Individuals have rights, and there are things no person or group may do to them (without violating their rights)' (p. ix).
5. A. Gewirth, *Reason and Morality* (Chicago, IL: University of Chicago Press 1978).
6. R. Dworkin, *Taking Rights Seriously* (London: Duckworth 1977).

7. C. Larmore, *Patterns of Moral Complexity* (Cambridge: Cambridge University Press 1987). Despite ostensibly seeking 'a *neutral justification of political neutrality*' (p. 53; original emphasis), Larmore acknowledges that his 'argument is not *morally* neutral. It relies upon a commitment to converse rationally about what ought to be collectively binding political principles, and ... several other normative commitments are involved as well' (p. 54; original emphasis).
8. See C. Geertz, *The Interpretation of Cultures: Selected Essays* (New York: Basic Books 1973).
9. I say more about this move, with respect to aretaic ethical concepts, in G.F. Newey, 'Tolerance As A Virtue' in S. Mendus and J. Horton (eds), *Toleration: Identity and Difference* (London: Macmillan 1999).
10. See D. Parfit, *Reasons and Persons* (Oxford: Oxford University Press 1984).
11. T. Nagel, *The Possibility of Altruism* (Princeton, NJ: Princeton University Press 1970), p. 7; my emphasis.
12. M.A. Smith, *The Moral Problem* (Oxford: Blackwell 1994), p. 12.
13. *Ibid.*, Chapters 5 and 6. This, of course, does not look much like a purely *ceteris paribus* clause. Moreover, it is quite consistent with a world in which *nobody* is rational, and therefore nobody's relevant beliefs and motivations are conjoined in fact. People believe morality says they should do this; they just don't *feel like doing it.* Would we *really* hold on to our view that the moral beliefs and motivations were 'distinct existences' in such circumstances, or conclude that they didn't really have the beliefs after all? What could guide us in making this choice, anyway?
14. B. Williams, 'Internal and External Reasons', in Williams, *Moral Luck: Philosophical Papers 1973–1980* (Cambridge: Cambridge University Press 1981).
15. In the text I use the following verbal formulations: '*A* has a reason to ϕ' states the existence of an internal reason for *A* to ϕ, while 'there is a reason for *A* to ϕ' states an external reason. Nothing substantive depends on the ordinary-language formulations themselves.
16. B. Williams, '*Ought* and Moral Obligation', in Williams, *Moral Luck.*
17. *Ibid.*, p. 122.
18. D. Brink, 'Externalist Moral Realism', *Southern Journal of Philosophy* 24 (supplement) (1986), pp. 23–41; p. 31f.
19. J.R. Searle, 'How to Derive *Ought* from *Is*', *Philosophical Review* 73 (1964) pp. 43–58, reprinted in P. Foot (ed.), *Theories of Ethics* (Oxford: Oxford University Press 1967).
20. D.Z. Phillips, 'In Search of the Moral "Must"', *Philosophical Quarterly* 27 (1977), pp. 140–57.
21. J.L. Mackie, *Ethics: Inventing Right and Wrong* (London: Penguin 1977), pp. 23, 26–7, 29, 40, 42, 49.
22. P. Foot, 'Morality as a System of Hypothetical Imperatives', in Foot, *Virtues and Vices* (Oxford: Blackwell 1978).
23. Phillips, 'In Search of the Moral "Must"', pp. 140–57; p. 148.
24. *Ibid.*, p. 152.
25. Williams, 'Internal and External Reasons', p. 102f.
26. P. Foot, 'Reasons For Action and Desires', in Foot, *Virtues and Vices.*

27. J. Dancy, 'Supererogation and Moral Realism', in J. Moravcsik, J. Dancy and C.C.W. Taylor (eds), *Human Agency: Language, Duty, Value* (Stanford, CA: Stanford University Press 1988).
28. In my 'Against Thin-Property Reductivism: Toleration as Supererogatory', *Journal of Value Inquiry* 31 (1997), pp. 231–49; for relevant remarks see also Williams, '*Ought* and Moral Obligation'.
29. For a justly celebrated statement of this view, see H.A. Prichard, 'Does Modern Moral Philosophy Rest on a Mistake?', in J.O. Urmson (ed.), *Moral Obligation* (Oxford: Oxford University Press 1968).
30. As I argued earlier with respect to attempts to 'ground' political obligation in supposedly more accessible types of reason for action, in Chapter 3.
31. There is no warrant for regarding moral (or other) properties as 'queer' if they do not motivate intrinsically, or at least in their own right (for this distinction see J. Dancy, *Moral Reasons* (Oxford: Blackwell 1993) Chapter 2).
32. See M. Stocker, 'The Schizophrenia of Modern Ethical Theories', *Journal of Philosophy* 73 (1976), pp. 453–66.
33. See Chapter 3; also G.F. Newey, 'Recent Political Philosophy', *Political Studies Association Conference Proceedings 1996*, vol. III, pp. 1310–21.
34. As I argued at greater length in Chapter 3.
35. See R. Dworkin, 'The Original Position', in N. Daniels (ed.), *Reading Rawls* (Oxford: Blackwell 1975), p. 18.
36. In my view this problem arises in a particularly acute form in Hobbes's political theory. Briefly put, the central crux (for example, in *Leviathan*) is that what is supposed to drive the argument justifying the Hobbesian sovereign is 'passions' (T. Hobbes, *Leviathan*, ed. R. Tuck (Cambridge: Cambridge University Press 1991), Chapter 6) or natural motivations, but that these passions make impossible what they are supposed to justify (whether because these passions give good reason for not joining the state, or because they drive people not to do what they have good reason to do). So from an apparently naturalised conception of political reasons for action, Hobbes is driven towards a normative or corrective account of those reasons; hence the ambiguous status of the laws of nature, and the loophole through which the 'Taylor-Warrender' thesis could pass. These remarks apply only to the sovereign created by institution, not conquest. I hope to argue this in more detail in my *Hobbes and Leviathan* (Routledge: forthcoming).

Chapter 6

1. Prominent works expounding versions of liberal neutrality in recent years have included the following: B. Ackerman, *Social Justice and the Liberal State* (New Haven, CT: Yale University Press 1980); T. Scanlon, 'Utilitarianism and Contractualism' in A.K. Sen and B. Williams (eds), *Utilitarianism and Beyond* (Cambridge: Cambridge University Press 1982); C. Larmore, *Patterns of Moral Complexity* (Cambridge: Cambridge University Press 1987); J. Rawls, *Political Liberalism* (New York: Columbia University Press 1993); B. Barry, *Justice As Impartiality* (Oxford: Clarendon Press 1995); J. Habermas, *Between Facts and Norms*, trans. W. Rehg (Cambridge: Polity Press 1996); J. Cohen, 'Moral Pluralism and Political Consensus' in D. Copp et al. (eds), *The Idea of*

Democracy (Cambridge: Cambridge University Press 1993); J. Waldron, *Liberal Rights* (Cambridge: Cambridge University Press 1993). See also R. Dworkin, 'Liberalism' in S. Hampshire (ed.), *Public and Private Morality* (Cambridge: Cambridge University Press 1978); Dworkin, *A Matter of Principle* (Cambridge, MA: Harvard University Press 1985) and T. Nagel, 'Moral Conflict and Political Legitimacy', *Philosophy and Public Affairs* 16 (1987), pp. 215–40. For more sceptical views, see for example, W. Galston, *Liberal Purposes* (Cambridge: Cambridge University Press 1991); G. Sher, *Beyond Neutrality* (Cambridge: Cambridge University Press 1987); T. Hurka, *Perfectionism* (New York: Oxford University Press 1993) and R. Kraut, 'Politics, Neutrality, and the Good', *Social Philosophy and Policy* 16 (1999), pp. 315–32.

2. Larmore, *Patterns of Moral Complexity*.
3. See G.F. Newey, 'Value Pluralism in Contemporary Liberalism', *Dialogue: The Canadian Philosophical Quarterly* 37 (1998), pp. 498–522, and Chapter 4 above; also G. Newey, 'Metaphysics Postponed: Liberalism, Pluralism and Neutrality', *Political Studies* 45 (1997), pp. 296–311.
4. Most notably, in *Political Liberalism*; see also Rawls's 'The Idea of an Overlapping Consensus', and 'The Domain of the Political and Overlapping Consensus', both in Rawls, *Collected Papers*, ed. S. Freeman (Cambridge, MA: Harvard University Press 1999).
5. With particular reference to Barry's *Justice As Impartiality*; for example, p. 8.
6. *Roe* v. *Wade*, 410 U.S. 113 (1973). On this issue, Ronald Dworkin's view (*Life's Dominion: An Argument about Abortion and Euthanasia* (London: HarperCollins 1993)) is that the protagonists in conflicts over abortion (and euthanasia) share a belief in the sanctity or 'sacred' quality (p. 13) of life, even though for 'pro choice' advocates (strangely enough) it is unexceptionable, and in fact morally required, that women carrying unwanted foetuses should be allowed to have them killed.
7. As Rawls himself argued explicitly in *A Theory of Justice* (Oxford: Oxford University Press 1971).
8. See R. Nozick, *Anarchy, State, and Utopia* (Oxford: Blackwell 1974), p. 29.
9. Brian Barry's argument in *Justice As Impartiality* is of this form. See pp. 146–50 below.
10. This need not mean that outcomes may *de facto* be neutral in their effect even though the justification for them fails to respect the side-constraint. For example, mutual-advantage considerations may dictate a *de facto* neutral settlement, even though the argument for it either violates the side-constraint or conforms to it only coincidentally.
11. This is to be taken as equivalent to saying that it is not the case that there is sufficient reason to favour one conception. This is true if, for example, the reasons for favouring one conception equal in strength to the reasons for not favouring it.
12. Larmore, *Patterns of Moral Complexity*, p. 23. For discussion of the VP version of the schema, see Newey, 'Metaphysics Postponed'.
13. Barry, *Justice As Impartiality*, pp. 26–7.
14. *Ibid.*, p. 163.
15. *Ibid.*, p. 169.
16. *Ibid.*, p. 168.
17. *Ibid.*, p. 8.

18. Charles Larmore ('Political Liberalism' in Larmore, *The Morals of Modernity* (Cambridge: Cambridge University Press 1996), argues that the non-neutralist liberalism of Joseph Raz (in *The Morality of Freedom* (Oxford: Clarendon Press 1986)) is mistaken in criticising neutrality for failing to rule out the possibility that unjust principles may arise through a bargaining process (Raz, *The Morality of Freedom*, p. 128). Larmore states that 'this ignores the point that liberal neutrality is a moral conception, not a matter of bargaining' (Larmore, *The Morals of Modernity*, p. 125). But the deeper point arising from Raz's criticism is surely that the bargaining process only makes sense if the protagonists have already had certain key issues decided for them, which cannot (however much we might like it to be so) be determined pre-politically.
19. This is why neutrality between actual religious creeds, for example, is held to be of political account, rather than neutrality between religious beliefs which nobody holds.
20. The status need not be equal in a relevant respect: cf. the remarks on handicapping at p. 142 above.
21. Ackerman, *Social Justice and the Liberal State*, p. 11; original emphasis.
22. *Ibid.*, p. 359; original emphasis.
23. For an interesting (if ultimately unpersuasive) attempt to apply Habermasian principles of dialogic neutrality to the conflict in Northern Ireland, see S. O'Neill, *Impartiality in Context: Grounding Justice in a Pluralist World* (Albany, NY: SUNY Press 1997); and O'Neill, 'Liberty, Equality and the Rights of Cultures: The Marching Controversy at Drumcree', *British Journal of Politics and International Relations* 2 (2000), pp. 26–45.
24. The point is underlined, rather than undermined, by the fact that a commitment to such a mechanism may obscure radical differences about the scope of the franchise (for example, whether it should include only the North or the whole island of Ireland). What is a neutral mechanism which could decide the issue even given a shared commitment to the value of democratic self-determination?
25. For further discussion of the issues raised by the *Satanic Verses* affair see G.F. Newey, '*Fatwa* and Fiction: Censorship and Toleration' and other essays collected in J. Horton (ed.), *Liberalism, Multiculturalism, and Toleration* (London: Macmillan 1993).
26. See B. Ackerman, 'Why Dialogue?', *Journal of Philosophy* 86 (1989), pp. 5–22; J. Habermas, 'On the Cognitive Content of Morality', *Proceedings of the Aristotelian Society* (1996), pp. 335–58; also S. Benhabib, 'Deliberative Rationality and Models of Democratic Legitimacy', *Constellations* 1 (1994), pp. 26–52.
27. B. Barber, *The Conquest of Politics* (Princeton, NJ: Princeton University Press 1988), Chapter 5.
28. For reasons why the facts of political power are liable to undermine dialogic neutrality, see S. Benhabib, 'Liberal Dialogue versus a Critical Theory of Discursive Legitimation' in N. Rosenblum (ed.), *Liberalism and the Moral Life* (Cambridge, MA: Harvard University Press 1989), for example, p. 156; also S. Chambers, *Reasonable Democracy: Jürgen Habermas and the Politics of Discourse* (Ithaca, NY: Cornell University Press 1996), p. 75f.

Chapter 7

1. J. Rawls, *A Theory of Justice* (Oxford: Oxford University Press 1971), pp. 48–51.
2. For the 'Overlapping consensus' idea, see Rawls, *Political Liberalism* (New York: Columbia University Press 1993), Chapter 4; also Rawls, 'The Idea of an Overlapping Consensus' and 'The Domain of the Political and Overlapping Consensus', both in Rawls, *Collected Papers*, ed. S. Freeman (Cambridge, MA: Harvard University Press 1999).
3. Rawls, *Political Liberalism*, p. 217.
4. *Ibid.*, p. 1. See also Rawls, 'The Idea of Public Reason', in Rawls, *Collected Papers*, p. 581, p. 591.
5. J. Habermas, 'On the Cognitive Content of Morality', *Proceedings of the Aristotelian Society* (1996), pp. 335–58, at p. 354 (original emphasis); cf. principle 'D' enunciated on p. 347. For similar formulations, see also Habermas, *Between Facts and Norms*, trans.W. Rehg (Cambridge: Polity Press 1996), p. 107. For yet a further formulation, cf. Habermas, 'Morality and Ethical Life: Does Hegel's Critique of Kant Apply to Discourse Ethics?' in C. Lenhardt and S. Weber Nicholsen (trans.), *Moral Consciousness and Communicative Action* (Boston, MA: MIT Press 1990), p. 197.
6. Cf. Chapter 6, pp. 146–8.
7. For this constraint, cf. Habermas, *Between Facts and Norms*, p. 107: 'just those action norms are valid to which all possibly affected persons could agree as participants in rationale discourses'.
8. In other words, that conception of neutrality which allows values or normative principles to be invoked in political design, as long as they are neutral between relevant conceptions of the good. 'Perfectionism' (a term also applied to Raz's theory) is sometimes contrasted with neutrality; but, again, a normative consensus about the supreme value of perfectionism itself (even if this could only be promoted by a wide variety of 'experiments in living') would satisfy neutrality in its weaker form.
9. For example D. Gauthier, *Morals By Agreement* (Oxford: Oxford University Press 1986).
10. See J. Gray, *Isaiah Berlin* (London: HarperCollins 1995) p. 141ff; and below, Chapter 8.
11. Habermas, 'On the Cognitive Content of Morality', p. 344; original emphasis.
12. I have taken this line of thought further in my *Virtue, Reason and Toleration: The Place of Toleration in Ethical and Political Philosophy* (Edinburgh: Edinburgh University Press 1999), Chapter 5. Of course, the remark in the text is not meant to imply that the notion of political justification is empty.
13. On this see my 'Gassing and Bungling', *London Review of Books*, 8 May 1997, pp. 14–15; see also Q. Skinner, 'Habermas's Reformation', *New York Review of Books*, 7 October 1982, pp. 32–5.
14. As Simone Chambers perhaps believes: cf. her *Reasonable Democracy: Jürgen Habermas and the Politics of Discourse* (Ithaca, NY: Cornell University Press 1996), p. 156f. A sceptical attitude towards value is equally capable of explaining these conflicts.
15. But, of course, in resolving the issues prior to political engagement, they contrive to pre-empt it.
16. Rawls, 'The Idea of Public Reason Revisited', p. 573.

17. It is, for example, accepted by Norman Daniels in his account of Rawls's later work. See Daniels, *Justice and Justification: Reflective Equilibrium in Theory and Practice* (Cambridge: Cambridge University Press 1996), p. 147, p. 151.
18. See for example Rawls, 'The Idea of an Overlapping Consensus', p. 425, where he talks of the 'diversity of doctrines – the fact of pluralism'. This is conflated with 'reasonable pluralism'.
19. See Rawls, *Theory of Justice*, Chapter 7; Rawls, *Political Liberalism*, p. 176f.
20. Rawls, *Political Liberalism*, p. 208.
21. *Ibid.*, p. 147.
22. *Ibid.*
23. J. Habermas, 'Reconciliation through the Use of Public Reason: Remarks on John Rawls's *Political Liberalism*', in *Journal of Philosophy* 92 (1995), pp. 109–31, at p. 131.
24. Rawls, *Political Liberalism*, p. 395.
25. *Ibid.*, pp. 103–4.
26. Rawls sets out the basis for the constructivist procedure in 'Kantian Constructivism in Moral Theory', in Rawls, *Collected Papers*.
27. Rawls, *Political Liberalism*, p. 104.
28. *Ibid.*, Introduction, p. xli.
29. *Ibid.*, p. xliv.
30. See for example *ibid. Political Liberalism*, p. 147f.
31. *Ibid.*, p. 10.
32. It is notable that Daniels, in his exposition of Rawls expresses 'a sense of philosophical loss' at 'the politicisation of justice' (Daniels, *Justice and Justification*, p. 151). This takes the description of Rawls's theory as a 'political' one at face value. A more apposite reaction might be to feel a sense of political loss at Rawls's purely philosophical account of justice.
33. Rawls, *Political Liberalism*, pp. 26–7.
34. For further argument in support of this, see Chapter 4.
35. As Raz appositely puts it, Rawls's overlapping consensus 'makes the doctrine of justice morality's department of foreign affairs': J. Raz, 'Facing Diversity: The Case of Epistemic Abstinence', *Philosophy and Public Affairs* 19 (1990), pp. 3–46, at p. 28.
36. Rawls, *Political Liberalism*, Introduction, pp. xxxix–xl. Cf. also p. 147: 'an overlapping consensus is quite different from a modus vivendi ... the object of consensus, the political conception of justice, is itself a moral conception. And second, it is affirmed on moral grounds, that is, it includes conceptions of society and of citizens as persons, as well as principles of justice, and an account of the political virtues.'
37. Rawls, 'The Idea of an Overlapping Consensus', p. 439: 'Faced with the fact of pluralism, a liberal view removes from the political agenda the most divisive issues', since these threaten 'the bases of social cooperation'. Roberto Alejandro, in his article defending a 'political' interpretation of Rawls's intentions describes this passage as 'baffling' (Alejandro, 'What Is Political About Rawls's Political Liberalism?', *Journal of Politics* 58 (1996), pp. 1–24, p. 13).
38. See for example B. Honig, *Political Theory and the Displacement of Politics* (Ithaca, NY: Cornell University Press 1993), p. 158; also J. Gray, *Endgames:*

Questions in Late Modern Political Thought (Cambridge: Polity Press 1997), Chapter 3.
39. Rawls, *Political Liberalism*, p. 85.
40. *Ibid.*, p. 85 n33.
41. *Ibid.*, p. 194. At p. 193 Rawls is at pains to distinguish neutrality of 'aim', to which he assumes political liberalism is committed, from procedural neutrality.
42. Rawls himself is, it seems, not very optimistic about this. He says that the projected consensus 'is highly speculative and raises questions which are little understood'; all we can do is hope to find such a consensus. Rawls, 'Justice As Fairness: Political, Not Metaphysical', in Rawls, *Collected Papers*, p. 414; cf. Rawls, 'The Idea of an Overlapping Consensus', p. 447.
43. A version of the idea of working 'from the inside out' appears in J. McDowell, 'Virtue and Reason', *The Monist* 62 (1979), pp. 331–50.
44. 'Quasi-discursive', since it is unclear how far the discursive model is thought of as being *essentially* dialogic. If it is, problems arise from the fact, noted by Gaus, that real dialogue is often characterised by inferential error. Perhaps Habermas has in mind an ideal dialogue model, which avoids inferential errors while remaining, in some sense, interpersonal.
45. G. Gaus, *Justificatory Liberalism* (Oxford: Oxford University Press), for example pp. 61–62.
46. Alejandro, 'What is Political about Rawls's Political Liberalism?', p. 20.
47. As I shall argue in Chapter 8, however, one consequence of recognising this distinction may be a move from a purely philosophical to a more political understanding of the aims of political philosophy itself. This can also be detected in the 'anti-foundationalist' work considered there.
48. Alejandro, 'What is Political about Rawls's Political Liberalism?', p. 17f.
49. For example: 'The focus of a political conception of justice is ... how those norms [that is, principles and standards of justice] are expressed in the character and attitudes of the members of society who realise its ideals.' Rawls, 'The Idea of an Overlapping Consensus', p. 423.
50. Cf. Honig, *Political Theory*, especially Chapter 5.
51. Alejandro, 'What is Political about Rawls's Political Liberalism?', pp. 22–3; original emphasis. Cf. also p. 12: 'his [Rawls's] philosophical method always abolishes tensions by placing them *outside the sphere of deliberation*. The end result ... betrays Rawls's conception of pluralism and the parties or the citizens end up displaying a disturbing sameness' (original emphasis).
52. Gaus, *Justificatory Liberalism*, p. 130.
53. *Ibid.*, pp. 4–5; original emphasis.
54. F.B. d'Agostino, 'The Idea and the Ideal of Public Justification', *Social Theory and Practice* 18 (1992), pp. 143–64, at p. 158.
55. *Ibid.*

Chapter 8

1. Gray has also changed his substantive political position from the defence of liberal free market capitalism enunciated in works such as *Liberalisms: Essays in Political Philosophy* (London: Routledge 1989). Cf. Gray's *Endgames:*

Questions in Late Modern Political Thought (Cambridge: Polity Press 1997), especially Chapters 6 and 10, for his espousal of 'green' ideology.
2. R. Rorty, *Contingency, Irony, and Solidarity* (Cambridge: Cambridge University Press 1989).
3. R. Rorty, *Objectivity, Relativism, and Truth: Philosophical Papers Volume I* (Cambridge: Cambridge University Press 1991), p. 44; original emphasis.
4. Rorty, *Contingency, Irony, Solidarity*, p. 20.
5. *Ibid.*, p. 190.
6. *Ibid.*, p. 192.
7. It could be said that the apparent intelligibility of the question 'Why should we do what we do do?' stems from error, just as G.E. Moore's 'open question' argument against naturalistic definitions of 'good' might be thought to ignore the possibility that the apparent 'openness' of a purported definition might stem from error. But if what is being offered is a genuinely *explanatory* analysis, we need to know how such an error could arise, if not through failure to understand that 'we' is always correlative with 'should': that is, that the pronoun is *defined* as that community which believes that this thing should be done.
8. R. Rorty, *The Consequences of Pragmatism* (Brighton: Harvester 1982), p *xl*.
9. Rorty, *Objectivity, Relativism, and Truth*, pp. 191–2.
10. S. Macedo, *Liberal Virtues: Citizenship, Virtue and Community in Liberal Constitutionalism* (Oxford: Clarendon Press 1990).
11. A.C. MacIntyre, *Whose Justice? Which Rationality?* (London: Duckworth 1988).
12. See A.C. MacIntyre, *After Virtue* (London: Duckworth 1981). See also his *Three Rival Versions of Moral Inquiry* (London: Duckworth 1990).
13. Herein lies, for instance, a well-known objection to the 'paradigm case' argument which aims to refute scepticism: the mere fact that a language-learner is initiated via the ostension of certain paradigmatic situations into learning the correct usage of a term ('free will', 'the external world', and so on) cannot show that these situations can be consensually picked out *even though* we collectively are systematically deluded about their true nature.
14. Rorty, *Contingency, Irony, Solidarity*, p. 90.
15. Rorty, 'Postmodernist Bourgeois Liberalism' in Rorty, *Objectivity, Relativism and Truth*, p. 199.
16. It is a noteworthy fact that despite this, the pressure to accommodate normative fragmentation often makes itself apparent in the work of 'communitarian' writers. So, for example, MacIntyre's common-good theory acknowledges the existence of a plurality of traditions, while Walzer's includes plurality at the level of 'spheres' within which goods are evaluated, and Taylor accepts the existence of plural but incommensurable 'hypergoods'.
17. For extended discussion, see B. Williams, *Ethics and the Limits of Philosophy* (London: Fontana 1985), pp. 174–96.
18. Rorty, *Objectivity, Relativism and Truth*, p. 23.
19. See C.L. Stevenson, 'The Emotive Meaning of Moral Terms', *Mind* 46 (1937), pp. 14–31, and *Ethics and Language* (New Haven, CT: Yale University Press 1945).

20. E. Laclau, 'Discourse' in R. Goodin and P. Pettit (eds), *A Companion to Contemporary Political Philosophy* (Oxford: Blackwell 1993).
21. L. Carroll, *Alice's Adventures in Wonderland and Through the Looking-Glass*, ed. R. Lancelyn Green (Oxford: Oxford University Press 1971), p. 190.
22. N. Chomsky and E. Herman, *Manufacturing Consent: The Political Economy of the Mass Media* (New York: Pantheon 1988).
23. J. Gray, *Post-Liberalism: Studies in Political Thought* (London: Routledge 1993).
24. B. Barber, *The Conquest of Politics* (Princeton, NJ: Princeton University Press 1988).
25. MacIntyre, *After Virtue*, p. 5.
26. Gray, 'Berlin's Agonistic Liberalism' in Gray, *Liberalisms*, p. 66.
27. Gray, *Liberalisms*, p. 287. Cf. *Endgames*, p. 54, p. 55. Gray also criticises Rorty for failing to follow through the implications of his anti-foundationalism for his defence of liberal values: once we have come to see that liberalism is contingent 'all the way down', we will come to recognise the contingency and local character of the justification of liberal irony itself. Cf. Gray, *Endgames*, p. 60.
28. J. Gray, *Isaiah Berlin* (London: HarperCollins 1995), p. 50.
29. *Ibid.*, p. 145.
30. *Ibid.*
31. *Ibid.*, p. 144.
32. *Ibid.*, p. 147.
33. *Ibid.*, pp. 154–5.
34. *Ibid.*, p. 168.
35. J. Gray, *Liberalism*, 2nd edn (Milton Keynes: Open University Press 1995), p. 86.
36. *Ibid.*, p. 88.
37. *Ibid.*, p. 95.
38. *Ibid.*, p. 96.
39. Most obviously, the green fundamentalism endorsed in Gray's *Endgames*, Chapter 10. *This* ideology does not seem to be regarded as prone to the same contingency as liberalism.
40. Cf. J. Gray, *Enlightenment's Wake* (London: Routledge 1995), pp. 69–70.
41. *Ibid.*, p. 70; original emphasis.
42. *Ibid.*, p. 73.
43. *Ibid.*, p. 136.
44. *Ibid.*, p. 73.
45. G. Gaus, *Justificatory Liberalism* (Oxford: Oxford University Press 1996). See also Chapter 7 above, Appendix.
46. John Horton argues this in his as yet unpublished paper 'Value-Pluralism and Agonistic Liberalism', to which I am indebted. This is a deliberately neutral formulation (that is, neutral between pluralistic views of value and rival accounts). The formulation is intended to allow for the possibility that there are value-based conflicts between practical alternatives involving only a single value.
47. Hence Gray's attack on 'humanism' (that is, anthropocentrism) in *Endgames*, Chapter 10. This accompanies an attack on the 'post-modernist' view that human dispositions are sufficiently labile to preclude any naturalised explanation of them.

48. See *ibid.*, Chapter 10, where Gray's antipathy to the 'hubris' of the 'Enlightenment Project' and 'humanism' fuels a call for the radical environmental political agenda favoured by so-called 'deep' ecologists and in particular mass (human) depopulation.
49. For an application of this to 'political obligation', see J. Horton, *Political Obligation* (London: Macmillan 1992), especially Chapter 6.
50. One manifestation of this is in the thought that there is an independent method of determining the scope of the community itself, other than the locus of affect itself. This is then thought to determine who count as eligible recipients, for example, for redistributed benefits, in arguments for restricting concern to the political community as a whole, rather than merely those with the relevant affects.
51. It is ironic that modern liberalism, which seeks to take seriously the 'fact' of value-pluralism, and sees a grounding for pluralism in practical regret, so seldom applies this insight to the regret endemic in politics itself.
52. It is of course a prime insight of Hannah Arendt's work. See for example her *The Human Condition* (Chicago, IL: University of Chicago Press 1958).

Bibliography

Abbott, P. *The Shotgun Behind the Door: Liberalism and the Problem of Political Obligation* (Georgia 1976).
Ackerman, B. *Social Justice and the Liberal State* (New Haven, CT: Yale University Press 1980).
Ackerman, B. 'Why Dialogue?', *Journal of Philosophy* 86 (1989), pp. 5–22.
Alejandro, R. 'What Is Political About Rawls's Political Liberalism?', *Journal of Politics* 58 (1996), pp. 1–24.
Altham J. and Harrison, R. (eds) *World, Mind, and Ethics: Essays on the Ethical Philosophy of Bernard Williams* (Cambridge: Cambridge University Press 1995).
Arendt, H. *The Human Condition* (Chicago, IL: University of Chicago Press 1958).
Arendt, H. *Eichmann in Jerusalem* (Harmondsworth: Penguin 1977).
Aristotle, *Nicomachean Ethics.*
Aristotle, *Politics.*
Aristotle, *Rhetoric.*
Audi, R. *Practical Reasoning* (London: Routledge 1989).
Audi, R. 'Acting From Virtue', *Mind* 104 (1995), pp. 449–72.
Ball, T. 'Power', in R. Goodin and P. Pettit (eds) *A Companion to Contemporary Political Philosophy* (Oxford: Blackwell 1993).
Ball, T. *Reappraising Political Theory* (Oxford: Clarendon Press 1995).
Ball, T. Farr, J. and Hanson R. (eds) *Political Innovation and Conceptual Change* (Cambridge: Cambridge University Press 1989).
Barber, B. *The Conquest of Politics* (Princeton, NJ: Princeton University Press 1988).
Barry, B. *The Liberal Theory of Justice* (Oxford: Oxford University Press 1972).
Barry, B. *Theories of Justice* (Berkeley, CA: University of California Press 1989).
Barry, B. *Justice As Impartiality* (Oxford: Clarendon Press 1995).
Benhabib, S. 'Deliberative Rationality and Models of Democratic Legitimacy', *Constellations* 1 (1994), pp. 26–52.
Benhabib S. and Dallmayr, F. (eds) *The Communicative Ethics Controversy* (Cambridge, MA: MIT Press 1990).
Berlin, I. 'Does Political Theory Still Exist?', in P. Laslett and W.G. Runciman (eds) *Philosophy, Politics, and Society,* 2nd series (Oxford: Oxford University Press 1962).
Berlin, I. *Four Essays on Liberty* (Oxford: Oxford University Press 1969).
Berlin, I. *Concepts and Categories* (Oxford: Oxford University Press 1978) .
Berlin I. and Williams, B. 'Pluralism and Liberalism: A Reply', *Political Studies* 43 (1994), pp. 306–9.
Blackburn, S. *Spreading the Word* (Oxford: Oxford University Press 1984).
Blackburn, S. (ed.) *The Oxford Dictionary of Philosophy* (Oxford: Oxford University Press 1994).
Bloor, D. *Wittgenstein, Rules, and Institutions* (London: Routledge 1997).

Bohman J. and Rehg, W. 'Discourse and Democracy: The Formal and Informal Bases of Legitimacy in Habermas' *Faktizität und Geltung*', *Journal of Political Philosophy* 4 (1996), pp. 79–99.

Brink, D. 'Externalist Moral Realism', *Southern Journal of Philosophy* 24 (supplement) (1986), pp. 23–41.

Broome, J. *Weighing Goods* (Oxford: Oxford University Press 1991).

Carroll, L. *Alice's Adventures in Wonderland and Through the Looking-Glass*, ed. R. Lancelyn Green (Oxford: Oxford University Press 1971).

Castoriadis, C. *The Castoriadis Reader*, ed. D. Curtis (Oxford: Blackwell 1997).

Castoriadis, C. *The Imaginary Institution of Society*, trans. K. Blamey (Cambridge: Polity Press 1997).

Chambers, S. *Reasonable Democracy: Jürgen Habermas and the Politics of Discourse* (Ithaca, NY: Cornell University Press 1996).

Chomsky N. and Herman, E. *Manufacturing Consent: The Political Economy of the Mass Media* (New York: Pantheon 1988).

Cohen, G. *Marx's Theory of History: A Defence* (Oxford: Oxford University Press 1978).

Cohen, G. *Self-Ownership, Freedom and Equality* (Cambridge: Cambridge University Press 1996).

Cohen, J. 'Moral Pluralism and Political Consensus', in D. Copp et al. (eds) *The Idea of Democracy* (Cambridge: Cambridge University Press 1993).

Collier, A. *Critical Realism: An Introduction to the Thought of Roy Bhaskar* (London: Verso 1994).

Collingwood, R. *The Idea of History* (Oxford: Clarendon Press 1941).

Connolly, W. *The Terms of Political Discourse*, 3rd edn (Oxford: Blackwell 1993).

Crisp R. and Slote, M. (eds) *Virtue Ethics* (Oxford: Oxford University Press 1997).

Crowder, G. 'Pluralism and Liberalism', *Political Studies* 43 (1994), pp. 293–305.

D'Agostino, F.B. 'The Idea and the Ideal of Public Justification', *Social Theory and Practice* 18 (1992), pp. 143–64.

Dancy, J. 'On Moral Properties', *Mind* 90 (1981), pp. 367–85.

Dancy, J. 'Supererogation and Moral Realism', in J. Moravcsik, J. Dancy and C. Taylor (eds) *Human Agency: Language, Duty, Value* (Stanford, CA: Stanford University Press 1988).

Dancy, J. *Moral Reasons* (Oxford: Blackwell 1993).

Daniels, N. (ed.) *Reading Rawls* (Oxford: Blackwell 1975).

Daniels, N. *Justice and Justification: Reflective Equilibrium in Theory and Practice* (Cambridge: Cambridge University Press 1996).

Darwall, S. *The British Moralists and the Internal 'Ought'* (Cambridge: Cambridge University Press 1995).

Darwall, S. Gibbard, A. and Railton, P. (eds) *Moral Discourse and Practice* (New York: Oxford University Press 1997).

Davidson, D. *Essays on Actions and Events* (Oxford: Oxford University Press 1980).

Deigh, J. *The Sources of Moral Agency: Essays in Moral Psychology and Freudian Theory* (Cambridge: Cambridge University Press 1996).

Dworkin, R. 'The Original Position', in N. Daniels (ed.), *Reading Rawls* (Oxford: Blackwell 1975).

Dworkin, R. *Taking Rights Seriously* (London: Duckworth 1977).

Dworkin, R. 'Liberalism', in S. Hampshire (ed.), *Public and Private Morality* (Cambridge: Cambridge University Press 1978).

Dworkin, R. 'What is Equality? Part 1: Equality of Welfare', *Philosophy and Public Affairs* 10(iii) (1981), pp. 185–246.
Dworkin, R. 'What is Equality? Part 2: Equality of Resources', *Philosophy and Public Affairs* 10(iv) (1981), pp. 283–345.
Dworkin, R. *A Matter of Principle* (Cambridge, MA: Harvard University Press 1985).
Dworkin, R. *Life's Dominion: An Argument about Abortion and Euthanasia* (London: HarperCollins 1993).
Edmundson, W.A. *Three Anarchical Fallacies* (Cambridge: Cambridge University Press 1998).
Falk, W. '"Ought" and Motivation', *Proceedings of the Aristotelian Society* 48 (1948), pp. 492–510.
Farr, J. 'Understanding Conceptual Change Politically', in T. Ball, J. Farr and R. Hanson (eds) *Political Innovation and Conceptual Change* (Cambridge: Cambridge University Press 1989).
Flathman, R. *Political Obligation* (New York: Atheneum 1972).
Foot, P. 'Morality as a System of Hypothetical Imperatives', 'Reasons for Action and Desires', and 'Are Moral Considerations Overriding?', reprinted in P. Foot, *Virtues and Vices* (Oxford: Blackwell 1978).
Foster L. and Herzog, P. (eds) *Defending Diversity: Contemporary Philosophical Perspectives on Pluralism And Multiculturalism* (Amherst, MA: University of Massachusetts Press 1994).
Frazer, E. *The Problems of Communitarian Politics* (Oxford: Oxford University Press 1999).
Freeden, M. *Ideologies and Political Theory* (Oxford: Clarendon Press 1996).
Furrow, D. *Against Theory: Continental and Analytical Challenges in Moral Philosophy* (Routledge: London 1995).
Gallie, W.G. 'Essentially Contested Concepts', *Proceedings of the Aristotelian Society* 56 (1955–6), pp. 167–98.
Galston, W. *Justice and the Human Good* (Chicago, IL: University of Chicago Press 1980).
Galston, W. 'Pluralism and Social Unity', *Ethics* (1989), pp. 711–26.
Galston, W. *Liberal Purposes* (Cambridge: Cambridge University Press 1991).
Gaus, G. *Justificatory Liberalism* (Oxford: Oxford University Press 1996).
Gauthier, D. *The Logic of Leviathan* (Oxford: Clarendon Press 1969).
Gauthier, D. *Morals By Agreement* (Oxford: Oxford University Press 1986).
Geertz, C. *The Interpretation of Cultures: Selected Essays* (New York: Basic Books 1973).
Gewirth, A. *Reason and Morality* (Chicago, IL: University of Chicago Press 1978).
Goodin R. and Pettit, P. (eds), *A Companion to Contemporary Political Philosophy* (Oxford: Blackwell 1993).
Gray, J. 'On the Essential Contestability of some Social and Political Concepts', *Political Theory* V (1977), pp. 385–402.
Gray, J. 'On Liberty, Liberalism and Essential Contestability', *British Journal of Political Science* 8 (1978), pp. 331–48.
Gray, J. 'Political Power, Social Theory and Essential Contestability', in D. Miller and L. Siedentop (eds) *The Nature of Political Theory* (Oxford: Blackwell 1983).
Gray, J. *Hayek on Liberty* (Oxford: Blackwell 1984).
Gray, J. *Liberalisms: Essays in Political Philosophy* (London: Routledge 1989).
Gray, J. *Post-Liberalism: Studies in Political Thought* (London: Routledge 1993).

Gray, J. *Enlightenment's Wake* (London: Routledge 1995).
Gray, J. *Isaiah Berlin* (London: HarperCollins 1995).
Gray, J. *Liberalism*, 2nd edn. (Milton Keynes: Open University Press 1995).
Gray, J. *Endgames: Questions in Late Modern Political Thought* (Cambridge: Polity Press 1997).
Griffin, J. 'Are There Incommensurable Values?', *Philosophy and Public Affairs* 6 (1977), pp. 41–59.
Griffin, J. *Well Being* (Oxford: Oxford University Press 1986).
Gutmann, A. *Liberal Equality* (Cambridge: Cambridge University Press 1980).
Habermas, J. *The Theory of Communicative Action*, vols I and II, trans. T. McCarthy (Cambridge: Polity Press 1984–7).
Habermas, J. *The Philosophical Discourse of Modernity*, trans. F. Lawrence (Cambridge, MA: MIT Press 1987).
Habermas, J. *The Structural Transformation of the Public Sphere* (Cambridge: Polity Press 1989).
Habermas, J. 'Morality and Ethical Life: Does Hegel's Critique of Kant Apply to Discourse Ethics?' in C. Lenhardt and S. Weber Nicholsen (trans.) *Moral Consciousness and Communicative Action* (Boston, MA: MIT Press 1990).
Habermas, J. 'Reconciliation through the Use of Public Reason: Remarks on John Rawls's *Political Liberalism*', *Journal of Philosophy* 92 (1995) pp. 109–31.
Habermas, J. *Between Facts and Norms*, trans. W. Rehg (Cambridge: Polity Press 1996).
Habermas, J. *Die Einbeziehung des Anderen: Studien zur politischen Theorie* (Frankfurt: Suhrkamp 1996).
Habermas, J. 'On the Cognitive Content of Morality', *Proceedings of the Aristotelian Society* (1996), pp. 335–58.
Hampshire, S. *Thought and Action* (New York: Viking Press 1959).
Hampshire, S. *Morality and Pessimism* (Cambridge: Cambridge University Press 1972).
Hampshire, S. *Morality and Conflict* (Cambridge: Cambridge University Press 1983).
Hampshire, S. *Justice Is Conflict* (Princeton, NJ: Princeton University Press 2000).
Hampton, J. *Political Philosophy* (Boulder, CO: Westview Press 1996).
Hare, R.M. *Moral Thinking* (Oxford: Oxford University Press 1982).
Harrison R. and Altham, J. (eds) *World, Mind And Ethics* (Cambridge: Cambridge University Press 1995).
Herzog P. and Foster, L. (eds) *Defending Diversity: Contemporary Philosophical Perspectives on Multiculturalism* (Amherst, MA: University of Massachusetts Press 1994).
Heyd, D. *Supererogation and its Status in Ethical Theory* (Cambridge: Cambridge University Press 1982).
Hobbes, T. *Leviathan*, ed. R. Tuck (Cambridge: Cambridge University Press 1991).
Hohfeld, W. *Fundamental Legal Conceptions as Applied in Judicial Reasoning* (New Haven, CT: Yale University Press 1919).
Honig, B. *Political Theory and the Displacement of Politics* (Ithaca, NY: Cornell University Press 1993).
Horton, J. *Political Obligation* (London: Macmillan 1992).
Horton, J. (ed.) *Liberalism, Multiculturalism and Toleration* (London: Macmillan 1993).
Horton J. and Mendus, S. (eds) *After MacIntyre* (Cambridge: Polity Press 1994).

Hume, D. *An Enquiry Concerning the Principles of Morals*, ed. P. Nidditch (Oxford: Clarendon Press 1975).
Hume, D. *A Treatise of Human Nature*, ed. P. Nidditch (Oxford: Oxford University Press 1978).
Hurka, T. *Perfectionism* (New York: Oxford University Press 1993).
Hutchinson, D. *The Virtues of Aristotle* (London: Routledge 1986).
Kant, I. *The Groundwork of the Metaphysics of Morals*, ed. J. Paton (London: Hutchinson 1972).
Kant, I. *Critique of Practical Reason*, ed. and trans. L. Beck (New York: Macmillan 1993).
Kant, I. *Political Writings* trans. and ed. H. Reiss, 2nd edn. (Cambridge: Cambridge University Press 1995).
Kavka, G. 'Why Even Morally Perfect People Would Need Government', in E.F. Paul, F.D. Miller and J. Paul (eds) *Contemporary Political and Social Philosophy* (Cambridge: Cambridge University Press 1995).
Kekes, J. *The Morality of Pluralism* (Princeton, NJ: Princeton University Press 1993).
Kekes, J. *Against Liberalism* (Ithaca, NY: Cornell University Press 1997).
Kleinberg, S. *Politics and Philosophy: The Necessity and Limitations of Rational Argument* (Oxford: Blackwell 1991) .
Klosko, G. 'Presumptive Benefit, Fairness, and Political Obligation', *Philosophy and Public Affairs* 16 (1987), pp. 241–59.
Korsgaard, C. *The Sources of Normativity* (Cambridge: Cambridge University Press 1996).
Korsgaard, C. *Creating the Kingdom of Ends* (Cambridge: Cambridge University Press 1996).
Kraut, R. 'Politics, Neutrality, and the Good', *Social Philosophy and Policy* 16 (1999), pp. 315–32.
Kymlicka, W. *Liberalism, Community and Culture* (Oxford: Oxford University Press 1989).
Kymlicka, W. *Contemporary Political Philosophy* (Oxford: Oxford University Press 1992).
Kymlicka, W. *Multicultural Citizenship* (Oxford: Oxford University Press 1995).
Laclau, E. 'Discourse', in R. Goodin and P. Pettit (eds) *A Companion to Contemporary Political Philosophy* (Oxford: Blackwell 1993).
Larmore, C. *Patterns of Moral Complexity* (Cambridge: Cambridge University Press 1987).
Larmore, C. 'Pluralism and Reasonable Disagreement', *Social Philosophy and Policy* (1994), pp. 61–79.
Larmore, C. *The Morals of Modernity* (Cambridge: Cambridge University Press 1996).
Laslett, P. (ed.), *Philosophy, Politics and Society*, 1st series (Oxford: Oxford University Press 1956).
Leftwich, A. *Redefining Politics: People, Resources and Power* (London: Methuen 1983).
Locke, J. *An Essay Concerning Human Understanding*, ed. P. Nidditch (Oxford: Clarendon Press 1975).
Lovibond, S. *Realism and Imagination in Ethics* (Oxford: Oxford University Press 1983).
Lukes, S. *Power: A Radical View* (London: Macmillan 1974).

Lukes, S. 'Making Sense of Moral Conflict', in N. Rosenblum (ed.), *Liberalism and the Moral Life* (Cambridge, MA: Harvard University Press 1989).
Macedo, S. *Liberal Virtues: Citizenship, Virtue and Community in Liberal Constitutionalism* (Oxford: Clarendon Press 1991).
McDowell, J. 'Are Moral Reasons Hypothetical Imperatives?', *Proceedings of the Aristotelian Society* (1978), pp. 13–29.
McDowell, J. 'Might There Be External Reasons?', in J. Altham and R. Harrison (eds) *World, Mind and Ethics: Essays on the Ethical Philosophy of Bernard Williams* (Cambridge: Cambridge University Press 1995).
McDowell, J. 'Virtue and Reason', in R. Crisp and M. Slote (eds) *Virtue Ethics* (Oxford: Oxford University Press 1997).
Machiavelli, N. *The Prince*, trans. G. Bull (Harmondsworth: Penguin 1961).
Machiavelli, N. *The Discourses*, trans. L. Walker, ed. B. Crick (Harmondsworth: Penguin 1970).
MacIntyre, A. *Against the Self-Images of the* Age (London: Duckworth 1971) .
MacIntyre, A. 'The Essential Contestability of Some Social Concepts', *Ethics* 84 (1973–4), pp. 1–9.
MacIntyre, A. *After Virtue* (London: Duckworth 1981).
MacIntyre, A. 'The Indispensability of Political Theory' in D. Miller and L. Siedentop (eds) *The Nature of Political Theory* (Oxford: Basil Blackwell 1983).
MacIntyre, A. *Whose Justice? Which Rationality?* (London: Duckworth 1988).
Mackie, J. *Ethics: Inventing Right and Wrong* (London: Penguin 1977).
McNaughton, D. *Moral Vision* (Oxford: Blackwell 1988).
Marx, K. *Theses on Feuerbach* XI, reprinted in D. McLellan (ed.), *Karl Marx: Selected Writings* (Oxford: Oxford University Press 1977).
Mason, A. 'On Explaining Political Disagreement: The Notion of an Essentially Contested Concept', *Inquiry* 33 (1990), pp. 81–98.
Mason, A. *Explaining Political Disagreement* (Cambridge: Cambridge University Press 1993).
Mason, A. 'MacIntyre on Liberalism and its Critics: Tradition, Incommensurability and Disagreement', in J. Horton and S. Mendus (eds) *After MacIntyre* (Cambridge: Polity Press 1994).
Miller, D. 'Constraints on Freedom', *Ethics* 94 (1983), pp. 66–86.
Miller, D. 'Linguistic Philosophy and Political Theory', in D. Miller and L. Siedentop (eds) *The Nature of Political Theory* (Oxford: Basil Blackwell 1983).
Miller, D. *Principles of Social Justice* (Cambridge, MA: Harvard University Press 1999).
Miller D. and Siedentop, L. (eds) *The Nature of Political Theory* (Oxford: Basil Blackwell 1983).
Morriss, P. *Power: A Philosophical Analysis* (New York: St Martin's Press 1987).
Mouffe, C. *The Return of the Political* (London: Verso 1993).
Mulhall S. and Swift, A (eds) *Liberals and Communitarians* (Oxford: Blackwell 1992).
Nagel, T. *The Possibility of Altruism* (Princeton, NJ: Princeton University Press 1970).
Nagel, T. *Mortal Questions* (Cambridge: Cambridge University Press 1979).
Nagel, T. *The View From Nowhere* (Cambridge: Cambridge University Press 1986).
Nagel, T. 'Moral Conflict and Political Legitimacy', *Philosophy and Public Affairs* 16 (1987), pp. 215–40.

Newey, G. 'Reasons Beyond Reason? "Political Obligation" Reconsidered', *Philosophical Papers* 25 (1996), pp. 21–48.
Newey, G. 'Recent Political Philosophy', *Political Studies Association Conference Proceedings 1996*, vol. III, pp. 310–21.
Newey, G. 'Philosophical Aromatherapy', *Res Publica* II (1996), pp. 215–21.
Newey, G. 'Value-Pluralism in Contemporary Liberalism', *Dialogue: The Canadian Philosophical Review* 37 (1998), pp. 498–522.
Newey, G. 'Against Thin-Property Reductivism: Toleration as Supererogatory', *Journal of Value Inquiry* 31 (1997), pp. 231–49.
Newey, G. '"Gassing and Bungling", review of Habermas, *Between Facts and Norms*', *London Review of Books*, 8 May, pp. 14–15.
Newey, G. 'Metaphysics Postponed: Liberalism, Pluralism and Neutrality', *Political Studies* 45 (1997), pp. 296–311.
Newey, G. 'Political Lying: A Defense', *Public Affairs Quarterly* 11 (1997), pp. 93–116.
Newey, G. 'Tolerance As A Virtue' in S. Mendus and J. Horton (eds), *Toleration: Identity and Difference* (London: Macmillan 1999).
Nicholson P. and Horton, J. (eds), *Toleration: Philosophy and Practice* (Aldershot: Avebury 1992).
Nozick, R. *Anarchy, State, and Utopia* (Oxford: Blackwell 1974).
Nozick, R. *The Nature of Rationality* (Oxford: Oxford University Press 1989).
Oakeshott, M. *Rationalism in Politics and Other Essays* (London: Methuen 1962).
O'Neill, O. *Towards Justice and Virtue* (Cambridge: Cambridge University Press 1996).
O'Neill, S. *Impartiality in Context: Grounding Justice in a Pluralist World* (Albany, NY: Suny Press 1997).
O'Neill, S. 'Liberty, Equality and the Rights of Cultures: The Marching Controversy at Drumcree', *British Journal of Politics and International Relations* 2 (2000), pp. 26–45.
Outhwaite, W. *Habermas* (Cambridge: Polity Press 1994).
Parfit, D. *Reasons and Persons* (Oxford: Oxford University Press 1984).
Pateman, C. *The Problem of Political Obligation* (Cambridge: Polity Press 1985).
Peacocke, C. *A Study of Concepts* (Cambridge, MA: MIT Press 1995).
Pettit, P. *Republicanism: a theory of freedom and government* (Oxford: Oxford University Press 1997) .
Philips, M. 'Weighing Moral Reasons', *Mind* 116 (1987), pp. 367–75.
Phillips, D. 'In Search of the Moral "Must"', *Philosophical Quarterly* 27 (1977), pp. 140–57.
Pitkin, H. 'Obligation and Consent', *American Political Science Review* 55 IV (1965).
Pitkin, H. 'Obligation and Consent II', *American Political Science Review* 56 I (1966).
Pitkin, H. 'Obligation and Consent', in P. Laslett, W.G. Runciman and Q. Skinner (eds) *Philosophy, Politics and Society*, 4th series (Oxford: Blackwell 1972).
Prichard, H. 'Does Modern Moral Philosophy Rest on a Mistake?', 'Green: Political Obligation', and 'Moral Obligation', in J. Urmson (ed.) *Moral Obligation* (Oxford: Oxford University Press 1968).
Quine, W. *From A Logical Point of View* (Cambridge, MA: Harvard University Press 1953).
Quinton, A. (ed.) *Political Philosophy* (Oxford: Oxford University Press 1967).
Rawls, J. *A Theory of Justice* (Oxford: Oxford University Press 1971).

Rawls, J. *Political Liberalism* (New York: Columbia University Press 1993).
Rawls, J. 'Reply to Habermas', *Journal of Philosophy* 92 (1995), pp. 132–80.
Rawls, J. *Collected Papers*, ed. S. Freeman (Cambridge, MA: Harvard University Press 1999).
Raz, J. *The Morality of Freedom* (Oxford: Clarendon Press 1986).
Raz, J. 'Legal Rights', *Oxford Journal of Legal Studies* 4 (1987), pp. 1–21.
Raz, J. 'Autonomy, Toleration, and the Harm Principle', in S. Mendus (ed.) *Justifying Toleration* (Cambridge: Cambridge University Press 1988).
Raz, J. 'Facing Diversity: The Case of Epistemic Abstinence', *Philosophy and Public Affairs* 19 (1990), pp. 3–46.
Rorty, R. *Philosophy and the Mirror of Nature* (Princeton, NJ: Princeton University Press 1979).
Rorty, R. *The Consequences of Pragmatism* (Brighton: Harvester 1982).
Rorty, R. *Contingency, Irony, and Solidarity* (Cambridge: Cambridge University Press 1989).
Rorty, R. *Objectivity, Relativism, and Truth: Philosophical Papers Volume I* (Cambridge: Cambridge University Press 1991).
Ross, W. *The Right and the Good* (Oxford: Clarendon Press 1930).
Sandel, M. *Liberalism and the Limits of Justice* (Cambridge: Cambridge University Press 1982).
Scanlon, T. 'Utilitarianism and Contractualism', in A.K. Sen and B. Williams (eds) *Utilitarianism and Beyond* (Cambridge: Cambridge University Press 1982).
Scanlon, T. *What We Owe To Each Other* (Cambridge, MA: Harvard University Press 1999).
Schmitt, C. *The Concept of the Political*, trans. G. Schwab (New Brunswick, NJ: Rutgers University Press 1976) .
Searle, J.R. 'How to Derive *Ought* from *Is*', *Philosophical Review* 73 (1964) pp. 43–58, in P. Foot (ed.) *Theories of Ethics* (Oxford: Oxford University Press 1967).
Selbourne, D. *The Principle of Duty* (London: Sinclair Stevenson 1994).
Senor, T. 'What If There Are No Political Obligations? A Reply to A.J. Simmons', *Philosophy and Public Affairs* 16 (1987), pp. 260–8.
Sher, G. *Beyond Neutrality* (Cambridge: Cambridge University Press 1987).
Shklar, J. *Ordinary Vices* (Cambridge, MA: Harvard University Press 1984).
Simmons, A. *Moral Principles and Political Obligations* (Princeton, NJ: Princeton University Press 1979).
Simmons, A. 'The Anarchist Position: A Reply to Klosko and Senor', *Philosophy and Public Affairs* 16 (1987), pp. 269–79.
Skinner, Q. 'Meaning and Understanding in the History of Ideas', *History and Theory* 8 (1969), pp. 3–53.
Skinner, Q. 'Conventions and the Understanding of Speech Acts', *Philosophical Quarterly* 20 (1970), pp. 118–38.
Skinner, Q. 'On Performing and Explaining Linguistic Actions', *Philosophical Quarterly* 21 (1971), pp. 1–21.
Skinner, Q. '"Social Meaning" and the Explanation of Social Action', in P. Laslett, W.G. Runciman and Q. Skinner (eds) *Philosophy, Politics and Society*, 4th series (Oxford: Blackwell 1972).
Skinner, Q. *The Foundations of Modern Political Thought*, 2 vols (Cambridge: Cambridge University Press 1978).

Skinner, Q. 'The Idea of a Cultural Lexicon', *Essays in Criticism* 29 (1979), pp. 205–24.
Skinner, Q. 'Language and Political Change', in T. Ball, J. Farr and R. Hanson (eds) *Political Innovation and Conceptual Change* (Cambridge: Cambridge University Press 1989).
Slote, M. *From Morality to Virtue* (Oxford: Oxford University Press 1995).
Smith, M. 'The Humean Theory of Motivation', *Mind* 96 (1987), pp. 36–61.
Smith, M. *The Moral Problem* (Oxford: Blackwell 1994).
Spinoza, B. 'Tractatus Politicus', in A. Wernham (ed.), *Spinoza: The Political Works* (Oxford: Clarendon Press 1958).
Stevenson, C. 'The Emotive Meaning of Moral Terms', *Mind* 46 (1937), pp. 14–31.
Stevenson, C. *Ethics and Language* (New Haven, CT: Yale University Press 1945).
Stocker, M. 'The Schizophrenia of Modern Ethical Theories', *Journal of Philosophy* 73 (1976), pp. 453–66.
Stocker, M. *Plural and Conflicting Values* (Oxford: Oxford University Press 1990).
Strawson, P. *Individuals: An Essay in Descriptive Metaphysics* (London: Methuen 1959).
Swanton, C. 'On the "Essential Contestedness' of Political Concepts', *Ethics* 95 (1985), pp. 811–27.
Taylor, C. *Hegel* (Cambridge: Cambridge University Press 1975).
Taylor, C. *Hegel and Modern Society* (Cambridge: Cambridge University Press 1978).
Taylor, C. *Philosophical Papers I: Human Agency and Language* (Cambridge: Cambridge University Press 1985).
Taylor, C. *Philosophical Papers II: Philosophy and the Human Sciences* (Cambridge: Cambridge University Press 1985).
Taylor, C. *Sources of the Self: The Making of the Modern Identity* (Cambridge, MA: Harvard University Press 1989).
Taylor, C. *Multiculturalism and 'The Politics of Recognition'* (with A. Gutmann et al.) (Princeton, NJ: Princeton University Press 1992).
Tuck, R. 'Why Is Authority Such A Problem?', in P. Laslett, W.G. Runciman and Q. Skinner (eds) *Philosophy, Politics and Society*, 4th series (Oxford: Blackwell 1972).
Tully, J. *Meaning and Context: Quentin Skinner and his Critics* (Cambridge: Polity Press 1988).
Tully, J. *Philosophy in an Age of Pluralism: The Philosophy of Charles Taylor in Question* (Cambridge: Cambridge University Press 1994) .
Waldron, J. *Liberal Rights* (Cambridge: Cambridge University Press 1993).
Walzer, M. *Spheres of Justice: A Defense of Pluralism and Equality* (New York: Basic Books 1983).
White, S. *The Recent Work of Jürgen Habermas: Reason, Justice, and Modernity* (Cambridge: Cambridge University Press 1988).
Wiggins, D. 'Truth, Invention and the Meaning of Life', 'Weakness of Will, Commensurability, and the Objects of Desire', and 'Deliberation and Practical Reason', in D. Wiggins, *Needs, Values, Truth: Essays in the Philosophy of Value* (Oxford: Blackwell 1987).
Williams, B. *Problems of the Self* (Cambridge: Cambridge University Press 1972).
Williams, B. *Moral Luck* (Cambridge: Cambridge University Press 1981).
Williams, B. *Ethics and the Limits of Philosophy* (London: Fontana 1985).

Williams, B. *Making Sense of Humanity* (Cambridge: Cambridge University Press 1995).
Williams, B. *Shame and Necessity* (Berkeley, CA: University of California Press 1996).
Wittgenstein, L. *Philosophical Investigations*, trans. and ed. G. Anscombe (Oxford: Blackwell 1953).
Wittgenstein, L. *Zettel*, ed. G. Anscombe and G. von Wright (Oxford: Blackwell 1967).
Wolff, R. *In Defense of Anarchism* (New York: Basic Books 1976).
Zagzebski, L. *Virtues of the Mind: An Inquiry into the Nature of Virtue and the Ethical Foundations of Knowledge* (Cambridge: Cambridge University Press 1996).

Index